Victoria: Where Dreams Come True

88 year autobiography of the life and times of

Morris Kersey

What it is like to fly with the Concorde, travel the Orient
Express, QE2 and South Africa's Blue Train

Order this book online at www.trafford.com
or email orders@trafford.com

Most Trafford titles are also available at major online book retailers.

Print information available on the last page.

ISBN: 978-1-5521-2836-7 (sc)

Trafford rev. 09/15/2022

 www.trafford.com

North America & international
toll-free: 844-688-6899 (USA & Canada)
fax: 812 355 4082

Preface

My Aladdin's Lamp of Life -- *To be born with an attached, computerized video of my entire future life, from cradle to grave, and, at birth, to have the option to look it over, knowing what I now know at age 75, and reprogramme it as I feel it should be or the way I would have liked it to be............*

This is the story of my life. I was born January 2, 1913 at 644 Speed Avenue, Victoria, B.C., Canada. Although perhaps unlucky for some, being born in the year 1913, with thirteen letters in my name, proved lucky for me -- in 1954, holding ticket number 13, I won a new Cadillac at a charity dinner. The Carmelcrisp shop I started in 1934 was located at 644 Fort Street.

My first six years of life were spent in my father's bakery on Alpha Street in Victoria, across from the present Mayfair Shopping Mall, where he needed the dough to survive. The pungent smell of hot bread was ever present.

The austere conditions that prevailed in 1913, followed by World War I, brought restraints to the economy. Parents could provide their children with only the bare necessities. Thrift became the top priority. I was too young to realize these conditions, but I feel sure I inherited some of the wartime restrictions which was a stepping-stone to my successful life.

Jobs I've held and businesses I've owned in my career include:

1.	Times and Colonist paper routes	*Age --* 7 to 14
2.	Standard Steam Laundry	14
3.	Helper to Electrician Harry Rowntree	15 to 16
4.	Victoria Cold Storage - Shipping Clerk	16 to 17
5.	Wholesale Fishing Business (Frank Lawrie)	17
6.	Royal Trust Company - Assistant to Building Superintendent	17 to 20
7.	Painter (offices and houses; after hours)	17 to 20
8.	Owner / Operator - Victoria Service Station, Douglas & Humbolt Sts	20 to 21
9.	Owner / Operator - Carmelcrisp and Morris Kersey Coffee Shop, Fort St.	21 to 28
10.	Apprentice to Carpenter Harry Rowse	28
11.	United Meat Packers - Wholesale Delivery	28
12.	Joined Army as Catering Officer	28
13.	Yarrows Ship Building - Full Journeyman Electrician	28
14.	Owner / Operator - Phonograph Recordings' Business	28 to 40
15.	Owner / Operator - Retail Nut Shop and Carmelcrisp	29 to 32
16.	Owner / Operator - National Wholesale Nuts and Bakery Supplies	32 to 40
17.	Manufacturer - Kersey's Peanut Butter *(Largest in Canada)*	32 to 40
18.	Manufacturer - Dirl Products Limited (Soaps, etc.)	40 to 42
19.	Real Estate Sales	42 to 43
20.	Flying Instructor and Charter Flying	40 to 61
21.	Owner / Operator - New Victoria Airport Coffee Shop	51 to 61
22.	Owner / Operator - Victoria Airport Duty Free and Gift Shop	51 to 73
23.	Totem Travel Services - Sales	51 to 81

Table of Contents

A biography tells a story. This person was born not an educated professional, born without skills, or knowledge, and he has worked at what he is today. One cannot help learning by reading a life story. It is one's ambitions, learning, working, sincerity, responsibilities, usually passing up discouragement and hard times, both in success and defeat.

Part 1: *1913 - 1929*

"In my youth I had fixed stars that comforted me with their permanence. They gave me a known horizon and they told me there was a loving, kind and just father out there looking down on me, ready to receive me, thinking of my concerns all the time. I am today what I am because of those beliefs. I wonder what happens to children who don't have those fixed stars, that known horizon -- those myths."   - Joseph Campbell

How did we get from here to there?

When I was a small boy, we lived in a barn at the edge of the bush about twelve miles from Victoria, B.C., Canada, with snow sifting onto my bed through the chinks in the walls. Now I live in a nice house with a heated indoor pool. My brother and my father (who passed away in May 1986) also have been comfortably off. While we were making our journey from poverty to a modest affluence, I seldom stopped to puzzle out what happened, and why. I am putting this story together for my own pleasure, for the family record, and for people who seek ways of solving their own poverty problems.

The main secret of my small-scale-success story is that I had parents and grandparents who knew how to survive, and how to be happy. Some of the survival techniques are universal principles which can be picked up by advice and example. Some must be painfully learned by trial and error. I didn't always make a good job of acquiring the survival techniques. Sometimes I fell flat on my face. However, I learned from the experience, and it was fun. What more can you ask?

I have been privileged to have lived through extreme poverty to extreme luxury. I did not need an education in schools, but I did need parents who cared. This lifetime covered most every condition known to a human being, and I was indeed fortunate to have been born and lived in such an era. I have lived possibly in the greatest one hundred-year period of the world. There has never been a time in history with such ever-increasing opportunities. We are presently saturated with them in all respects, and in recent years the government came with aid and an abundance of cash to most of those who asked for it. Before the government intervened it was necessary to make your own way, which had its benefits. It built character, self-respect and self-learning, and an employee always worked in the best interests of his employer. The wages, whether ten cents per hour or one dollar per hour, made no difference to the job you did or to your efforts or attitudes towards your employer.

There have been such dramatic changes in almost everything from schooling, working, morals, science and inventions. It is only in the last couple of decades that our society has denied youth the opportunity to develop into responsible people. By being given so much from my generation, youth cannot possibly comprehend or understand. If our generation has done anything to destroy values, ambitions or morals, it is because of our denying youth the opportunity to take responsibility in all walks of life. In spite of this, there is a very small percentage that it didn't affect, and they will have to shoulder the future if we are to carry on.

Vision and enterprise

Father began his life in the days of the horses, but he soon became an enthusiast for the automobile. Earlier than most people, he foresaw the brilliant future of the car, and the way it was going to shape the city and suburbs.

Since he had emigrated as a fifteen-year-old boy from England to work on farms and in mills in Ontario, and seek his fortune in the West, my father had sharpened his survival skills in good times and bad. One of those survival skills was the ability to see a trend quite early, and profit by it.

It started when he was still courting my mother, Nellie Brown, another immigrant from Bromley, Kent. He travelled by rail from Ontario to Victoria in 1906, hoping to make enough money to marry Nellie. He went to work with a shovel line, a road gang at one dollar and twenty-five cents a day, six hours after he arrived in Victoria. Canada's population then was ten million and Victoria's was thirty thousand and growing rapidly.

Father worked in a grocery store and a lumber mill, then went to work as a rough carpenter during a land and building boom that escalated real-estate prices and sent carpenter's wages up to an unprecedented four dollars a day.

When his fiancee came to Victoria with her family and went to work as a housemaid, she and Father pooled their savings, bought a lot and built a house on Princess Avenue. They sold the house for three thousand five hundred dollars (nearly double what it had cost) and used the profit for a honeymoon in England. My uncles, Father's brothers Albert and Aleck, came back to Canada with them, and later my grandparents emigrated to Victoria also.

Uncle Albert went to work as a carpenter for Father, helping him build another house on Queens Avenue, while Father worked at the bakery in the day time and on the house evenings and weekends.

In 1911, at the height of Victoria's real-estate boom, Father sold his Queens Avenue house for five thousand five hundred dollars, again at a substantial profit. This was the year my brother Raymond was born.

Father took a job as a wagon driver for Lawrence Goodacre, the butcher. As he trundled along with loads of meat between Goodacre's rural slaughter house, where St. Michael's University School now stands, and the store at the corner of Johnson and Government Streets, he had time to look around and think about the way that wheels and population growth were changing the face of the city.

Semi-rural Maywood district on the outskirts of Victoria (where Mayfair Shopping Centre now stands) was then beginning to build up. It had a post office, a meat market and a grocery store. In 1912 Father built a bakery, hired a baker, and started the first bread delivery in the area by horse and van.

He had timed the enterprise exactly right. It was an instant success. Then he looked beyond the city to distant rural and bush places in Saanich, Colwood and Luxton. Why couldn't he deliver bread to stores in these places by automobile? Experts said it couldn't be done; it wasn't practical. But Father's vision told him otherwise.

He bought a second-hand Ford van and delivered three days a week to stores in outer Saanich, three days a week to Colwood and Luxton. That was the year I was born -- 1913.

Again his timing was right. Rapid delivery of fresh bread was exactly what the stores wanted. Soon Father's Maywood Bakery was producing between seven hundred and one thousand loaves a day.

Then he came to one of those crucial decision points that challenge a new, growing business. Demand was rising rapidly, but costs were rising even faster. Two answers were to cut costs and work harder. He could have started to mechanize and industrialize his bakery, expand the market and produce more bread at lower cost.

But Father never took that next step. Instead, he angled off in another direction, pursuing a different dream. While he had been building and expanding the bakery, he had bought five acres with a house and barn on Stelly's X Road in Keating. Now, instead of putting more effort into the bakery, he planted strawberries at the Keating place, sold the bakery and moved us all into the country.

He said he did it to protect his family from the flu epidemic which reached its height in 1918. The country would be healthier than the city, he thought. He also hoped for big profits from strawberries. In 1920, the year we moved to Keating, strawberries were selling at a record-breaking twenty cents per pound.

Changing down to low gear

Father knew it was time to get out. After the slump in the strawberry market he accepted an offer from a wealthy Englishman, Mr. Geidt, to supervise the purchase of farm lands and manage a farm near Courtenay.

He sold the five-acre Keating farm for five thousand five hundred dollars, which was top price. The buyers were a couple newly retired from China, who had not heard about the disastrous decline in farm income.

We all moved to Courtenay but, within a year, we were back in Victoria. Part of the job in Courtenay was teaching the two, spoiled, young Geidt sons how to farm. After they had crippled the work horses by riding them to exhaustion, had caused a pregnant cow to abort by riding her like a rodeo steer, and had refused to wash their hands at milking time, Father's patience had run out. Once more he knew when it was time to quit.

He paid two thousand dollars for seven acres of forest and bush land and one acre of clear bottom land in Keating, on the right of way of the old Victoria and Sidney railway, nicknamed "The Cordwood Limited", which had ceased running three years earlier.

The railway ties were still in place. Father ripped them up and used some for firewood and some for the foundation of a new barn. We lived in a neighbour's drafty old barn while Father was building us a new house.

Patiently and laboriously he cut down trees, blasted and grubbed out the stumps and planted crops. The railway right of way, graded and gravelled, became

Veyaness Road. This was our address while my brother Raymond and I were growing up.

With a cow, some chickens, a horse, a vegetable garden and slightly improved prices for strawberries, our family was barely surviving. Father wanted to do better than that. He wanted to save some money.

The main transportation link between our rural area and downtown Victoria had been the old Victoria and Sidney Railway (by then defunct). There was a story about a lady that got on in Victoria and, about every fifteen minutes, asked the conductor how long it would be before they got to Sidney. The conductor finally got so tired of her asking and said, " What is your rush?" She said, "I am pregnant and am going to have a baby." The conductor told her she should not have gotten on the train in that condition. She replied, "I wasn't when I got aboard!"

Father had a lively, inquisitive mind. He liked to talk to all kinds of people and find out what they were thinking. He learned that a lot of people were irritated by the sluggish delivery service of the morning Daily Colonist newspaper, which meandered out by mail on the interurban railway, and often arrived a day late.

So Father went to the Colonist in 1924, and proposed to pick up newspapers in bulk by automobile and rush them to carriers in rural Saanich, where no carrier service yet existed. After three months of negotiations, he secured a contract to deliver papers to carriers all the way from Marigold district to Deep Cove.

Many boys wanted to become paper carriers and many people were willing to subscribe. Father and his Model T Ford pick-up linked the product to the market. The time was exactly right for his delivery enterprise.

Every day for thirty-seven years he picked up the papers at four a.m. and delivered them in Saanich. For twenty-one years of that time he also put in a full day's work on the farm, from eight a.m. until late in the evening.

The money from the Colonist gave us a period of relative prosperity during the remaining years of the 1920's, when strawberries went up in price and Father got a good return on the loganberries he sold to the newly-established Growers' Wines Company. So I learned from Father's stories and memoirs.

Father's newspaper income allowed him to protect his small savings during the depression of the 1930's when berry prices went so low that the fruit was barely worth harvesting, and many growers were forced to go on relief at two dollars per day.

But why did Father give up the bakery and move to Keating in the first place? He said he did it to escape the flu and in the hope of making a profit on strawberries. I think his real reasons were different, although he may not have been aware of this himself.

He changed down into low gear to survival mode when the depression started. That was how he had been brought up -- to save his pennies, work hard, live cautiously and wage a lifelong struggle in a difficult world. That was the kind of world in which he felt comfortable. There was a lot to be said for his outlook. It brought us security and peace of mind when he needed those goals. It gave us a step to stand on when we wanted to reach for a bigger share of goods and money.

Keating School

This was where I received my early education and graduated from Grade Eight on 26 July 1927.

The following article about the school was written by my father:

Before the turn of the century, there were three one-room schools in the area now known as Central Saanich. The first was at Mt. Newton X Road, a log cabin built by William Thompson, the first white farmer, in 1855.

In 1862 Captain Stephen Butler emigrated from England and went to work for Alex Thompson, son of William Thompson. The Captain's wife taught eight pupils in this log cabin.

Another was built around 1875 at the corner of Clarke Avenue and the West Road. Robert Sluggett, one of the first settlers in the area now known as Brentwood, taught there more than 100 years ago. Frank Lindsay who attended this school at the turn of the century, still living at Brentwood, remembers his teacher, Miss Ruby Tubman, and says there were eight classes in one room.

Another was on Veyaness Avenue, just north of Stelly's X Road. The land was donated by Fred Turgoose who lived at the corner of Mt. Newton and the East Road. He farmed 100 acres of land and was postmaster when it was known as Turgoose.

Mr. Turgoose was fond of saying anyone could write a letter addressed Turgoose, B.C., and it would find him.

In 1906 district municipality of Saanich was incorporated and in 1913 built the two-room schools, one on Mt. Newton X Road and one on the brow of the hill at Central Saanich and Saanich X Roads at Keating.

In 1920 Mrs. Lila Parberry was appointed principal of the school at Keating. She was a strict disciplinarian, aided by a rubber cane, which was seldom, if ever, used. The fact that it was there was enough.

There were no frills. A basketball hoop in the gravel playground was the only equipment. In this two-room school many successful students were grounded in integrity, fair play and three R's.

The success of the boys between 1920 and 1930, who left school to face a depression and a war, deserves to be mentioned as an example of results obtained by disciplinary teaching without frills and other amenities of the elaborate schools of today.

During the summer holidays the boys picked fruit and in the winter months they helped clear land for further production. Their education was enhanced by this important subject -- Agriculture.

The girls did not have the same opportunity to establish themselves. At school they got high marks and often surpassed the boys in many subjects.

Dorothy Butler won two scholarships and several others earned honor rolls for proficiency. Most married and gave their time to improve the rural welfare of the ward.

Miss McKenzie taught the junior classes and prepared them well for their entrance into the top grade under Mrs. Parberry.

Space will not allow all successful students to be mentioned, who also made a success of their lives and now look back at the little Keating School where they were seasoned to meet the problems of a competitive and complicated world.

Here are some brief biographies of some of the students who, without any financial aid, made a success of their lives and who give Mrs. Parberry credit for her dedicated teaching.

Claude Butler and his brothers built a million-dollar business in gravel, cement and the lumber industry. Caude flew his own aeroplane in a race across the Atlantic and has built a solar-heated house at Brentwood. His wife was Mayor of Central Saanich for several years. It was a sad day when Claude passed away in 1987.

John Young joined the air force and took a course at Cambridge University in England where he earned a doctoral degree in economics. For several years he was economic advisor for the federal government in Ottawa. His valuable services were lost when he died in the prime of life.

Fred Sutton was a top salesman for a paper company and later in real estate. He is now in semi-retirement and living on his five-acre estate with no financial worries.

Murray Bryce, whose mother was a school trustee for the area which was then known as Ward Six, went to Washington to take a position in the World Bank. The B.C. Government has called on him for advice on intricate matters. He is active today in Vancouver in the business of industrial relations.

There were three Chinese boys in the class -- Wong, Chew and Keith. Wong went into the wholesale produce business. He is now living in Sooke and financially well off. Chew operates successfully in Vancouver in the produce business. Keith had a grocery business at Cadboro Bay and is now retired.

Ray and Morris Kersey were both successful in their careers. Ray started work for the provincial government at $40 per month, finishing as Industrial Commissioner for B.C. Morris promoted several business enterprises, including Kersey's Peanut Butter which became well known throughout Canada. He lives on his eight-acre estate at Keating and operated the gift shop at Patricia Bay Airport for 21 years until 1986.

Karl Young held an important position at Boeing Aircraft in Seattle. His mother taught at the one-room school on the corner of the West Road and Clarke Avenue.

Jackie Thompson had a large commercial fishing boat and made himself financially secure. He lives on Martindale Road with acreage on the waterfront.

The Scott-Polson family included 13 children, seven boys and six girls. The boys all worked through the depression and were self-employed in the trucking business and other enterprises.

Ken Stanlake, after completing his education at Victoria High school, saw the need for a meat market at Keating and did a thriving business for several years. Keeping up with the times he installed one of the first refrigeration plants in the ward. Ken served as alderman on the Central Saanich Council and takes an active part in many of the major improvements in the area. Now retired he is busy with his herd of beef cattle on his 25 acres of pastureland at Keating. The dedicated teaching he received at the two-room school at Keating, he says, was an important factor in his success.

George McCarthy quit school at 14 and, not being handicapped with a college education, worked on his dad's farm and others in the area for several years. During the depression he hauled cordwood in the Highland district. One winter, when the snow was three-feet deep, he hauled 1,200 cords, which were sold in Victoria for $3.50 a cord. By 1936 he had saved $500; with it he purchased 16 acres of land on Oldfield Road and planted strawberries. With 40 pickers, in one day he harvested three tons of berries and became one of the largest growers in the area. He sold his acreage and is now living in a new home overlooking Patricia Bay.

Those who stayed on the farm are all on easy street today.

Dixon Holloway still grows strawberries and loganberries and could retire if it were not for the land freeze.

James Wright has prize-winning cattle and horses which are consistent winners at the fairs.

The Mitchell family, Willard (now deceased), Bud, Tom and Ralph are all financially secure. Willard played a big part in forming the Pioneer Society at Saanichton. (His son Maurice is carrying on the tradition.)

In 1960 a reunion of former students was held to pay respects to Mrs. Parberry and Miss McKenzie for their dedicated part in molding their students' lives so efficiently.

Mrs. Parberry, who passed away recently, lived a stone's throw from the little two-room school where she taught. Looking back over the years she said, "There was no vandalism, never a broken window or a violent, unruly student. How proud I am of my pupils."

The passing of the countryside

My boyhood days were spent in the Keating district of the old Ward Six, now the district municipality of Central Saanich, twelve miles from downtown Victoria.

While the farmers were still clearing bush and taking over the Indians' hunting grounds and berry-picking places, a second invasion was already under way. The city had started to invade the countryside. Being born in Victoria in 1913, I lived in the right time and place to see it happen.

Ward Six was an area of about twelve thousand acres, heavily treed and, as mentioned previously, alive with birds. There were thousands of pheasants, quail, blue grouse, willow grouse, blue jays and ducks. The sky was alive with skylarks and, as a boy, I could sit on the ground when dusk was approaching and watch them climb to great heights. They would then make a very fast descent with a sound of its own, never to be forgotten. Apparently they kept their mouths open and gathered insects for food on the way down. The vividly-coloured jays were a pest to the apple growers. They would move from one apple to another, pecking a small hole in each and causing untold damage to the crop.

Today there are no blue jays in the area, and I seldom see one anywhere. There are a few pheasants and quail in some wooded zones, but they are dwindling in numbers each year because of the urban invasion.

There used to be an unwritten law of sportsmanship which required you to flush the bird, let it take wing, before you fired your gun. This was a conservation measure.

With the coming of the motor car, this conservation principle was pushed aside by thousands of city people who had never heard of the sporting code. Hunters in cars toured Ward Six and shot at sitting pheasants and quail from their cars.

When my father told Mr. R.L. Pocock, Country Editor of the Daily Colonist, what was happening, Mr. Pocock was sceptical. He was an ardent sportsman himself; he found it hard to believe what my father said.

To prove his point, my father placed a stuffed pheasant in his fields about forty yards from the roadway and in view of the house. The hunters soon found it. The same scene was enacted again and again -- a car cruising past, an arm and a pointing finger projecting out the car window, followed by a shotgun blast. Some people stopped and got out of the car, crawled through the grass to the fence line, and let the stuffed pheasant have it with both barrels.

Mr. Pocock, now convinced, named the bird "Archibald" and ran an account of these events in the newspaper. Archibald was blown to bits, except for the head. My father then stuck a stiff wire in the head and fastened the wire behind a clump of bracken, so that the head could be seen. Archibald's head was soon destroyed.

Mr. Pocock used to write a weekly sporting story entitled, "Yarns they spin in the old shack". He said he never had the same enthusiasm for writing these stories after the pheasant episode.

Covies of quails twittering on the roadside met the same fate as the pheasants, along with the blue and willow grouse. Often, farmers' chickens were shot and killed, and there were instances of pigs being shot.

The countryside was no longer a place on its own. The automobile had made it part of the city. In some ways we profited by the change. My father had the first contract to pick up bundles of Daily Colonist newspapers with his car in the city, and deliver them to carriers in rural Saanich. The start of carrier service there was Dad's idea; the income was a welcome addition to our family budget. Now there is a large warehouse where the house and fields used to be, and the general area is all commercial properties.

It was in this setting -- farm and bush land linked with a small city that was invading the countryside and taking it over -- where I grew up and learned the lessons that allowed me to achieve a small-scale prosperity. Father was my main teacher. He had the vision and enterprise to see the changes coming, and profited by them in a limited way.

Was the urban invasion worthwhile? Did we gain more than we lost by the passing of the countryside? Such questions have no answer. But, in my mind, I can still hear the songs of the birds.

Living in a grown-up world

My brother and I didn't really live in a separate kids' world. You could say we were apprentice grown-ups right from the start. The same applied to most of the other children we knew. Even our ways of having fun were closely connected to the farm and our parents' lives. When Father killed a pig, we used the bladder for a football. I think we had as much fun with that as kids of a later generation might have had with expensive toys.

Close to our farm and house we also had fifteen acres of bush that Father paid the taxes on for the right to use it. He cleared and cultivated this bush land and grew delicious strawberries on it for many years. Sometimes we went with him and helped. It was strenuous, physical effort but it could be exciting, so I don't know whether you'd call it work or play. Father would dig a hole under a stump and put in a few sticks of dynamite. He'd light the fuse and we'd all run back until it blew. Then we'd take a team of horses and pull it out. It all had to be done by hand.

Mr. Gale, our neighbour, devised a way of pulling stumps. He had a tripod with a big worm gear down the middle and he put a horse on the outside, walking him in a circle to turn the worm gear. He'd have the worm gear chained to the stump and it would pull the stump out. It was an efficient operation.

We had grown-ups around who knew how to solve practical problems. We learned a lot from their example. The same Mr. Gale built a press out of logs to crush apples and make cider. He also made all the horses' equipment, including whipple trees hewn out of birch trees.

Mr. and Mrs. Gale had lost two sons by drowning on the prairies before they moved here, and had one daughter, Pat, who was ten years older than us. She played the piano and gave us some singing lessons at a very early age. When we were at the Gales, Mrs. Gale would give us cookies. My mother would say, "You can't go up to the Gales," but we were always wanting to go because we would get cookies.

My Uncle Aleck, my father's youngest brother, had a milk run, and he had his eye on Pat Gale, but the closest he got to her was talking over the fence. I guess Mr. Gale didn't like Aleck or, for the matter, anyone who had an eye on Pat. One day, when Aleck was talking to Pat trying to make arrangements to meet somewhere, Mr. Gale came out with a shotgun and said, "If I ever see you talking to her again, I'll let you have it." So Uncle Aleck went away from the Gales' place and never went back. Years later, when Uncle Aleck was living in Australia, a man in his eighties with children and grandchildren, and Pat Gale was married with a family, we visited Uncle Aleck and he gave us a message to bring back, "Tell Pat Gale I'm still interested."

The rooster trick

"Twenty-five cents that my rooster can beat yours," my dad said.

"Done," said the owner of the big white bird.

"I'll make the same bet with anyone here," my dad said, looking around the circle of spectators. A dozen more men took up his offer.

You might have asked yourself, "Is he crazy?" How could Dad's little scrawny bird stand up to that giant?

That was what I thought. The bets were placed. Dad and the other farmer let loose their birds and, in thirty seconds, it was all over. Dad's tiny rooster flew at the giant in a whirl of spurs and feathers, and sent it away beaten. The owner of the big bird had to intervene to save its life.

My dad's bird was a fighting cock, bred and trained for duelling. The other bird was an ordinary farmyard rooster. It was no contest. I saw my dad do this trick several times. Of course, he didn't repeat it until he found another bunch of fellows who had not heard of the fighting cock, or didn't believe what they heard.

He had a couple of tricks of strength and skill that he always collected money on. He would bet maybe ten people a dollar each that he could lift a hundred-pound sack of potatoes ten times from the ground to over his head.

There was a strong fellow we knew, a Saanich Indian named Baptiste Paul who became famous as a wrestler under the name of Chief Thunderbird. He used to be a runt until he took a Charles Atlas Course and built himself up lifting the heavy bales on the hay baler. However, he could not do the potato lift more than three times. Father had practised it so much and, if necessary, could lift a hundred pounds from the ground to over his head with extended arms, up to twenty times.

My enemy the gander

A very large gander moved towards me, hissing and bobbing his head. I was seven years old and small for my age. The gander probably was about my own height but, in memory, he seems the size of an ostrich.

"Show him you're not afraid," my father ordered. His word was law. He never beat me or my brother Raymond but we knew we must obey him. So I marched as bravely as possible towards the menacing tower of feathers.

The gander bit me on the stomach and hung on with his beak clamped into my flesh. My father and one or two others grabbed and twisted the gander, and flailed him with sticks and boots until he let go of my belly, scattering blood all around.

I was afraid of geese for some time after that, but I grew out of it. My father's lessons in courage did not always succeed. On the whole, however, we absorbed his guiding ideas -- face the risks, find ways to deal with them, and keep moving forward.

Animal tactics

We always had a spirited horse and a balky cow. When I was a boy I used to wonder why Father brought home these troublesome animals. Later I understood that it was one of his thrifty ways to save money.

The Soldier Settlement Board would let you have a horse for next to nothing, just to get it off their hands. But that horse could pull a plough, and my father nursed it along and induced it to work. Once we had a horse that would always be lying down in a large mud hole and couldn't get up. There was no way he could get out of the hole on his own, so Father would take a large chain, put it around the horse's neck, hitch the other horse to the chain and pull him out. Apparently this does not hurt the horse because this is the correct way to get him up, but it is a little bit difficult to watch the goings-on.

For a very small amount, a neighbour would give us a bad-tempered cow that he had written off as not worth feeding, because nobody could milk her. Father either charmed or bullied her into surrendering -- maybe both. Quite soon she was calmed down. From that time on, we had our own milk.

Scratching for money

Gathering beer bottles was one of the ways I earned money for the family treasury. One time I found a bonanza of bottles at a place on Stelly's X Road, where a drinking man had been burying the evidence of his habit. I mined that beer-bottle Klondike for months. Father would take the bottles into town on a Saturday and sell them to the brewery at twenty-five cents per dozen.

We would haul in discarded stoves and sell them to a junk deaker for a couple of dollars as scrap iron. We would pick mushrooms and sell them to the Empress Hotel at two dollars for quite a small bag. We peeled Barbery Bark off the trees and dried it; this was sold to the National Wholesale Drug Company on lower Yates Street. Not only did we work in the fields on our own place, we also worked for neighbours, picking loganberries and cherries, and doing other jobs.

Harvesting and baling season was our big earning time. They would pay me twenty-five cents an hour. They would be shoving the hay in with forks, and they needed a kid to clamp together the wires on the bales as they came off the baling machine. I got that job sometimes. The baling equipment belonged to the Bates' boys. Like most of the machinery in those days, the old hay balers were cranky. They'd run for three hours and break down for eight.

During baling season, when we were living in our neighbour's floorless barn, my mother somehow would cook up a huge meal of potatoes, vegetables and meat on an old wood and coal stove for the workers. It is amazing the quality of food and pies processed in this fashion, and remember -- no electricity and no water, except in a well outside.

A lot of the workers at baling time were Indians. They were a hard-working bunch. They'd always find some way to make a dollar. Sometimes they'd go down to the sea at Brentwood Bay and bring in a boat load of salmon, which anybody could do in those days, because the salmon were so plentiful. They'd sell the salmon door-to-door at twenty-five cents each.

There was a fellow called Captain Baker who ran a boat rental place at Brentwood. He must have liked kids, because he'd lend any of us kids a boat, and he'd give us a line and an abalone spoon. We'd go out a little way and we'd soon catch four or five fish on a hand line. If you hooked a really big fish, you'd have trouble bringing it into the boat, so you'd pull ashore in Mackenzie Bay and haul in that eighteen or twenty pounder onto the beach. Then you'd take the fish home, or sell it and take the money home.

Once we found two dollars on the road, and we took that home too. When our neighbour Mr. Shearing wanted a horse brought out from town, a distance of twelve miles, he hired my brother Ray to ride it, and he gave Ray twenty-five cents for that job.

Toughing it out

It was four a.m. on a freezing cold Saturday morning. Ray and I were on our way into town with Father in our old Ford pick-up truck with the side curtains, to fetch the bundles of Daily Colonist newspapers which Father delivered on contract to the carriers of Saanich. This was one of his ways of making money.

Just as we got to Elk Lake, the radiator started boiling over. The lake had ice on it, which was unusual in Victoria's mild climate. But somehow the winters always seemed colder when I was a boy. As for Father, he never took any notice of the temperature. He stomped down to the edge of the lake with a lard pail, and began smashing the ice to get water for the radiator.

As he kicked downward with his boot, the ice crumbled more readily than he had expected, and he lost his balance and fell full length into the water. He climbed out dripping wet and showering down splinters of ice as he walked. He filled the radiator and drove to town without saying a word or making a complaint. It never fizzed on him.

I never knew him to have a cold or any kind of illness. He just didn't allow himself to be sick. My father was physically tough, and he saw life as a struggle in which strong people survive and weak people go under. He boxed, and he made my brother and me box with the gloves on. When I was six, the year before my encounter with the angry goose, my brother and I were matched in a bout which my father arranged in Saanich Agricultural Hall. The fight went three rounds. Then the referee held up both our hands.

The arbutus vendor

One mild winter day just before Christmas, I was sitting in the cab of an old flat-bed truck parked on Broad Street in Victoria, waiting for my father, who had gone off on some business errand. I was eight years old. The truck was loaded with arbutus limbs, foliage and red berries, which my father had contracted to deliver to the city market.

The southern coast of British Columbia is the only place in Canada where the broad-leafed evergreen arbutus tree grows. The clusters of red arbutus berries were fresh and bright. They would make good Christmas decorations.

A fellow poked his head in the cab window and asked, "Can I buy some of that?"

I hoisted myself up on the truck's deck and broke off a bunch.

"How much?"

"Twenty-five cents."

When Father came back, he found people lined up waiting to buy arbutus foliage. I had taken in several dollars. The arbutus wasn't mine to sell, but my father gave me a tolerant grin, and I knew that in his eyes I had done the right thing.

I learned early in life that enterprise pays off and earns approval if it succeeds. I also learned that you can bend the rules a little, provided that you don't get too greedy. We delivered most of the arbutus to the market. As for the branches that I had sold, they were never missed.

Memories of the farm

How clearly I remember my boyhood days on my father's fruit farm -- the long green rows of strawberries with their white blossoms dancing in a light breeze in the spring, and the trellised acres of loganberries that landscaped the countryside.

Life was peaceful and orderly. I have carried the memory of that life in my mind ever since. It has helped me feel comfortable through many changes.

Our faithful horse Topsy never had a whip or a cross word used on her. She lived the longest of all the horses that my father brought home. There was no farm job that she could not do efficiently. She cleared land with the aid of a block and tackle. Also she pulled the cultivator between the rows of loganberries and strawberries.

I could ride her bareback to fetch the mail two hundred yards down the road. During a heavy snow she pulled a sleigh to deliver the Daily Colonist. She was really one of the family. When my father was cultivating the land at twelve o'clock noon, she would prick up her ears and give a welcoming neigh when she saw me coming home from school. She knew it was time to quit for lunch. Sometimes, when there was another row or two to finish the job, she could be coaxed to continue. She would put her ears back and walk a little slower to show her disapproval of overtime.

Trellising the loganberry vines was a tedious job. Tying the vines and cutting off the weaklings took many hours. As early in the year as February, Mother would wrap her legs with sacking to protect them from the heavy dew which hung on the vines, and she would start work on the loganberry patch. She took breaks of fifteen to thirty minutes from the loganberries to do the housework.

Mother made jam from the fruits, and butter from our Jersey cow. Father grew all the vegetables. Our free-roaming chickens provided us with brown eggs, which were relished with milk direct from the cow.

I never heard Mother complain about the work. To this day I am amazed at the amount of work that she did faithfully and well.

Waste not, want not, was her motto. With one wood stove, she could whip up a tasty meal in short order for the family, and sometimes, in hay-baling season, for the baling crew as well.

During fruit-picking time she would co-ordinate the work of as many as fifteen or twenty pickers, weighing the fruit, and giving each picker a slip for the amount picked. Each picker was allotted a row, and Mother would inspect the row to see that berries fit to be picked were not left behind. She carried a basket and picked the neglected berries. The poorer pickers overlooked as many berries as they picked.

At eleven-thirty she would run over to the house (a couple of hundred yards), stoke the fire in the stove, put on the vegetables and then run back to the loganberry patch to catch up on the weighing. At twelve noon the pickers were checked off, and Mother was back in the house to prepare lunch.

At five p.m. picking stopped for the day, and Mother was in the house to prepare the evening meal and do the evening housework. I can see her across the years, smiling at us in the warm light that glowed from the stove as she opened it to stoke the fire.

Leftovers for my birthday

We were poor, and we wore darned and mended clothes, but we always had enough to eat. The fields around our place were alive with pheasants. These imported birds found the country so much to their liking that they multiplied by the thousands. We had a cow and chickens, so we always had milk and eggs. But bread sometimes was a problem. Flour or bread cost money.

For a time Mother helped our meagre budget by working in Victoria as a servant in the household of a doctor. I remember one time when I was allowed to invite my friend Ivan Randall to dinner on my birthday. All we were going to have for dinner was boiled eggs, but my mother would provide a treat by bringing home a bag of leftover crusts and raisin bread which the doctor's wife let her have. That night it happened that they kept her working later than usual. When she finally arrived by the "Flying Line" express bus, it was quite late in the evening. But I enjoyed that birthday dinner of eggs and leftover raisin bread as much as any feast with iced cake and candles.

Ducks or dollars

Something was missing from our farmyard when I came home from school one afternoon. There was no sign of the six half-grown ducklings or their mother. I had fed and half-tamed and protected them ever since a pair of wild mallard ducks had hatched their brood from a nest in the brush by the swamp. They were something like friends and something like children, the first creatures that had been mine to look after.

I found my father at work ploughing in the field. "What happened to the ducks?" I asked.

"I sold them for two dollars," he said calmly. "The Chinese pedlar took them away in his basket."

I was going to complain but something in the set of my father's face told me to keep quiet. And yet a question began taking shape in my mind, "How could you get enough money so that you didn't lose the things you really liked?"

I have never forgotten how I felt that day. Every so often, for no special reason, my memory screen brings up pictures of the duck family and my father's resolute face.

The two faces of money

Two ideas about money were planted in our heads from early childhood.

Firstly, you can have fun making it by enterprise and hard work, and secondly, it doesn't fully belong to you; it belongs to the whole family. Since it is not fully your own you spend it with caution, where you think spending will yield the best returns.

My brother Raymond and I were well acquainted with the process of making money, which was often a source of pride and satisfaction. Spending money was a less familiar process, wrapped in mystery and hedged about with safeguards. Father had charge of that department. Until I was nearly fifteen, I never had any money of my own. If Ray and I went out and worked, Father took charge of the money and used it for us to live on.

My brother and I shared two paper routes. It was a year-round source of money -- the morning Daily Colonist and the afternoon Times. I pedalled along a fourteen-mile route every day for many years, and in all those years I never saw a cheque. Father would pick up the cheques at the newspaper offices and add them to the family budget.

We delivered in sunshine, rain or snow, and used the horse in heavy snow, and no one needed to give you a push. It was a job, so you just did it. If you didn't want the job, there was a line-up of boys and some girls waiting in the sidelines. Today it is difficult to get a paper boy. He is paid over one hundred dollars per month to deliver to a very small area of houses. They are mollycoddled by parents, who drive them around the routes, let them sleep in and protect them from society. I was listening to a radio phone-in talk show, and mothers by the dozens were phoning, bitterly complaining how ruthless the paper company was to make their boys responsible for collecting payment for the paper and having to cope with people. The mothers are denying the children the opportunity to learn what life is all about in this world; some customers don't pay, some could care less how many times the paper boy has to come back for his money.

One of my customers on the afternoon route was Butchart Gardens. It was an exciting place, with the rainbow colours of the flowers and the rich people who came there. Butchart's management and employees were really good to the kids. When we delivered the paper, they would often give us food.

Usually I took the food home, the way Father had taught me. But one day the Chinese kitchen man called me in and gave me a paper bag full of oranges and cookies that were left over from a party. On the way home I couldn't resist sitting down and eating an orange. I felt guilty about that for a long time afterwards. My conscience told me I was stealing it from the family and, in a way, I was.

Those two ideas about money -- that you can have fun working out ways to make it, and that money doesn't fully belong to you -- are useful in business.

Ray had a fellow named Mr. Stokes on his paper route. He lived down in the valley. If you rolled and wired the paper, threw it over his fence, his collie dog would come up and get it. When you went to collect at the end of the month, he would always give you twenty-five cents, which was a huge tip. Ray wouldn't go; he was too shy to go because of the twenty-five cents, so he sent me to collect. The money didn't go into any piggy bank; it became part of the family survival fund, like the rest of our earnings.

Learning to play the game

We received our first lessons in dishonesty on those trips in the mornings when we went with Father to town to pick up the papers for delivery. We would go into the White Lunch on Yates Street. Father would have coffee and we would have chocolate pie. It was unbelievable how good that pie tasted.

Well, I don't know whether Father knew the man at the counter or not, but he would pay for the food and, somehow, when we took the tray to a table, we would find the money under the plate. This would have nothing to do with Father; his honesty was unquestionable. However, thinking back, we looked so poor; I presume the attendant was trying to help us out.

We used to go to the hockey game to see Lester Patrick play. Again, I don't know whether Father knew the man at the gate, but I think he did. He would send us ahead, and tell us to go through and say to the man at the gate, "Father is coming." When we were safely inside Father would come alright, but he had just enough money to pay for himself, not for us. So we usually got into the hockey game free of charge.

The Patricks were a Victoria family, and we grew up with Lynn and Muzz. It was odd that many years later in life, when I was returning from eastern Canada after leaving some Chinese that I had escorted from Vancouver as a guard, the Patricks invited me to their training session in Winnipeg for the New York team. I put on some skates and the first player to pass me practically blew me to the ground. That was the extent of my skating.

I sometimes feel that history has not given Lester Patrick quite the fame he deserved. He really was the founder of the National Hockey League, both in Canada and the United States, and left us this legacy; maybe being in the Hall of Fame is sufficient.

Obeying the rules

"Good morning, Miss McKenzie," I called out from my bicycle, as I teetered along early one morning with a satchel full of newspapers.

"Good morning," said the teacher, as she rode her bicycle past me, and I thought she gave me a frosty stare for a moment before she turned her head and hurried towards the school. What had I done wrong? I was only delivering my papers.

When I arrived at school she called me to her desk and asked, " Didn't you forget something this morning?" I tried to look polite, but I didn't know the answer.

"The next time you see me go by," she said stiffly, "remember to tip your hat."

Respect for authority was one of the pillars of the world. It began at home and it continued in the two-room Keating School, where Miss McKenzie was the ruler of Grades One to Four, and Mrs. Parberry was the absolute monarch of Grades Five to Eight.

The school day began with examination of ears, teeth, hair and shoes. If any of these crucial areas showed signs of dirt or neglect, then you were issued a solemn warning, "Don't come to school in that condition tomorrow."

Usually the warning was enough. But there were a few kids whose fathers kept them busy right up to school time with chores on the farm, and they didn't have the time to clean their shoes and change their clothes.

When they came back on the second day with dirty shoes or clothes, the teacher would send them home. If you had a perfect record of attendance and cleanliness for thirty days, which was marked up on the blackboard beside your name, the teacher would present you with a toothbrush or some other prize.

The odd thing was that we were afraid of our teachers, but we weren't really afraid of the police chief, although we had a lot of respect for policemen in general.

The Saanich Police Chief was a sociable drunk. He would ride out to our neighbourhood once a week on his Indian motorcycle to drink the loganberry wine that many growers made. While he was tippling, he invited us to ride his motorcycle. I learned to ride a motorcycle by trial and error during the Chief's visits.

At one place he found the grower away, so he went into the basement and helped himself, and then forgot to turn off the tap. The basement flooded an inch deep with loganberry wine. The angry grower warned him never to enter his premises again.

One of his favourite calling places was Frank Verdier's at the corner of Stelly's and West Saanich Roads. Mr. Verdier was a timber cruiser who had blazed the first trail over the Malahat Mountain for the Island Highway. He always had a supply of hard apple cider, which was the main reason for the Chief's visits.

In later years the Chief would tour the ward in a police car, and, after several hours of drinking and visiting, he was often seen slumped over his steering wheel, passed out.

The Police Commission knew about his heavy drinking, but out of compassion for his wife and family, knowing that he only had a short time to retirement, the commissioners let him finish his term and he received his pension.

How could he get away with such gross neglect of duty? What were the criminals doing when he was swigging wine and sleeping at the wheel? The answer is that there were very few criminals. Crime and vandalism were almost unknown in our district in those far-off times.

So we didn't fear the police chief in the same way that we feared the teachers. But we showed respect for all grown-ups.

Mrs. Parberry, the former teacher of the upper grades who passed away in the 1980's, became a widow and remarried. Her old pupils still call her Mrs. Parberry. She liked to reminisce about school days.

One time she was relaxing at home about six-thirty in the evening, when she suddenly remembered that she had left Ozzie Shearing locked in the broom closet for punishment. He had been in there since three o'clock. She hurried to the school and let him out. He didn't say a word. As far as she knows, it didn't do him any harm.

There was only one fellow from that school that gave any trouble to the community. He ran afoul of the law at quite a young age. He stole a car just after he left school, and then he went to Vancouver and held up a service station. They gave him three months in jail and nine lashes. As kids we were interested in talking to him after he came out of jail, and finding out how he felt. He said, "There's one thing for sure; I'll never go back to jail again." And he never did. He went to work, got married and raised a family, and he's never given any trouble to the community since. It was the lash that calmed him down. He just wouldn't go back and face it again.

Maybe our behaviour is caused by forces outside ourselves, as some of the psychologists now say. But the old-time teachers, parents and police made us behave as if we were responsible for our actions. In some ways, they did us a favour. Instead of using up our energies on rebellion, we could concentrate on work and pleasure.

The system of authority and discipline carried over from school to the work place. When we left school and went to work, nearly all of us practically stood to attention when we saw the boss.

Dinner for three

John Steed was a young English sailor who deserted from the Royal Navy gunboat Columbo, when the ship was visiting British Columbia waters. He found his way to our place, and Dad put him up for three years in exchange for work. He was like another older brother to me. Sometimes we were business partners. Each Christmas we would cut Christmas trees, borrow Jack Brook's truck and sell trees from door to door. John Steed or my brother Ray would drive. We split the money; John kept his share and I gave mine to Father.

Once we knocked on the door of a luxurious house on Craigdarroch Avenue. A butler admitted us and took us to see his employer, who was an elderly lady. She must have taken us for starving orphans. She bought a tree, and invited us to come for dinner the next week. Father said it would be all right to go. On the appointed day we took our seats at a long walnut table, just John and I and the lady of the house. We were scared into silence by the armoury of knives and forks, the gleaming dinner service, and the maid and butler who waited on us.

Which knife, fork and spoon were we supposed to use out of all that array? We were too nervous to enjoy our food, or answer our hostess' gracious attempts at conversation. I can't remember a word that was said, or a single item from the menu of several courses. But the Dickensian scene sticks in my head -- two frightened young fellows at a long table with an old lady who was trying to be kind. When we knocked on the door the following Christmas, there was no answer, so we presumed she had gone to heaven.

John Steed certainly held up the English tradition of hard work for no pay, and was never heard to complain. Equally as well, Father was good to him. Further on in this story I tell of the unusual reunion in England in 1986, after not hearing from John for approximately sixty years.

Jimmie Little's store

The store had everything. Jimmie Little's store closed 31 May 1969 after forty-nine years of business at the corner of Quadra and Pembroke in Victoria. These folks were an institution, and became good friends of mine from my early years on the farm. I would saw and cut truck loads of Christmas trees, and Jimmie would always purchase them from me at a fair price and pay cash.

Jimmie was a very short gentleman and very much overweight, in the three hundred-pound class. The weight never seemed to bother him. He and Mrs. Little were on the run about eighteen hours a day. He told me, when he first started business in a very little store, his motto was -- anything a customer asked for, if he didn't have it, for sure he would have it the next time they asked. The business and store grew into what would be the beginning of our departmental stores.

During his latter years, he found a Chinese doctor in Hawaii who treated him for weight problems. He told me he felt so good that, rather than go all the way to Hawaii to see a doctor, he and Mrs. Little moved to Hawaii. They built a beautiful home on Oahu on the sea. Jimmie told me that now he felt so good, he gave up his Chinese doctor and went on his own diet. He was a fully-trained chef, had worked in Europe and could really put on a dinner.

Both the Littles have passed on now, but they left a large part of history with all the older Victoria folks. No matter if it was Sunday or ten p.m. at night, if you were working on something and needed materials, you just dropped your tools and went over to Jimmie Little's store. He was sure to have what you required.

Farewell to my Buick

One spring day in 1924, a strange contraption laboured uphill from Elk Lake towards the Kersey place on Veyaness Road. It was a 1906 Buick with our horse Topsy harnessed to the front end; Father had loaned Topsy to me to haul the car home.

Until that morning the Buick had been the property of a fellow named Sandy Smith, whose perceptions had been somewhat clouded by a head injury he suffered several years earlier, when Point Ellice Bridge in Victoria collapsed under the weight of a crowded street car, throwing the passengers into the inlet. Sandy Smith had a silver plate in his skull.

Although he had just bought a new chain for his chain-driven vehicle at a cost of eighty-six dollars, he couldn't make it run. When he saw me inspecting the car in his yard at Elk Lake, he impulsively offered to sell it to me for five dollars.

I hustled home to beg my father to provide the horse and release the money from my earnings as a newspaper carrier and bottle collector.

The Buick was a remarkable vehicle. It had a two-cylinder engine in the middle of the frame, a gas tank in the front, and an exhaust system at the back. You started it at the side with a crank which was linked to a huge flywheel. One cylinder had seized up. When we got home, I enlisted the help of my brother and two friends. We borrowed wrenches and pliers, removed the frozen cylinder, and heated it over an outdoor fire to expand the metal, until we could free the moving parts. We lubricated the cylinder, reassembled it and got the car running again.

For several years after that, we ran the car in all the May 24th parades. I wrote twice to the Buick company, offering the car for sale, but some official wrote back to say the company already had several specimens of that model.

That ended another hope of making some quick money. I drove the old Buick chugging and popping into Father's barn and left it stored there.

When I finally did get a full-time job and went to live in Victoria, the car was still in the barn. It stayed for years among the chickens and the bales of hay, and I thought of it as a landmark of my boyhood that would always be there, but nothing is permanent. One day I came back for a visit and the Buick was gone.

"Pete Whitehouse took the entire engine for a pump and the rest of it went to the junk man for aluminum," my father said. "It fetched fifteen dollars."

Nowadays the value of that car as an antique would be many thousands of dollars. But you can't find fault with my father's judgement. He sold it for three times what I paid for it.

Wells....wells....wells

For the benefit of those who have never lived on a farm, it was necessary to have water. Most farm houses had a drain pipe from the roof gutter that ran into a rain barrel. This water was collected and used for general purposes, other than for drinking.

At the age of eight, my job, along with my brother, each morning at six a.m., was to take the wheelbarrow and two ten-gallon cans to our neighbours (a return distance of approximately one and a half miles), and fill the two cans from their well by hand pump. This was precious water and only used for drinking and cooking.

It was to our delight when Father decided to have a well on our own property, which consisted of eight acres and a roughed-in house. For years, tradition has been to use water diviners, and, lo and behold, one turned up to tell us where to dig. The idea is to take a willow tree and cut out a "y" stick, like a sling shot. By holding this with two hands, single end pointing towards your body, and walking around, the stick will start turning and revolving in your hands until it is in a reverse position. This means there is water at that point. An alternative is to take a willow bough, about four or five feet long, and walk around with it in one hand. When you are over water, it will start to beat. If the water is twenty-seven feet deep, it will only beat twenty-seven times, telling you the depth. Our diviner finally found the spot and we set up an operation to dig.

The idea is to dig a round hole and, after it is about five feet deep, set a windlass, with about one hundred and fifty feet of rope around it, over the hole. A windlass is made out of a tree about eight to ten inches in diameter, cut to approximately six feet in length; a crank handle is put in one end and a cradle arrangement is fitted over the hole for the well.

The person doing the digging is let down the hole on the rope; he digs and fills the bucket, which the windlass operator pulls up and empties. This is a long and slow procedure, and the deeper the well, the slower you go down.

The soil at the start is top soil, generally followed by a layer of gravel, but about three to six feet down you usually hit hard pan, which is almost like concrete, and really takes a lot of muscle swinging the pick to get through it. Depending on the type of ground, you might go through ten or twenty feet of hard pan and then reach sand. Digging in the sand is relatively easy and puts a lot more work on the windlass operator at the top of the well, who is going steadily, pulling up the bucket and emptying it.

A great problem after you are about six feet down in the sand layer is that the walls keep caving in, so cribbing of two-by-six lumber is installed around the walls in a square to stop the caving-in. Also a two-by-six wood shelving is laid parallel around the well edge just above where the digger works. This is for protection from the bucket when it swings around as it's being pulled up and hits the walls. Stones and debris get knocked down the well. The idea was to stand under the shelf for protection.

On most farms in the early days the farmer seemed to have had a helper; this man was usually a little backward. He was hired for ten dollars per month, plus room and board, but he never got paid as there was not any money.

One story told is that our neighbour hired a hand on such a basis, and after ten years he went to the farmer and said, "I haven't received any pay. What about it?" The farmer said, "How about if I give you the farm in payment, and I work for you for ten dollars per month?", which was agreed upon. After ten years the farm hand said to the farmer, "I haven't been able to pay you, so how about taking the farm back and I will again work for you?", which they did.

We had such a hired hand, and I was assigned the job of going down the well with him to help put the bucket on the hook. I well remember the experience at nine years of age. Father, operating the windlass, would occasionally drop the bucket while taking it off the hook, and we would hear this coming down eighty feet, hitting the walls of the well. Scared to death, we crouched under our two-by-six shelving until the bucket landed at our feet.

Another near catastrophe happened every fifteen to twenty minutes. The sand would cave in behind the cribbing and cover us to above the knees, scaring us half to death wondering whether it would go right over us. I would holler up to Father, "Let me up; I am hungry."

The first well, one of seven that we dug, was a dry hole at eighty feet. Father decided it was deep enough after the diviner had said twenty-seven feet.

I would judge my father as above-average intelligence, and a good worker and provider; however, how anyone could be so hypnotized by a diviner seems hard for me to believe.

Calling on the diviner when we didn't get water, he re-divined for us, but decided that we had just missed water by about ten feet away from where we had dug. Lo and behold, we set up operations ten feet away and hacked away another eighty-foot depth, taking the dirt from number two well and throwing it into number one well. We were now left with two eighty-foot dry holes and recalled the diviner.

First, he said, "Where is the most convenient place to have a well?" Father picked out a spot and the diviner said, " Just keep digging until you get water." At one hundred and twenty feet there was all kinds of water. This last well, when about half dug, started a humming noise and carried on like a musical interlude until we finished it. I presume it was trying to tell us something.

Waiting for Grandfather

Where was Grandfather? Ever since eight o'clock we had expected to see his battleship-grey beard and thick, unbending figure at the door. Now it was nearly noon, and he still had not arrived.

Mind you, Ray and I weren't scared or worried by his absence. We didn't particularly look forward to his visit. We had only recently met our grandfather, although we knew him second-hand from Father's tales of boyhood in England.

Real-life Grandfather was much like my mental picture of him -- stern, remote, pious, given to long silences alternating with prayers and quotations from the Scripture.

We were more interested in Grandfather's tool box than in Grandfather himself. He was an old-time joiner, or precision carpenter and cabinet-maker. When he built a house, he made all the mouldings and the door sashes. He didn't buy them in a store.

In his tool box he had some specialized planes and some other joiner's tools with strange curves and angles. We had already caught a glimpse of some of them at a house that Grandfather was building. Maybe we would even get a chance to handle some of them, when he brought them out to work on our house.

Father took all kinds of thrifty short cuts to save money and materials, like putting the cardboard page mats from the stereotype room at the Colonist newspaper into the walls for insulation, and using old ties from the abandoned V. & S. Railway for foundation timbers in the house and barn.

But his most serious problem was shortage of time. He was busy clearing land, delivering newspapers and growing fruits and vegetables. So the work on the house went forward slowly, year by year.

Now that Grandfather and Grandmother had come out to Victoria from England, and settled down to live on Carey Road, about eleven miles from where we lived, the house should soon be finished with Grandfather's expert help. He was soon invited out to start work on it.

Father instructed him to stand on the side of the road and flag down the Flying Line bus which operated a couple of times a day. At noon he had not arrived, but soon there he was, tool box in hand, plodding up the path between the rows of strawberries. Grandfather nodded and grunted as he came through the door. He was more than four hours late.

"Did you miss the bus?" my father asked. The Flying Line bus came out from town morning and evening.

"The bus missed me," Grandfather said. "Went by without stopping."

"Did you hold up your hand?"

Grandfather ignored the question. Evidently he had forgotten that you were supposed to flag it down.

"The bus didn't stop, so I walked here," Grandfather said. He didn't seem at all tired from the eleven miles on the road carrying the tool box. He opened the box and began taking out the mysterious tools.

But Father didn't give us a chance to hang around as spectators or helpers. "Time to hoe the strawberries," he said.

Our investigation of Grandfather's tools would have to wait until another day.

Father's incentive system

"Just finish hoeing that row of strawberries," Father said, "and after that I'll drive you over to Elk Lake for a swim."

On a hot day the row seemed to stretch to the horizon, and you thought your back was breaking. But you pictured the fun of splashing in the cool lake, and the job would go faster. That was one of the ways my father got my brother and me to work hard, when we were quite young.

There would often be something to look forward to. He would give us a certain amount of work, and after that we were free to do what we wanted. Sometimes we chose to go off on revenue-producing jaunts, fishing or bottle collecting. Out of two dollar's worth of beer bottles that we had gathered for my father to sell to the brewery on a Saturday, we would get fifteen cents each to go to the Columbia Theatre and see Tom Mix in a western movie. The rest of the money went to living expenses. When we were gathering bottles, we knew the larger part was earmarked for family revenues, the smaller part for the Tom Mix movie.

Future reward was only one side of Father's incentive system. He also put the idea of work and thrift in our heads by example. He didn't seem to need much sleep. He'd be up at four in the morning to fetch the Colonist papers from town, and he didn't go to sleep until ten o'clock at night.

He worked something like a sixteen-hour day and was careful how he spent money, but he made sure we had food, clothes and recreation. He'd go to the auction sales. One time he came back with several pairs of skates of the old clamp-on type. He'd bought the whole lot for fifty cents. A few hundred feet behind our farm house was a large swamp that froze over in the winter, and here we learned to skate.

Mother took Ray and me with her on grocery-bill-paying day. Mr. Colwell, who operated the general store, would give each of us a chocolate bar. We looked forward to that day with excitement. When the day came, we walked along quietly and stood to one side without a word as Mother paid the bill. Then Mr. Colwell would come over and give us a chocolate bar each. We didn't wolf the bar down, but nibbled it slowly, as if we could make the flavour last a month, until the next bill-paying day. This was a great event in our lives, and remembered today as if it was just yesterday.

A slow start for my musical career

I don't know where I got the idea that I could be a musician, but somehow it became my major goal. Maybe it came from listening to the dance bands, or the piano and organ music that accompanied the old silent movies, or maybe I was inspired by the music on the radio. My dad brought home his first radio in 1924, a battery-operated model with three peanut tubes. He and his friends were in the habit of boasting to one another about the far-away stations they could bring in.

"I got Chicago," Dad would say, or "I got Mexico."

"Sure," said our friend Maurice Tubman, who was tired of hearing this. "I stuck my bare bottom out the window and got 'Chilly' ! "

Sometimes you couldn't listen to half a minute of jazz or military marches without crackling and roaring, but we thought it was a marvel. Other times the reception was good.

Maybe it wasn't the radio or the silent-movie music that set off my ambition to play a musical instrument. Maybe I just had an inner drive to charm the world and earn people's applause. Applause didn't come easily in our house. You were supposed to be hard-working and enterprising; you didn't get praised for it.

My dad saw that I was in earnest about music, so he actually came up with a dollar a week for ukelele lessons with the music teacher, Lillian Atwell.

I turned out to be a slow pupil. After a few weeks of discordant strumming, the teacher and I abandoned one another. But I didn't give up my ambition. Maybe this wasn't the right instrument for me, or the right time to learn it. So I made up my mind that I was going to try again.

"If you really want to learn music, I'll lend you an E-flat saxophone," said my friend Oscar McComb, who played in the Empress Hotel orchestra and taught music. "You can take it home and try it out for a few weeks."

I was music-struck and hung around the musicians at concerts, dances, and jazz sessions, gulping in the melodies as if talent could be inhaled and absorbed into the blood. Oscar took pity on me. He saw that I would have no peace of mind until I made a serious effort to become a musician.

True enough, my ukelele lessons six years earlier had been a failure, but maybe I had been designed by nature to play a reed instrument, rather than strings. Oscar took some time to run through some sheet music, and show me how to relate the marks on the paper to sounds, rhythms and finger positions.

Some days later I carried the silvery instrument out to the farm and into our barn, and blew a volley of notes that sent the chickens fluttering away in terror for their lives. Wow! I could make music! Once again I floated into a day-dream of musical achievement. Then I woke up to the real audience of panic-stricken hens, kicking up the dust as they rushed back and forth trying to escape, and my father came in holding his hands over his ears.

I began to realize that my fingers were not going where I wanted them to go. Did that matter? My father and the hens appeared to dislike my playing, but what did they know about music?

A week later I gave the saxophone back to its owner. Maybe this wasn't my instrument either. Maybe I should be trying to sing or play the piano. I was still determined to learn to be a musician. It was my ambition, even higher than the pursuit of money.

    As a matter of fact, why couldn't I do both at the same time -- pursue money and play music? I made up my mind to look for a way to do this.

My favourite composers are: *George Gershwin*
                                       Irving Berlin
                                       George M. Cohen
                                       Cole Porter
                                       Richard Rogers
                                       Michael Feinstein

"Love Letters in the Sand" was the song which stayed longest in the number one position on the song charts.

"Embraceable You" was the song most used in movies.

Morris' Memories of the Farm

As I sit alone on a quiet day,
I think of the days now far away --
I see the peaceful countryside
With lines of berries side by side;
Their blossoms white, danced in the breeze,
And birds made nests in the rustling trees.

Topsy, our horse, was a faithful friend,
Her long life happy until its end.
She cleared the land and pulled the hoe,
Carefully treading row by row.
I'd ride her bareback to fetch the mail;
In heavy snow she would never fail.

My mother worked hard, night and day,
But never a grumble did she say.
She picked the fruit and made the jam.
She taught me how to be a man.
Waste not and want not -- her motto firm,
And from her ways I'd watch and learn.

So, as I grew in height and age,
My memories now fill many a page.
No possessions, wealth or praise
Could take the place of bygone days --
My life with loved ones, free from harm,
A happy lad down on the farm.

- Ursula Thomas (2001)

Part 2: **_1930 -1940_**

Fast times	*Work is fast*
	Play is fast
Run, run all week	*Food is fast*
	Cars go faster
Rebirth of competition	*Boats go faster*
	Aeroplanes go faster
Respectability of wealth	*Never sit down* - Author Unknown

A job with a future

I went to Victoria High School for six months, but it didn't seem to be teaching me anything useful or pointing me towards a job with a future, so I left school at the age of fifteen and joined the labour force.

I started working for an electrician named Harry Rowntree at fifteen cents an hour. He had all the contracts to wire the houses and other buildings at Cordova Bay, where B.C. Electric was extending power lines. My job was to go up into the attic and bore holes all day with a sort of triangular brace and bit. Clay-type tubes went through the holes for Number 14 wire to pass through. It was as hot as an oven in those attics.

I didn't learn much about electrical work, but it was a job. After a time I quit for the same reason I had quit high school; there didn't seem to be much future in it. I made sure of other employment before quitting.

I secured a job at the newly-opened Victoria Cold Storage plant on Dallas Road. Living at Keating twelve miles from Victoria, with no transportation, meant I had to move to the city to a boarding house on Vancouver Street at forty dollars per month and do my own wash.

My title was Shipping Clerk (at sixty dollars per month), which entailed keeping records of ice and fish sold. I am still looking for a fish boat that gave me one of my first lessons in dishonesty. The captain purchased one dollar's worth of crushed ice; I reached down from the dock and was handed a folded one dollar bill. When I returned to the shipping office, I realized it was only one half of a bill. For this I could only get fifity cents from the bank, and so I put my own dollar in the company cash box.

The manager of the plant was an American refrigeration expert by the name of Mr. H. Brown, about five feet four, maybe one hundred and sixty pounds, always immaculately dressed, always wore a turned-up fedora, and smoked a small cigar. He would come over from the offices, which were about one hundred yards from the plant, to see that the fish were properly glazed and frozen. If you saw him coming, you worked at top speed.

You were scared to death of your boss in those days. I think Mr. Brown always treated me right, but I just naturally was nervous of the big boss. If you lost your job how would you survive? There was no such thing as unemployment insurance, and nobody ever heard of welfare. So you showed respect, and kept a good hold on your job until you had another one. I was still looking for a job with a future, and this did not seem to be it.

My Uncle Tom Brown was friendly with Mr. Jim Bennell, the Property Manager for the Royal Trust Company, and he arranged a job for me with the Royal Trust at fifty dollars a month. This was a big cut in pay, but I thought it was worth taking the loss because the Royal Trust seemed to offer a better future. By this I mean the chance for advancement, more money, more freedom and responsibility. At least I think that was what I had in mind. It's hard to get a good look at your younger self in the rear-view mirror!

Fish business

The Royal Trust job was not immediately available. I had to wait for it. Meanwhile, I could have continued working for the Victoria Cold Storage, but a Mr. Lawrie gave me a chance to go into business. When you are young, people sometimes take a liking to you and give you a chance to get started. I was lucky this way.

Mr. Lawrie and his partner Mr. Clifford had five boats under charter, hauling fish from Prince Rupert and selling it in Victoria and Seattle. He said to me, "While you are waiting for the Royal Trust job, would you like to join our company as a partner?" I readily accepted.

"You can try it out for a few months. I'll give you sixty dollars per month." It's good to know there are such generous people in the world. I had no money and nothing to offer except my labour.

The fish boats were loaded on the west coast of Vancouver Island and carried about sixty thousand pounds of fresh fish each. When they arrived in Victoria, I would go down to the dock and see that the fish were unloaded by winch, weighed in and stored in the Victoria Cold Storage locker. I would sell to the local retail fish stores and fish and chip shops, like the famous Old British Fish and Chip Shop. They would purchase up to a ton of ling cod at one time. Any fish we did not sell in Victoria went to Seattle to be sold.

Mr. Lawrie's partner, George Clifford, was a prairie man who also ran the Amphion Hall; this was a dance hall located above the Standard Furniture Store on Yates Street in Victoria. It had an all-girl orchestra and admission cost about twenty-five cents, but Mr. Clifford was always there to welcome me for no charge. That was how the system worked in those days, and that is how it still works. Friends give special treatment to one another.

If the bottom hadn't dropped out of the economy, it would have been a nice business to continue in. But hard times became even harder, and the end was in sight for the fish business. When the Royal Trust job came up, I parted company on good terms with Mr. Lawrie, with a lot of respect for him.

My boss at the Royal Trust Company, Mr. James Bennell, was a tremendous influence on my future development. I owe him a great deal for his direction and for treating me as a fully-qualified adult, learning the facts of life. One might call it luck to have such an educator, something that could not be learned from books or school.

Moonlight painting

"Here are the three bids for that Campbell Building job," I told my boss Mr. Bennell, as I laid the papers respectfully on his desk.

"You don't have to ask me," said the Royal Trust Property Manager. "Go ahead and arrange the contract for the lowest bidder, the way you've been doing."

"Thank you, Mr. Bennell," I said, "but I know a way it can be done for ten dollars cheaper."

"You're going to get four bids this time?"

"Yes, sir. The fourth bid is my own bid. I can get a helper and do the job myself at night."

Jim Bennell looked up from the desk like a driver switching his headlights to high beam. He gazed at me in silence for two or three seconds. "I'll look at the figures and let you know," he said.

He had already done me a big favour. When I went to work for the Royal Trust at the age of seventeen, he gave me a load of responsibility, and left me to carry it. He assigned me to arrange the contracts for repair and painting jobs, on buildings that the Royal Trust was looking after. Nobody ever suggested that I was too young or not wise enough, so I just went ahead. But now I had taken a bolder step. Maybe he would fire me for being so insolent.

There was only one problem with my situation. I didn't have enough money to live on. My salary was fifty dollars a month, with fifteen-dollars-a-month car allowance, and I was paying forty dollars for room and board on Vancouver Street. There was no way I could live on ten dollars per month. My salary remained at fifty dollars a month for the whole time I worked for the Royal Trust.

This may seem strange in the 1980's, when the guiding slogan is 'more for me, now'. During the depression years 1931 to 1934, when I worked for the Royal Trust, there was no thought of asking for a raise, the way it seems to happen in comic strips and cartoon panels, where junior employees gather courage to put their demands to the boss. There was no individual or collective bargaining for money in our office.

You didn't dare ask for a raise. You were glad enough to have a job. The pay for workers like me was fifty dollars if you were single, one hundred and twenty-five dollars if you were married. The rules were rigid. If you were hired as a single man, you couldn't get married. You had a choice, marriage or your job. You couldn't have both.

You had plenty of encouragement to take your job seriously. It came from your fellow workers, eager to please the management as they were, hard working and careful to show an image of devotion to duty. The office opened at nine o'clock and closed at five, but you wouldn't walk in at five minutes to nine. Nobody did. I got there at eight or eight-fifteen to start work. You didn't just go out the door at five o'clock and say good night. I might be there until five-thirty or quarter to six. You'd lose your job if you left at five. They had no use for clock watchers.

You spent a lot of your spare time improving yourself and making sure your employer got good value for his money. On many evenings we took courses in book-keeping and typing at Sprott Shaw Business School. It was insurance against losing your job, and an investment in the hope of a better job some day.

It was in this setting that I had dared to offer my services as a painting contractor for my own employer. But the gamble paid off.

"All right, you can do the painting job," Jim Bennell said. Characteristically, he never questioned my ability to get the job done properly, and on time.

I recruited my friend John Steed to help me, and we worked through the night painting several floors of the Campbell Building on the corner of Fort and Douglas Streets in Victoria, to make the place ready for occupancy by the U.S. Immigration. I had rented out these offices for the Royal Trust and negotiated with Mr. Monaghan, the U.S. boss. Now I was painting them as well.

John Steed and I did a number of other painting contracts for the Royal Trust. If you can get an inside track, why not use it? John Steed was now working for my old employer, Victoria Cold Storage. I had helped him to get a job there. John travelled to work from Father's farm on a motorcycle that he had bought for a bargain price.

The moonlight-painting contracts solved my cost of living problem, and provided enough money to buy a car for one hundred and fifty dollars. Then Mr. Bennell gave me an allowance of fifteen dollars a month to run the car on company business.

The key to it all was trust. If Mr. Bennell had treated me like a teen-aged Bob Cratchit, and had stood watching every move while I did minor clerical chores, I would have done no more than routine things. But he gave me a lot to do, and he trusted me to do it properly. Also, he trusted me to earn my own rewards through enterprise. My father had done the same. I have them to thank for building my confidence.

Turning hard times to advantage

Although I survived by off-duty painting, and even bought a car, there still wasn't much money to spare for having fun. The budget was tight. I found other ways of turning hard times to advantage, There were all kinds of empty stores, apartments and buildings. Mr. Bennell would let me live free of charge in one of the Royal Trust's apartments until it was rented.

My first free shelter was a furnished apartment in the Adelphi Building, where the main Victoria Post Office now stands on Government Street. The apartment was on the market for thirty dollars a month, but, for the time being, there were no takers. As each apartment was rented, I moved to another. Most of them were free of charge, but for one apartment in the Hibben-Bone Building I had to pay nine dollars a month. I cut the expenses in half by sharing with Bill Sylvester. I'll tell you more about Bill later. He worked at night in a U-Drive business and I worked during the day, so we shared the apartment quite harmoniously.

Johnny Garrard was my room-mate for two years. He had the up-bringing and manner of a young gentleman in the English style. His father was rich and owned a big yacht, or so I heard, but he had married again and had a new young family. Most of his attention went to the new family. Johnny was having a hard time, just as I was.

Johnny was the manager of the Columbia Theatre on Government Street. The pay for this fine-sounding executive job was fifty dollars per month, the same as mine. However, there were extra privileges. The theatre used to offer cups, saucers and plates as prizes to customers. Johnny brought home eight or ten dinner sets. In bachelor tradition, we piled the dirty dishes in the bathtub until the tub was full. Then we would invite a couple of girls to come and visit us, and trick them into helping us wash the dishes.

Entertainment was provided by a red-faced fellow from Famous Players (I think he was an ex-alcoholic) who used to come around with posters advertising the shows. In return for putting the poster in the window of an empty store that was for rent, he would give us a couple of tickets to first-class visiting performances, like Harry Lauder, Showboat, Billy Burke -- the best seats in the house as these were hard to sell. I received Mr. Bennell's permission to put up these posters and collect and use the tickets.

When the show left town, I would tear down the posters and destroy them; never once did I realize that, if I had kept them until now, their value would be in the thousands of dollars. Watching an auction on TV, I saw a similar old poster sell for seven thousand dollars.

In this way we lived quite well on very little money during the Great Depression.

But my dream of a job with a future had now taken a definite shape. I wanted to work in my own business. Thanks to that arrangement with my employer, which was a profitable exchange for both parties, I had been able to move sideways and duck out from under the restrictions on my income. I began to feel that I could go further and become my own boss, and this opportunity was getting closer.

Feeling ashamed on Cormorant Street

Mrs. Beatrice Hudson, who ran a house of prostitution on Cormorant Street, swept into the Royal Trust offices one day to see the big boss, Mr. Winslow.

We spoke Mr. Winslow's name with awe, but his high office meant nothing to Mrs. Hudson. She was a favoured client. The roof was leaking in the Olive Rooms, the ancient building that she rented through the Royal Trust from an owner who lived in Seattle. She wanted it fixed right away, and we had better carry out her wishes. If she moved out, who else was going to rent that rickety fire trap?

"Morris," the big boss said, "will you take Mrs. Hudson in your car and see what the trouble is?"

Well, you may not believe this, but I was afraid to be seen going in there. As I escorted Mrs. Hudson from the car and through her front door, I caught myself scrunching down and away from her, and turning my face to the wall, as if I hoped to become invisible.

Mrs. Hudson was a tall, slender woman, about four inches taller than I. I thought of her as quite old, but she must have been in her middle forties. I'm sure she sensed my panic. She looked down at me with quiet amusement. I slunk past all the girls who were lying around sleeping, and looked at the roof.

Then I had the problem of getting out. I stood behind the door for maybe five minutes, trying to focus a searchlight of intuition through the woodwork and along the street, to see if anybody I knew was in sight. Finally I got the nerve to poke my head part way through the doorway and squinted in both directions. Then I ran to the car and drove back to the office.

I had to fetch a fellow called Harry Dean from Pacific Sheet Metal to fix the roof, and that meant several more trips in and out of the building on Cormorant Street. On each occasion I made these furtive duck-and-run entrances and exits, like an actor in a low-grade movie.

The world has changed a lot since then.

Dr. Clem Davies

I met Dr. Davies in my Royal Trust days. I suppose he was one of the first "Billy Grahams" of America. He had an outstanding following, both on radio and in personal appearances. He was actually one of the first to use such mediums for religion in Canada and the United States, and finally was associated with the famous Aimee Semple McPherson in Los Angeles.

It was my early impression of religion. As a youth I had attended many different services of most religions; these were usually set up on a vacant lot in a large tent, with seats and a pulpit. I do not know how educational this attendance was, but it certainly gave me an insight into religion; I feel it did nothing to "save" me, but it was entertaining.

I had rented office space on Fort Street to Dr. Davies, also an apartment in the October Mansions. Like most church leaders of that time, his collections were not always enough to pay the rent, consequently he became pretty familiar to me with my monthly calls to collect the rent.

In my many dealings with Dr. Davies, he seemed always to have an entourage with him, a man who worked in a stationery store and a blue-eyed girl, who later became an evangelist in Los Angeles. Sometimes my contact with him was almost daily, trying to collect some rent.

I had endeavoured to see if he would move to some other apartment not handled by the Royal Trust, and he finally advised me he was moving. Previous to this, one of the Royal Trust clients had a very large house in Oak Bay, and she listed it for rent with us. It was most difficult to rent, and almost weekly she would phone me to come to the office and almost demand to know why we hadn't found a tenant. One day she phoned and informed us that she would like us to look after the collection of rent. She had rented it herself to Dr. Davies. My troubles were not over.

Chinese guards in 1931 train travel

Most young people of my era could only fantasize or dream about travel. The average wage was fifty dollars per month; out of this, it was necessary to pay forty dollars per month for room and board. The severe tragedy of being unemployed was constantly on your mind and it was necessary to bank as much as possible of the ten dollars left over, in case it was needed for an emergency. There was no such thing as welfare and hand-outs; if you wanted to eat, you had to be working. Unless you were born with a legacy, it was almost impossible to do much travelling, so I devised a method. When my annual holidays from my employer came up, I found a way of seeing a large part of Canada for just a few dollars.

During the First World War thousands of Chinese landed at William Head, Vancouver Island, B.C., on their way to labour battalions in France. Old records show that eighty-eight thousand went through the station and across Canada by train on the way to France, and forty thousand passed through on the way back home after the war. The rest returned by other routes. In all, there were about three hundred thousand overseas. Not all of them fought; they were behind the lines digging trenches, making ammunition dumps and latrines, constructing light railways and doing other jobs. Nearly all were from northern China and every one wore a pigtail. British interests in Hong Kong sent them over, and affluent Chinese in the community put up money at this end.

This migration continued for some years. In 1930, at seventeen years of age working at the Royal Trust Company, I became acquainted with Mr. Earl, Manager of the C.N. Railway in Victoria, at the time these Chinese were arriving in Victoria by ship. He advised me they were "in bond" and the railway company required guards to escort them across Canada for world destinations. I was hired by the railway to take them from Victoria to Vancouver, then from Vancouver to Montreal, P.Q., where I would be met by an official of the C.N.R. who would take charge of my group. My boss, Mr. Jim Bennell of the Royal Trust, kindly agreed to let me take my holidays to coincide with their arrival.

I was given passports, pictures and documents, etc., of the group entrusted to me, also one young fellow as my assistant, and was instructed to make sure no one jumped off the train. My assistant and I shared the twenty-four hour shift. I don't think any of the Chinese in my care ever thought of leaving the train. They were mostly in their middle years and not one spoke any English.

Both the Chinese and their guards were crowded into what was known as a Colonist Car. These cars had wooden slotted seats, bunks that pulled down at night, a coal stove at one end, and oil lamps for lighting. The lavatory was a seat built over a hole in the floor of the railway car and, when sitting in use, you could watch the rail ties go by. The cars were built in 1880, and it would be difficult to exaggerate the terrible filth, dirt and soot.

I would leave Victoria in a white shirt, tie and suit and, for the entire five-day trip east, would sit on a bench-type seat, never going to bed. There was no point in changing my clothes; I just stayed in them. Upon arrival in Montreal, it was necessary to dispose of the shirt; no laundry could clean it. I paid seventy-five cents for a new shirt, plus the cost of cleaning the suit.

The Chinese carried their own food, mostly dried fish, which they cooked en route; it smelled to high heaven! They also entrusted small sums of Canadian money to me to make additional food purchases at various train stops.

The terms of my agreement with the railway gave me a return ticket but no expenses and no berth. I would leave Victoria with approximately ten dollars; this was usually gone by the time I left Montreal for home. In those days there were lunch counters at most stations; as guards, we ate sandwiches and pie, with milk. Being out of cash, I, along with other experienced guards, figured out a way to neglect paying for our food. Sitting at the counter nibbling on the last small fragment of a ham sandwich, I would wait to hear the sound of the conductor's cry -- "All aboard", then wait about thirty seconds for good measure. As the steam locomotive puffed and whistled, I rushed out the door, ran along the platform and swung aboard the last-but-one car of the Transcontinental Train, as it moved along at ten miles per hour towards Vancouver. I had just given my famous impersonation of a man catching the train at the last minute and forgetting to pay for his meal! I am sure that I have taken care of those few, unpaid lunches many times over in the past years. I cannot recommend this practice; however, in some circumstances, mild hunger seems to surpass honesty.

The railway also had Silk Trains which crossed Canada travelling at much higher speeds. The guards on these trains carried loaded revolvers, but I was too young for this.

My paths crossed with many young fellows who were doing the same thing, but I never heard from them again. This experience was part of our education in growing up, and gave us a much broader sense of Canada.

The mystery of Joe Wilson

On one return trip from Montreal to Victoria, I took my brother Ray with me as an assistant. The rail tickets we were given as guards allowed us to sit in the Parlour Car on our return home, but didn't include food or anything else.

When the train stopped in Saskatoon to pick up passengers, one of the people boarding was dressed in slacks and open shirt; he had no coat and no luggage, except for a club bag. He was so drunk he needed assistance at all times. He sat with us, telling us his name was Joe Wilson and that he was head chef at the Multinomah Hotel in Portland, Oregon. His club bag was literally packed with loose American paper money of all denominations and liquor. It would be hard to estimate the amount of cash; it had to be several thousands of dollars. We wondered if he was a bank robber. He lavished all those on board with sandwiches, chocolate bars, etc., purchased from the newsboy's stand on the train coach.

On arrival in Vancouver he asked Ray and me to accompany him to his reserved hotel; the next day he was leaving for Portland by bus. He paid all our bills. The next morning I left for Victoria but Ray stayed on and took him to the bus, and then returned to check out of the hotel. Before Ray could check out, Joe returned as they would not let him into the U.S.A. in such a drunk condition. The next morning Ray again took him to the bus, and this time he didn't return.

Some months later I was driving to Portland, Oregon, and decided to look Joe up. I went to the front desk of the Multnomah Hotel and asked for him. No one had ever heard of Joe Wilson; this included one person who had worked at the hotel for over thirty years. Joe had also given me his residential address; this was in a very exclusive neighbourhood but the street number he gave me turned out to be between two houses. Joe's house didn't exist.

One secret of success - Be useful to a millionaire!

"Get me a room at the Strathcona Hotel," said the voice on the telephone, "but I won't pay more than six dollars a week."

The caller was P.J. Hobson of Ventura, California, whom I knew as one of the wealthiest men in the United States. He got Bill Sylvester and me to do his organizing and errand-running when he came north to look after his Victoria properties. The usual price of the economy-style hotel room that he wanted was nine dollars per week. I would have to haggle with the hotel management to get the price down.

I told them that this rich man was eccentric about saving small amounts of money, but if they humoured him they might put themselves in line for a big reward later on. I don't know if they believed that. I wouldn't have believed it. But they always let me have the room for six dollars. You might wonder why a thrifty American millionaire would want help from a junior employee of a trust company. The answer is simple enough. Mr. Hobson had an eye for an under-valued property, and the under-valued property was me. I would do a lot of work scheming for very little money. Mr. Hobson knew a bargain when he saw one. That was how he became rich.

A few days later I was ushering P.J. Hobson into the Poodle Dog Restaurant on Government Street. He was a lean-faced, somewhat shabby man.

"I guess you know Bill Morrow has gone on a drunk and disappeared again," Mr. Hobson said, as he laid down his battered hat, inherited from his late brother, on the seat beside him.

Yes, I knew. In a small city like Victoria, you heard about these things. Bill Morrow was one of P.J. Hobson's tenants. He ran a U-Drive business on Douglas Street and a garage diagonally opposite the Empress Hotel. Mr. Morrow was a successful entrepreneur, but he had a weakness for liquor. Now that he had disappeared, the business had no proprietor and Mr. Hobson had no tenant. Actually Mr. Hobson really owned the business for moneys advanced.

"Bill Sylvester is taking over the U-Drive," Mr. Hobson said. "I want you to take over the garage."

"But I'm working for the Royal Trust," I said. In the 1930's you didn't jump out of a job unless you had a safe place to land.

"How much are you making?" Mr. Hobson asked.

"Fifty dollars a month."

"I'll guarantee you fifty dollars a month for a year. If you don't make that much through your share of the profits, I'll pay it to you. Put that in writing," P.J. Hobson said, "and I'll sign it."

After winning an argument with the restaurant cashier about whether he owed twenty cents or twenty-five cents, the visiting millionaire went back to his six-dollar room, leaving me to walk to my apartment to ponder my next move.

Within the hour I was back in the Poodle Dog with Norman Whittaker, the lawyer. He drew up the agreement guaranteeing me fifty dollars per month. We sat in the cafe until four o'clock in the morning drawing up the document. Mr. Whittaker (who later became Chief Justice of British Columbia) charged me fifteen dollars for the job. I was just twenty-one years old.

Mr. Hobson also made a deal with Bill Sylvester to take over the U-Drive for nothing down and twenty per cent interest until he had the business paid for. In Bill's case he made another condition. Part of the contract was that Bill had to rent a house that P.J. Hobson owned, for fifteen dollars per month rent. It was situated where the Medical Arts Building is now, on Cook Street.

In a small sleepy city like Victoria, at the depth of the depression, a downtown business location was no prize. Half the stores in town were empty. But the booming automobile and gas market was beginning to take off, despite the bad times. After I had been pumping gas for three months and doing quite well -- better than the fifty dollar minimum -- a man offered me two thousand dollars for the business. That was a large sum for 1934. I accepted, taking Mr. Hobson off the hook for his fifty dollars per month.

I am sorry to say that I forgot the principles of thrift that I had learned on the Keating farm, and went on a spending spree.

Bill Sylvester went on to build the U-Drive into a large business, and became the owner of a regional airline. He married the daughter of Bill Morrow, who had opened an opportunity for both of us by dropping out.

Hard work may help make you rich, but by itself it isn't enough. You need the knack or good fortune to be in the right place at the right time. It also helps if you can gain the trust of a millionaire and be useful to him.

If these opportunities don't occur by natural good luck, you have to look for ways to make them happen.

Starting small

A young fellow named Foster sold me his Carmelcrisp business at 644 Fort Street, Victoria, for five hundred dollars, which was all the money I had left. (644 was also the number of the house where I was born on Speed Avenue.)

Carmelcrisp was made by mixing popcorn with brown sugar, glucose and butter. At twelve cents a bag, it was good value for the customer's money. However, people were buying less of everything due to the depression. Foster was an intelligent and hard-working operator, but he hadn't been able to meet his expenses in the small town of Penticton, and after he moved to Victoria, his sales were still so low that he couldn't pay his eighty-five dollars a month rent. So he sold out.

It was hard to find a way to make the business profitable. The solution, I decided, was to increase the revenues by putting in a coffee shop.

It's hard to understand how it was to be a new businessman in the 1930's unless you went through it. You didn't have a dime, and you owed everybody. You got by on hard work, credit and friendship. One of these alone wasn't enough; you needed all three. I got in touch with a Jewish fellow from the Ideal Showcase Company in Vancouver, and I said I wanted to put in four stools and a little bit of a counter. That was one hundred and some odd dollars which I didn't have.

He said, "You don't have to pay me anything now. I'll put it all in and you can pay me five dollars a month." This was agreed upon by both of us.

He'd come over once a month and get his five dollars. Sometimes he'd take a pound of butter and some cigars with him, and deduct it from his account.

Well, I got the counter paid for, but the number of customers kept growing, and the place wasn't big enough. So I kept expanding it again and again, and each time added another five or six stools on the same paying basis from the Ideal Showcase Company.

Looking back on what happened, that was a big mistake. I should have stayed the same size for a longer time. A lot of small businesses die because they grow beyond their strength too rapidly.

Benny Chan

Our Chinese chef never could get to work on time. He always overslept. I would open the restaurant at seven, and the place would fill up with customers, and I'm cashier, cook and waiter, and Benny hasn't turned up.

When he finally wandered in, I'm ready to hit him on the head with a saucepan. I'd have twenty stacks of hotcakes on, there's a guy waiting at the cash register to pay; I'm back in the kitchen; and there is another guy who hasn't been waited on and he looks impatient.

So I invented a way to wake Benny in the mornings. His father owned the Panama Cafe on Government Street. The family lived upstairs in the three-storey building in which the cafe was located. In behind it there was an alley.

Well, we put a cowbell on Benny's bed. We hooked it to a rope and ran the rope out the window to the ground. On my way to work at a quarter to seven, I'd drive by, stop and pull this bell rope, and go on to the restaurant. By the time I had the coffee made, Benny was there. I did this for a long time.

We had some fun, but I now owed fifteen hundred dollars in back rent, and that was serious. I always found Mr. Fletcher, the landlord, to be a real gentleman, but I was scared of him.

He used his son Walter as the enforcer. I tried to keep out of sight when Walter came in, but one morning he loomed up in the doorway before I had time to hide, and I was trapped.

"I can let you have fifty dollars on account next Monday," I volunteered.

"That's what you always say, but I've had enough of it," he said ominously. "You'll have to come in and talk to my father."

This was the event I had feared for a long time, a confrontation with Mr. Fletcher in the back of the music store. I felt like a condemned man going to his execution. However, looking at him across his desk, he did have a depth of reality and actually was, down deep, kind and considerate. Some extensions and adjustments by him always carried us over the financial troubles.

Stan Laver from Courtenay applied for work in the coffee shop. He was very young, full of vitality, clean and dependable. About this time we were making ice cream with a machine in the Fort Street window and selling it to passers-by. We also made ice-cream sundaes in a funnel-shaped plastic container. We would put a tablespoon of strawberries, chocolate or cherries in the bottom and fill it with ice cream. When it was frozen hard, it could be turned upside-down, to make a beautiful ice-cream sundae selling for ten cents.

We tried to teach Stan to ride a motorcycle and sidecar, and on his first lesson along Dallas Road, he flipped it and landed in the Animal Shelter. From then on Stan washed dishes, and we had another rider establish our delivery service. People would phone in for a few sundaes or a ten-cent sandwich to be delivered. We didn't have a minimum charge and I didn't realize that we couldn't economically deliver six sundaes, a total of sixty cents, all over town, but we did it until I discovered it was a losing proposition.

The dishes Stan washed were manufactured in England and were badged, meaning they had "Morris Kersey Coffee Shop" imprinted on them. Their cost was very little; I believe a cup and saucer landed in Victoria for about fifteen cents. They were shipped in a square, lattice-type box made out of small tree limbs, hickory or something. Apparently, when the dishes were put into the containers in England, straw was placed between each plate and cup; then it was watered down. On arrival in Victoria, there would be enough straw to fill a container four times the size of the original, even after the dishes were removed. Quite a few live rats made a free trip across the Atlantic and scattered down Fort Street. It was an ingenious way to ship and seldom was there any damage.

Stan nearly broke his neck washing these dishes, and when he joined the navy, he told his cousin Cliff that he could see them in his sleep. Cliff joined the army and went to Aldershot, England. One night, in a canteen, he really thought he had passed out of this world -- having coffee and doughnuts served on "Morris Kersey" dishes; he couldn't believe it. It appears that, during World War II, the dish manufacturers sent all their samples to be used in canteens in England.

Growing bigger and poorer

"Do you think we can get all the work done in time to open the restaurant on Monday morning?" I asked anxiously.

"Sure, we'll do it," said Ed Pridham, the plumber, who had just arrived with his tools and a helper.

Thanks to friends and creditors, I kept making the restaurant bigger. This was the latest and most ambitious of a series of expansions. The restaurant had just closed for the weekend at eleven-thirty p.m. on a Friday, and had to open Monday morning. Most of the work crew, carpenters, electricians and labourers had already arrived. Others came on Saturday.

My earlier expansions had been easier to manage. At first I had been able to add stools and counter space by pushing back a partition and invading the storage space. The phone company people, who came in every morning for coffee, would unhook the phone for me, and hook it up again in a new location further back; all this work for just a cup of coffee.

The man at Ideal Showcase let me have the fixtures on credit. Just as I had the debt nearly paid off, I felt the need to expand again to deal with the increased volume of business.

At one of the earlier expansions, when I was increasing the size of the restaurant to twenty-five stools, I needed to lay linoleum and make some other changes. The Victoria Police Chief, Mr. McLennan, and his Deputy, Mr. Caldwell, thought I was somebody special; I don't know why. They came over at eleven-thirty p.m. closing time and helped me lay the linoleum. That's how small a town it was, and that was how helpful they were.

The volume of business continued to grow. This time I was going to increase the size of the restaurant more than double. We had a bake shop next to us. There was a hollow tile wall between the two stores. Mr. Fletcher, who owned Fletcher's music store, owned the building. For once I was doing fairly well -- slightly better than breaking even, I mean. So I had the rent paid up.

The bakery shop moved out, and Mr. Fletcher agreed to rent me the store next door. I arranged with Ideal Showcase to buy a sixty-seat, horseshoe-style counter on the usual terms, nothing down and pay when I could.

Most of the workmen stayed until Monday morning, until we had pulled the wall out, put in the counter, stools and some tables, laid the linoleum, and put in the electrical work and the plumbing. On Monday morning I was open for business. Ed Pridham was right -- we had done it.

I was young, and I didn't know what credit was. The business wasn't bad, but there was no way I could make all those payments. But none of the creditors ever bothered me. They said, "If you can't pay the twenty dollars, pay five dollars." And so the restaurant precariously kept going. It was running on borrowed time.

Our personnel policy

When I opened the bigger restaurant, I worked from seven a.m. until eleven-thirty p.m. Sometimes I got away in the afternoon, but it was a regular sixteen-hour day, seven days a week.

I never made any more money than the girls, probably less. We started a girl on a forty-eight hour week at nine dollars per week. After three months she went to twelve dollars, and after six months she got fourteen dollars. This was the government minimum wage.

Each customer was valuable. You couldn't afford to drive away even one person by bad service. So, if you hired a new girl, you wouldn't just turn her loose on the next customer who sat down. You'd get some friendly, patient fellow who came in every day for lunch, and you'd say, " Is it all right if this new girl serves you?"

So the customer helped to get her broken in, and if she did fairly well, she stayed.

If a girl came into work and her fingernails weren't clean, her hair wasn't combed, her smock wasn't clean, and her shoes were dirty, you'd be ruthless. You'd say, "I'm sorry; we don't need you any more."

There were plenty more people waiting to be hired.

You couldn't do that today. There are unions and laws that make it harder to fire employees. So you have to manage differently. But the principle is still the same. In a small, struggling enterprise, every employee has to give full value for the money.

I didn't know much about business in the restaurant days, but I learned that lesson quite early.

Running for the ham

"I'll take the ham and potato salad," the customer said. Our finances were such that we did not have any ham on hand, so I took ten cents from the till, slipped out the back door without the customer seeing me, and ran across the street to Charlie Dale's delicatessen shop.

"A couple of slices of ham, please, Charlie," I said, and sprinted back to the kitchen to make up the salad, and presented it to the customer for fifteen cents, without the customer ever knowing the predicament I was in.

The take was so small and the prices were so low that we never had the cash to store up sufficient food. The butcher and the baker wanted their money right away. They weren't like my friends the workmen who helped me expand the restaurant, and told me to pay when I could. The butcher and the baker weren't going to give credit.

We were going further into debt every month. I lived in fear that Mr. Fletcher, the landlord, might close me down for back rent.

I don't know whether I was making any profit or not. My bookkeeping was hazy. I hadn't yet learned that careful record-keeping can mean the difference between surviving and going broke. My restaurant was a self-taught course in how not to run a business.

Some people actually complained that our prices were too high, although we shaved them down as far as we could. In 1933 we'd give a breakfast special -- choice of prunes or applesauce, one poached egg with toast and coffee -- for fifteen cents. For luncheon we would offer soup, a grilled cheese sandwich and coffee for fifteen cents. The club special sandwich was twenty cents. Genuine hamburger with chili sauce cost ten cents.

Looking back on those days, I marvel at what an amateur, shoestring operation the restaurant was, and in these times of slick merchandising, I marvel at the innocent gimmicks we employed to draw customers to our place, and to keep the staff producing.

It was a different world, before television and before the days of transistor radios and radios in every car. People were keenly interested in the news, and a newspaper office was a glamorous place.

The people from the Victoria Times used to come into the restaurant for coffee. We were located just along the street from the Times office at the corner of Fort and Broad. The Times always had a news bulletin in the window, hand-lettered on a sheet of newsprint. I asked one of the Times men if they would run off a duplicate every time they printed a news bulletin.

From then on they brought me news bulletins, which I displayed in a row on the wall. It made the restaurant seem like an exciting place, in that simple time before television and between the wars.

A swim in the ebb tide

"Do you want to buy a house?" the real-estate man asked as he paid for his coffee.

Just because I owned a restaurant, some people thought I must have money. That was a big mistake.

"We have a house down on Earl Street," he persisted. "It belongs to a man called Mr. Trench in Duncan. He has foreclosed on the two-thousand-five-hundred-dollar mortgage he held, and he wants to sell."

The year was 1935, I owed everybody, and I was struggling to stay alive. But the restaurant was still small; I hadn't yet made the mistake of over-expanding and plunging deeper into debt.

"Anything I'd pay you for that house would be so little, it wouldn't do you much good," I said.

"Take a look at it and let me know."

It was a nice solid house in the Fairfield district, although the front steps had caved in, the rest of the house needed paint and repairs, and the garden was a jungle.

"If I can pay you fifty dollars a month, I'll pay twelve hundred dollars for it," I told the real-estate man. "That's clear title with the mortgage written off."

"Will you pay the sixty-dollar commission?" he wanted to know.

"Yes, that would be all right, if I can pay it on time, along with the payments for the house." It turned out that the owner would be happy to take twelve hundred dollars.

Then I went to work and put in new steps with wrought-iron railings, which I made at the Victoria Night School; the material cost about ten dollars. I painted the stucco, sanded the oak floors, painted the house throughout, and cleaned up the garden as best I could.

A friend of mine used to work for Esso, and he had a lot of old oil burners. For twenty-five dollars he gave me an oil burner and a forty-five-gallon drum for a storage tank. We ran a line through the basement window, and we had automatic oil.

I kept the house for a year and a half, and then I sold it to a Mr. King for three thousand five hundred dollars. At the peak of real-estate prices in the 1980's, the same house was worth about eighty-five thousand dollars. If you're careful and lucky, you can make a profit in a depression. You have to find which way the tide is running, and swim with it. But I didn't keep my small estate profit for long. The restaurant and my living expenses swallowed it up.

Showboat

The Carmelcrisp at 644 Fort Street, where the candied popcorn was made, was located on a sort of pathway, which went down Fort Street and along Government Street, ending in front of the Parliament Buildings. Thousands of local people would walk this path one night a week in the summer when, I believe, the Chamber of Commerce set up a floating stage for a vaudeville and musical night. This was a well-organized show with a lot of professional-type entertainers, and no one was going to miss it. After the show ended these people would walk back to the town, passing my shop.

There were no stop-and-go lights or parking meters in Victoria, and just the odd streetcar. In order to capture this weekly trade, I would set up a three-piece band on the sidewalk in front of the store. The band members were all part of our staff. A counter with an ample supply of Carmelcrisp was also outside. We entertained the passers-by, and most of them parted with twelve cents for a bag of our product. This became a profitable night. It also brought the tourists our way.

Victoria was a small city, and I would estimate that I knew by name ninety per cent of our lunch trade. They came from all walks of life, many from the Parliament Buildings. If someone died or didn't turn up for lunch, they were missed like one of the family.

In the summertime, most of the out-of-town teachers going to summer school in Victoria would eat with us daily. One day, when I was away in Vancouver at the exhibition selling candy, the cashier in the restaurant couldn't get the safe open. I don't know why we locked it, as it hardly ever had any money in it. However, when she was trying to open it, one of the school teachers came to her assistance. She did not want to tell him the combination, so gave a wrong one. After half an hour he gave up and suggested it needed a repairman.

The silent borrower

I never meant to get into the small-loans business. It just happened, because of a real gentleman, Tommy Bowden, the bookmaker, who came into the restaurant six or eight times a day.

You have to know something about Tommy to understand how it worked. He was one of two or three big bookmakers in Victoria -- a practice which was illegal. Another was Jack Freer. The original bookie in Victoria was Tommy's brother-in-law Babe Harris, a big fellow with horn-rimmed glasses who operated the Boilermakers' Hall in Esquimalt. You might call them wholesalers. They handled all the bets on horse races from a number of small bookmakers who didn't have enough money to finance the bets. Even though bookmaking was against the law, these same bookmakers had to file income-tax forms in Canada. I understand this is also a must for ladies of the night. Even if it was illegal, the government required its share.

Tommy Bowden ran his business from a headquarters which shifted at intervals from one downtown location to another. His locations were quite well known -- there were wires and telephones bringing in bets and race results -- but, to my knowledge, he was never raided by police, nor gave any trouble.

He undoubtedly made a lot of money from gambling, but was always broke, because he gambled on his own private account. I don't think he watched the odds as carefully when he took a flyer as he did when working as a bookie.

One of the small-fry bookies was Tommy's brother Jerry, who rented the front window of my restaurant as a news-stand. Tommy frequently came to see Jerry and to have a coffee.

Sometimes Tommy would come in for coffee and leave me a plain envelope, which he handed over in silence. The envelope never played any part in the conversation. After he left, I would open it and read, "Dear Morris, I need fifty dollars for three days, and I'll give you back seventy-five dollars, if you can help me out."

So I left the fifty dollars in an envelope for him when he called back later in the day. Not a word was exchanged about the loan. It was always paid back in a few days as promised. This was extra income, and many loans of different amounts were made through the year, and always paid up as arranged.

In sickness and in health

As with many young people in my day, when you needed to see the doctor, it was necessary to be practically flat out before you made a visit. There was no free medicine or anything else. Everyone paid cash long before the monthly payment plan came into being. It was sometimes pretty difficult to have the money, so visits to doctors and dentists were rare.

I had a ruptured appendix and was rushed onto the operating table. Dr. George Hall, one of the Victoria Gentleman Surgeons, did the work, and some months later I received a bill for one hundred and fifty dollars. The shock of this nearly put me back in hospital; however, it could not be neglected. I phoned Dr. Hall's house and arranged to see him. When he saw how impossible it was for me to pay one hundred and fifty dollars, he said, " How much do you want to pay?" Well, I could get fifty dollars within a month. He said that would be OK for full payment. When I went in to pay the nurse, she said the doctor had told her he had collected already and I didn't owe anything; I had been taken off their accounts. However, I did give her the fifty dollars, with many thanks.

During the oncoming years the Kinsmen Club I belonged to had several doctors as members. Rates were always reasonable enough so that you could pay, or there was no charge.

Many single young doctors would come into the restaurant for our early fifteen-cent breakfast, and, usually, one of them would look all of us over in exchange for a coffee. However, one morning, when Dr. L. Ptak was having breakfast, our cashier, a hefty woman, took off her shoes and stockings, and went over to his breakfast table and said, "What can I do for this toe?" He later told me he would rather have coffee in a little different atmosphere.

Originally two girls and I worked in the restaurant kitchen. However, it had become necessary to make a change, so I decided to put in a Chinese crew. Most restaurants in Victoria employed Chinese as they were very competent. I had a Chinese friend, Benny Chan, whose father owned the Panama Cafe on Government Street. I asked him if he would come to work for me. At that time he had never worked anywhere other than in their own restaurant, and his father's permission was necessary for him to change jobs. After getting the required authorization, Benny hired a complete crew of three, including himself. I paid Benny only one wage and, out of that, he paid the others. I do not know how much. However, I do know that the very old Chinese dish-washer, who worked forty-eight hours a week, received only six dollars per week.

The day that Benny was to take over I had arranged for him to come alone at seven-thirty in the morning, made an urn of coffee, and one girl had arrived to serve customers. When Benny arrived, he was extremely nervous. Never having worked outside the family restaurant before, he had dressed up and was wearing a leather jacket while I showed him around the kitchen. All of a sudden, when he had his back to me, he fainted, falling backwards onto me. I was then as nervous as he was. The waitress rushed over with cold water and got us all operating. This was my introduction to a Chinese kitchen. Benny proved to be a terrific asset, and is a friend to this day. He has now retired.

The restaurant opened at seven a.m. daily and closed at eleven-thirty p.m. This made a long day but, in your youth, you can get accustomed to most things. On the night shift we made bread rolls by hand. A good baker can roll with both hands; I could use only one.

Wing, Benny's assistant, was an expert. He had worked in Fan Tan Alley and ran a Keno game at night. One day he burned his arm severely. This meant he could only roll buns with one hand. Now, with two of us one-handed, we were going home later every night. The burn didn't heal, so, when Dr. Ptak came for breakfast one morning, I asked him if I could bring Wing to his office across the street for a check-up. I took him in through the back door of the doctor's office. Almost immediately Dr. Ptak said Wing had gonorrhea. Never had I been so shaken up in my life; here I had been working side-by-side with Wing all these days. I asked for an immediate check-up for myself. The doctor just laughed and said it would be impossible to catch anything. I came out in the clear, and he treated the cook.

I phoned Dr. Felton, the city health doctor, and asked what I should do. He suggested that there were many cooks like Wing working in restaurants, and just keep him on; there could be no harm. You can be assured, I immediately hired a new night chef.

After selling the peanut-butter business, I considered, in a very small way, going into medicine. Dr. Jack Stenstrom, a long-time friend and member of the Victoria Kinsmen Club, suggested I come to the operating room at St. Joseph's

Hospital and have a first-hand look at surgery. By this time, Jack had become one of our leading surgeons. He had experimented for a long time on dogs, and was unpopular for doing so. However, when he picked up a stray dog, it was treated exactly as a human, and there was no suffering or ill-treatment. Through this experimentation, he became pretty expert at treating "blue babies" of that era.

The first operation I attended was on an older gentleman with a broken hip. I went directly to the operating area, scrubbed down, put on a gown and all the paraphenalia, and sat on a stool next to the operating table with three or four doctors. First, Jack and his assistants drove four or five twelve-inch steel-type needles into where they thought the fracture was located. The hip was then x-rayed, and the surgeon could see where to insert the scalpel. After the area was opened up, with very little blood or mess, a rack of tools, which included screwdrivers, hammers, and brace and bit, was wheeled in, and a steel plate was attached to the bone with stainless screws. The patient was up the next day and had a pretty good fix.

I also observed operations on two other nights, one operation for an appendix and another for a bowel obstruction. To me it was most interesting, but, without much schooling, it would take many years to complete and finish up with a degree. At my age I would have been almost too old to practise when I graduated, and I really wasn't that interested.

The following article appeared in the Medical Records of Thoracic Surgery:

Dr. Jack Stenstrom fits the pioneer mould of the early settlers in Fort Victoria perhaps better than the more gentle culture of the modern city. A McGill graduate in 1938, he began postgraduate training in graduate surgery at the Montreal General Hospital, but this programme was interrupted by army service in World War II (1942-1946) with No.24 Canadian General Hospital in England, and with No.6 Casualty Clearing Station in Northwest Europe. Following the war, he spent much of the time between 1946 and 1948 in Baltimore (Johns Hopkins Hospital), where his special interests in thoracic surgery were aroused by the opportunity to work with Dr. William Reinhoff and, also, by his association with Drs. Alfred Blalock, Henry Harkins, and Rudolph Bing (who was already exploring the potential of cardiac catheterization). During this period, he assisted in cardiac operations and worked in the dog laboratory learning the techniques of cardiac and vascular surgery.

When he established a practice in Victoria in 1948 -- as a Fellow of the Royal College of Physicians and Surgeons of Canada, a Fellow of the Royal College of Surgeons of Edinburgh, and Diplomate of the American Board of Surgery -- he was the first in the community to conduct a purely consultative practice dealing only with referred patients, although combining his thoracic surgical interests with a primary general surgical orientation. At no time in his career did the proportion of thoracic surgical referrals exceed 10 to 15 per cent of the total volume of referred case material. However, the indoctrination he had received in investigative medicine was to stimulate a life-long interest in animal research, which had great impact on the development of cardiac and vascular surgery on the West Coast.

For 12 years, he conducted intensive studies on myocardial revascularization in dogs, with supporting grants from the Medical Division, National Research Council. Between 1947 and 1960, these were the only grants made by the NRC to investigators working in non-university centres. Actually, it was his application of the Blalock procedure which first brought him an international reputation.

Without the benefit of education, I assisted the veterinarian in delivering a colt at three a.m. A close friend, Bob Shanks of Indian Motorcycle fame as a franchise dealer, got tired of motorbikes and went "horsey". His life became nothing but horses, some of which he raced; they did fairly well at the track. Bob would breed a mare every year and sell the offspring. One particular mare, who had foaled a couple of fast horses, was really getting too old to have youngsters. The last time she was having a foal I was visiting Bob, and the mare-in-delivery laid down, which I understand is almost fatal. Bob called a vet. My job was to pull on two chrome chains, which had been fastened to the colt before it was born, as the mare could not discharge him. Eventually, after many hours and with my arms aching, the colt arrived, but did not live very long, even after feeding from a child's milk bottle. I learned an interesting thing in medicine that night. The mare had to be destroyed, and all the vet did was take liquid Epsom salts and inject it into the main neck vein. My job was to rub the horse's eyes until it didn't blink any more. In a short time, without pain or struggle, it had gone to "Horse Heaven".

I suppose I am about average but, when I list all my illnesses from birth to present day, it makes me wonder how much more I could have achieved if not detoured and delayed by health problems. It has been said that the world's greatest bore is a fellow who you ask how he is and he tells you. At any rate, if you are young enough, the following gives you some idea of what the future holds.

I started early life with all the usual ailments -- the odd cold, flu, mumps, whooping cough and most other kids' diseases. Going to hospital is another story -- first a broken wrist, then German measles, removal of tonsils, removal of ruptured appendix, peptic ulcer and stomach surgery. I was in a cast due to back problems, which seems to befall most people. Tearing my Achilles tendon put me on crutches and, later on, on crutches once again due to a knee injury from sliding into third base. This was followed by gall-bladder removal, prostate problems, repair to an elbow injured during bowling and now shingles. It all adds up to many months of lost income. I feel it would be better when we are born to remove all these parts that seem unnecessary.

I do feel that, in some way, doctors of medicine are interferring with our Maker, and have no right to try to improve upon the human body. If we were all left alone, there would be fewer of us around depending on others to care for us.

Money sticks to my feet

My Carmelcrisp machine saved me from financial collapse. I took it to the exhibitions in Victoria and Vancouver for one week in each place, and returned with enough money to pay most of the urgent bills and the back rent.

My father came with me on the Vancouver trip. We saved money by checking into a skid-row hotel at six dollars a week for a room with bath. It was a rough place, frequented by loggers and prostitutes out on a spree. One morning, when we came down in the elevator, there was a dead man riding with us. I think he rode up and down a number of times before anybody removed him.

We went into the Pure Foods Building at the Pacific National Exhibition and built our own stand. A cigarette company decorated it with crepe paper, in return for advertising.

The popcorn machinery consisted of two pieces of equipment. One piece was a chrome metal upright designed like a TV set but, instead of a TV screen, there was a gas-fired revolving drum that would pop the corn. After popping, the corn was stored in a large container. Before popping this special type of imported corn, we laid it out on trays and soaked it overnight, whenever possible. It not only popped better, with less waste, but it was also a better product. The other piece of equipment was a large aluminium pot, about twenty-gallon capacity, which sat on a gas-fired frame. Into this we put three-quarters of a pound of butter, two pounds of brown sugar and a large two-fisted handful of glucose from a four-hundred-and-fifty-pound barrel. When this sweet goo was cooked, we would add a bunch of popcorn and mix it all together with a long, oak-hardwood paddle; the mixture would come out as Carmelcrisp. My father had the job of mixing the candy, and to the day he left us, he had a large callus in the palm of his hand from stirring the pot with that oak paddle. He never got any pay, and he was always kidding that he was going to sue for the damage to his hand.

We'd go over to the Pure Foods Building about nine o'clock in the morning, and started making and storing candy for a ten a.m. opening. There was no way of eating during working hours because we were too busy. We'd take several quarts of milk with us and put them behind the booth, hoping we'd get a break long enough to take in some nourishment, but we seldom ever did. We worked without stopping until ten o'clock at night.

When we started in the morning, we'd have a reserve supply of candy made and stored under the counter of our booth. We worked on the scarcity principle. We needed to have five or six people standing in front of the booth, so that onlookers could see that there were people waiting. If we ever did get everybody served so that there was nobody waiting, we wouldn't do any business after that. I guess the people thought the stuff wasn't worth having if there was nobody lined up, so we always kept a line waiting. We'd make them wait until we had a freshly-cooked batch ready.

It would finally build up to fifty or more people waiting, and then we'd start using up the reserves from under the counter. We poured the candy out so fast that we didn't have time to stow away the money in a cash drawer. We tossed the coins into a couple of twenty-five-pound jam tins. Some of them missed the target. With the glucose on the floor making everything sticky, we'd find twenty-five or fifty-cent pieces stuck to our shoes at the end of the day. But the secret of success was to have a crowd in front of our stand at all times.

It wasn't quite such a desperate hustle at the Victoria Fair. We served sandwiches at the stand, and I usually had time to eat.

There were some interesting characters who worked the fairs. There was one gentleman who drove up in style in a fancy Cord car, and he always arrived late, after everybody else had set up. He would rent quite a large piece of ground outdoors at the Victoria Fair, and he'd go right to the back of it and set up a little stand that looked like an outhouse. On the counter of this little stand he would put a Bunsen burner and a package of Aspirin.

Each night he'd move out about two hundred feet and walk backwards to the stand, planting lighted candles every few paces in the grass, with a dollar bill folded under each candle. Everybody would be standing around wondering what was going on. Finally he'd back up into his little stand and start his spiel.

"Do you know what killed Jean Harlow (the movie star)?" he'd ask, and then he'd answer his own question.

"Aspirin," he said, spitting it out like a dirty word. He'd light up his Bunsen burner, and he'd put an Aspirin tablet in a teaspoon, and hold it over the burner. It would go black, and he'd say, "That's just coal tar. It filled her kidneys, and that's what killed Jean Harlow."

Then he would talk about breakfast cereals, and how they were supposed to be bad for your health.

And he'd say, "Do you know what I'd do if I was an undertaker? I'd get a frying pan, and I'd frame it. I'd hang it at the bottom of the stairs, and every morning, when I got to the bottom of the stairs, I'd stand and bow and say, ' There's my meal ticket.' " By this he meant fried foods were so harmful that they killed people.

At last you'd find out what he was selling -- herbs. Little packets of herbs at one dollar each. They were supposed to keep you healthy and strong. He'd sell herbs like crazy after he got all these hundreds of people standing around. He was the original herb and natural-foods man. But the same fellow would come over to our stand and eat anything we had. When the fair was over, he'd drive away in his fancy Cord car with a sack of money.

Getting into music by the side door

"Sold to Morris Kersey for one hundred and fifty-four dollars," the auctioneer said, and I became owner of a Presto twin-recording machine, which made seventy-eight and thirty-three-and-a-third r.p.m. discs.

A man who worked for the old radio station CFCT Victoria (now defunct), had imported the machine from the United States, and failed to pay Customs duty. Customs officials seized the apparatus and put it up for auction. It was worth about five hundred dollars brand-new. I estimated its used value on the Victoria market at one hundred and fifty dollars, and I accepted the advice of a friend in the Customs service who said, "Never bid an even amount of money. A lot of people do that. You can get ahead of them by adding one dollar or one dollar and twenty-five cents." He turned out to be right. At least two other people bid exactly one hundred and fifty dollars.

I had a reason for buying the machine. The years were going by, and my musical career still had not started. During my long hours of drudgery in the restaurant, I still day-dreamed about becoming a musician. Now I had a chance to enter the world of music through a side door, by recording what other people played and sang. I pirated music and talk from the broadcasts of other radio stations, put it on phonograph records, and sold the records to Station CFCT. There was nobody enforcing copyright laws in such a remote city as Victoria. I never thought about such a thing.

I also began making three-minute records for amateur singers and musicians. Tape recorders were yet to be designed; I had the field to myself. I didn't make much money though. I would pay one dollar and thirty cents for a blank acetate record and on this, with the equipment which had an expensive diamond needle, I would record the entertainer. The finished product was three dollars and thirty cents per record, which didn't leave much profit. In some cases, I would put the one hundred and ten pounds of equipment in an old car and drive to a home, set up and make the record. One night I packed this equipment alone to the very top of the Catholic Church on Blanshard Street to record the organist and a solo singer.

During the war I made dozens of records for families with the father overseas. All the family would send a message on the record, and there were many sad nights listening to the love that was sent on that record.

I had a bonanza -- an East Indian girl phoned me and arranged to make about one hundred copies of records from India that couldn't be purchased. With my musical ear, I couldn't tell one side from the other and, after delivering this large quantity, the lady phoned to tell me I had recorded the same song on both sides of the record, forgetting to turn it over.

I did many weddings and certainly listened to a variety of quality and non-quality folks. Usually I would record all the church services and special events, especially at the Centennial Church on Gorge Road, and sold them to the participants.

One of my clients was a Mrs. Jamieson, of the Jamieson tea and coffee merchant family. She was a music teacher, and she would set up recording appointments for her pupils.

In the meantime, I worked hard to keep the restaurant afloat, and I recorded other people's music and songs on weekends and any night I could get away.

Jury Duty

Another educational help was being called for jury duty for the Spring and Fall Assizes. This paid four dollars per day; however it was difficult to both run a business and be on a jury. There was no way of not serving.

There were about fifty people summoned for jury duty, and, after lining up and passing through questioning by the defence and prosecution legal representatives, you could be challenged and possibly let off. To be challenged, you would have to be prejudiced or political or have some other bias.

I usually had to serve as one of the twelve jurors. As I was quite young, the lawyers would feel I had no fixed ideas one way or the other, and could be more easily swayed into a decision.

I served on many juries. One involved a bank robbery in Victoria West; the robber was found guilty.

One case, where I was not on the jury, involved a car driver who ran over and killed a Chinese man in the middle of Government Street. For years, Chinese vegetable peddlers would take two-wheeled carts door to door selling merchandise. The cart had two shafts where you could harness a horse to pull it, but, if you didn't have a horse, you pulled it yourself. This accident happened close to Christmas; it was just after dusk and the Chinese man was crossing the middle of Government Street with his head down. The lawyer for the Chinese man proved without a doubt that the car driver had been stopped by the police two hours before the accident, and told to go home because he was under the influence. He did not go home, and said at the time of the accident that he never took another drink from the time the police stopped him two hours earlier. This was my first lesson in so-called justice. The drunk driver was found not guilty. In my mind, I felt it was because the old Chinese man was considered not too important, and the jury made a poor decision.

Tax auditor

My Uncle Ephram liked a few drinks and betting on the horse races. He ran a wood door-frame manufacturing company, and had quite some experiences with the federal-government sales-tax auditors.

Being in the restaurant business in my early days, I also made ice cream for sale. This manufacturing process necessitated paying the federal government a twelve per cent sales tax each month.

I received a notice of audit, so I phoned Uncle Eph for information. I had nothing to hide from an audit, as everything was one hundred per cent as far as my operation and bookkeeping. However, an audit is a lot of work for a businessman and very time consuming.

The government auditor, who I presume is now deceased, was a war veteran with a gimpy leg and an excess liking for booze. Eph said all I had to do was to keep the auditor supplied with booze for three days, and after the celebration my audit would be finished. Eph, as mentioned, liked a few drinks and would do the town with the auditor, but I didn't have the constitution or the wish to burn up the town.

However, the day the auditor arrived, I supplied one twenty-six ounce bottle of rye. This was followed by two more, at which time I discovered this was a great mistake. He didn't carry out an audit but hung around my back office for those days, and was completely in the way.

The next year, when audit time came, I refused the continual request for booze, and found it easier to let him carry out his audit in the regular way.

Tuxedo

The early 1930's was a time of major social events, such as Firemen's Balls,

Police Balls and other functions. Usually one could get gratis tickets for the events, as most businesses felt it necessary to purchase several tickets, which they gave to their employees and others.

To attend one of these dances, it was mandatory to wear formal dress, or you would not be admitted. A new tuxedo was out of the question as it would cost me a couple of month's salary to purchase.

While working at the Royal Trust, I had rented a vacant store to a gentleman who ran a costume rental business. After discussing my predicament with him, he sold me a complete, used tuxedo for nine dollars. At the time I purchased this tuxedo I didn't realize the costume shop purchased a lot of deceased people's clothing, and that was the reason for such a bargain.

I wore this tuxedo for three years. At this time I could afford to buy a new double-breasted one, so I sold the used tux to a friend for twelve dollars. I couldn't argue with the profit, as inflation in the few years I owned it went from nine to twelve dollars.

Someone to care

The greatest gift that is given to man
Is someone to care.
When you hope and dream, when you work and plan,
Someone to care.
Someone to care when the day is long.
Someone to care when you're glad with song.
When the world goes right, when the world goes wrong,
Someone to care.

For never a loss will seem such a loss,
With someone to care.
And never a cross will seem such a cross,
With someone to care.
Someone to care when your heart is sad.
Someone to care when your heart is glad.
Those who have won are the ones who had
Someone to care.

We feel not cold if we have but this,
Someone to care.
We shall have our joy though the goal we miss,
With someone to care.
What is the good of all unless
There's someone to share your happiness,
Someone to care when you win success,
Someone to care?   - Fred McGregor

He Has Not Served

He has not served who gathers gold,
Nor has he served, whose life is told
In selfish battles he has won,
But he has served who now and then
Has helped along his fellow men.

The world needs many men today,
Red-blooded men along life's way,
With cheerful smiles and helping hand,
And with the faith that understands
The beauty of the simple deed.

Teach me to do the best I can
To help and cheer our fellow men;
Teach me to lose my selfish need
And glory in the larger deed,
Which smooths the road and lights the day
For all who chance to come my way.

- Clare Thacker, 1944 National Kinsmen Convention address

Part 3: *1945 - 1953*

"I am a part of all that I have met. Though much is taken, much abides. That which we are, we are on equal temper of heroic hearts, strong in will. To strive, to seek, to find and not to yield." — Tennyson's *Ulysses*

Selling out and settling up

World War II was on and the Great Depression had ended. But my cash register still hadn't heard the news. In the restaurant, it was still hard times. I had been in business for seven years, and I was sick of the never-ending hard work and worry about debts.

So I decided to join the army and put my restaurant up for sale. It came as a happy surprise when a real-estate agent said, "I think I have a buyer for you. Name of Bill Taylor. He's a meat man from Edmonton who wants to move to the coast."

I met Taylor with the real-estate man on a Sunday. He gave me a one thousand dollar deposit, and agreed to take over in ninety days' time, when he would pay the balance. The full price was seven thousand dollars, which happened to be very close to exactly the amount that I owed my creditors.

Getting free from debt was a cheerful prospect. A faint alarm bell rang in the back of my head to warn me that I might be making the wrong move. But I was too excited to pay any attention.

The day Taylor was supposed to take over, he never turned up. About a week went by, and I felt sure the deal must be off. Then I had a phone call from Taylor, who asked me to meet him at the Churchill Hotel.

"I've been here in Victoria for a week, and I'm nervous about this deal," he said. "I don't want to go through with it. Can you do anything for me?"

I didn't know what to say, so I waited to see if he would explain why he had changed his mind.

"Look," said Taylor, "I'm so worried that I've started smoking cigarettes again, after quitting for a month." He lighted up a Sweet Caporal and took several quick puffs.

"I was President of the Chamber of Commerce in Edmonton," he said, and pointed to a pile of papers. "I sold my business and said goodbye. Look at all these letters wishing me luck on my move to the coast and my new business venture. How can I go back and say I'm staying in Edmonton after all?"

"I'm sorry, Mr. Taylor," I said. "What do you want me to do?"

"Cancel the deal for me," he said. He was obviously having an argument with himself. He inhaled with a heavy breath, and blew out a cloud of smoke.

"All right," I said. "Just pay me the money I've spent for legal expenses in drawing up the agreement. Then I'll sell the restaurant to someone else." Three days later he came back and bought the restaurant for the same price. He still seemed worried.

For most of my years in the restaurant, Ed Pridham and several other creditors had held off collecting their money. I still owed Ed for the work he had done that week-end when we made the huge renovations.

One time I scraped together a little money and sent him a cheque for fifty dollars. He sent it back. "That's all right," he said. "Pay me when you can."

When I received payment for the restaurant, I went to him and said, "Ed, I've got to pay you now."

He dug out the itemized bill from some old cabinet, and I paid him in full. It was time to move along. The little restaurant was receding into the past.   But I carried with me the bright memory of friends like Ed Pridham and all the others, whose trust, patience and understanding allowed a young businessman to survive his apprenticeship.

A few months afterwards I heard that Bill Taylor had sold the restaurant at a solid profit and had bought Terry's big ice-cream parlour. He was an able businessman, but he had gone through a period of self-doubt.

How do you succeed in business? First of all, you need good hunches, because business is an art, not a science. Then you need a mixture of luck and judgement, plus hard work, knowledge and some help from your friends.

My judgement told me that I was getting out of business at exactly the wrong time -- from a financial point of view. The economy was beginning to boom. When I advertised the restaurant for sale, I was already picking up the signals of the trend. In the three months that passed between the time I signed the agreement and the time I received the money, my profits began to increase.

That was the reason for the alarm bell that rang in the back of my head when I agreed to sell. I could have kept the restaurant and watched it grow into a valuable property. And yet I was impatient for a change of scene. I would never have any peace of mind until I got free.

My short army career

"As soon as you sign the papers and take the oath, you'll be in the army," the recruiting officer said.

I knew something about food service, so I had applied to be a messing officer.

"Of course, you'll have to spend thirty days at Little Mountain Camp as a private," he told me, and that seemed all right. I had sold the restaurant; the war was on; I had to do some kind of work; and messing officer seemed as good a job as any.

They gave me a long bureaucratic form to fill out. There were questions about operations and illnesses. What was I supposed to say about that operation for peptic ulcer? It could get me rejected. So I asked a doctor, who had operated on me, to write a letter on my behalf, saying that the operation was only a small thing which did not affect my fitness.

Little Mountain Camp in Vancouver was crowded with disgruntled conscripts. They were being herded in masses through the corridors and dumped into rooms, to wait for hours and days for medical examinations. Some of them were suffering from self-inflicted wounds, which they hoped would be their ticket out of the service. One man boasted that he had cut his own leg with an axe.

The officer commanding, who was a Victoria man, told me, "I want you to go to Gordon Head Officers' Training Centre for two weeks, then I'm sending you to Halifax to be messing officer on a ship."

"I can't stand ships," I told him. "I would have joined the navy if I'd wanted to be on a ship."

"In the army you do what you're told," he said.

When I had been in the camp at Little Mountain for a week, I was called into the hospital. I waited in the corridor for a couple of days. On the third day, a doctor called me in, and started ranting and lecturing as soon as I entered.

"I checked your medical records," he said, "and it's people like you who cost the government money. All you want to do is collect a pension. You'd be no good to the army. You're out."

Apparently it was the healed ulcer that had set off his tirade. A few days later I was back on the street. I never even picked up my pay.

Losing the battle with bureaucracy

Yarrow's shipyard was my next stop. Because I had worked as an electrician's helper (mainly boring holes in ceiling rafters) when I was a kid, they made me a journeyman electrician at eighty cents an hour, which was an extremely high wage for the time. I had two female helpers.

I was absolutely unqualified, but anybody could have done the job. The wiring was easy to install. We would get a ship all wired with this lead electrical wiring. Then, a few days later, the foreman would come along and say, "This wiring has to come out. It's in the wrong place."

The amount of wasted time and effort was depressing. None of the people in charge seemed to have any idea of where they were going. They tried to do too many things in too much of a hurry. Later on they did produce ships efficiently, I believe, but just then it was a mess.

I spent a lot of my time sitting and waiting. If you have any aggressiveness in your nature, that's enough to drive you up the wall. I went around to other tradesmen and tried to learn to weld, so I could put the time to good use.

Finally, I couldn't stand it any longer. I said to my boss, "I'm getting out of this." He was hesitant, but finally Yarrow's agreed to let me go.

My one week in the army and my few weeks at Yarrow's were my only real experience of living inside bumbling, bureaucratic organizations. When you're a businessman, you have to learn to cope with bureaucracies. They're a fact of life, like winds and tides. But becoming part of the bureaucratic system, and accepting its waste of materials and manpower -- that was more than I could stand.

Skirmish with a dragon lady

After my two losing encounters with wartime bureaucracy, I went back into business. The Carmelcrisp enterprise had not been part of the deal when I sold the restaurant. Now I took the aluminium pot, oak paddle and the cooker out of storage in the basement of my house, found a new mini-store in one corner of a restaurant on Douglas Street in Victoria, and started selling candy and peanuts.

Soon after this, the restaurant changed hands. The new owner was Lydia Arsens, who later became well-known in provincial politics as a Social Credit member of the B.C. Legislature for Victoria and an early advocate for garbage recycling.

My lease contained a sale clause. It allowed the new owner to evict me, which Mrs. Arsens tried to do. She was a tall, stiff-necked woman with a sharp tongue.

"I want you out of here by this time next month," she said.

Where else was I going to get a downtown cubby-hole on the street for fifty dollars a month? This was all I could afford.

Once again my friend, the lawyer Norman Whittaker, did me a good service. He found that the written notice to vacate was dated two days late. I had rented the place on the twenty-ninth of the month; she had given me notice on the thirty-first. The notice was not legally valid. So I just stayed on.

Mrs. Arsens took the rebuff to heart. She launched a campaign of nagging and harsh words.

The law courts were on summer holiday. This gave me another three months, during which time I found another place just down the block. I bought a news-stand in front of a barber-shop owned by a Mr. Green, and put the candy stall in with the news-stand.

Mrs. Arsens left my old place vacant for a year after that, so I don't know why she was in such a hurry to get me out.

Every so often she would drop in to my new location to offer an insult. Her favourite put-down was, "Why aren't you in the army?"

I tried to tell her that I had already been in the army and out again for medical reasons, but she didn't listen.

A few days later she would ask me the same question. It wasn't really a question. It was a ritual of harrassment. After a time I learned to throw my mind out of gear and think about something pleasant when Mrs. Arsens came in sight.

The ten-foot step

Getting rich seems a mysterious process. The business world looks like an escalator that might carry you to fortune, if only you could reach the first step, which happens to be ten feet above your head.

But, when you look closely, there often are some handholds that will allow you to climb those ten feet. The key point is that you listen for changes in the world, and make those changes pay you a profit. In changing times, when most of the big companies are too slow, rigid or unimaginative to deal with new patterns of demand, the fast-moving, small operator finds his best chance to climb and grow.

That was how it was for me in the nut business. I did not see the situation in such a clear and cold-blooded way as I have just outlined. That is hindsight. I groped my way to the answers by a series of hunches, as part of the struggle for survival.

The first rule of merchandising is "give 'em what they want". People were lining up to buy my roast peanuts and my chocolate-and-peanut confection. Obviously there were more people out there wanting peanuts and candy than I could reach through my retail hole-in-the-wall on Douglas Street, Victoria.

So I started wholesaling. I bought peanuts in bulk from a Vancouver wholesaler, and hired two girls to work in the back of the store weighing nuts, packing them by hand into cellophane bags, and sealing the bags with a heat sealer.

I bought a truck and delivered nuts to a few local outlets, including the Capitol Theatre in Victoria, which was managed by the Fontana sisters. But I still wasn't producing enough nuts to meet the demand.

The year was 1945. The war was still on. There was money to be made in processing and wholesaling nuts on a large scale. In order to do this, I would have to solve problems of supply, financing, organization, processing, sales and distribution.

How could I climb ten feet to the bottom step of the escalator? I found that I couldn't do it all by myself. Other people boosted me part-way up on their shoulders. Then I climbed the rest of the way using my wits.

The first problem was supply. The larger the quantity of anything you buy, the lower the price. The nuts I sold in my store and peddled to the other stores came from the Vancouver wholesaler. But I wasn't making enough profit, and I was operating on too small a scale. I needed to buy the nuts more cheaply and in much larger quantities from a broker who marketed them on behalf of the growers in the southern United States.

My biggest upward boost came from a firm of brokers who let me have carload lots of peanuts on ninety days' credit without carrying charges, when everyone else was paying cash.

Donald H. Bain Limited was a brokerage firm owned by a wealthy bachelor, who had been an eminent figure in hockey. I believe he was the first person in the Hall of Fame. Although his firm did a large volume of business and had branches all across the West, it was still run in a personal style by Mr. Bain's managers, who received a percentage of profits. Even in those days, most of the dominant brokerage firms were already becoming impersonal and bureaucratic; Donald H. Bain Limited was an exception. I met some of Mr. Bain's Vancouver executives socially over drinks, and got to know them quite well. Partly out of a desire to increase their sales, they let me have ninety days' credit for a carload of peanuts at ten thousand dollars a carload and up.

Perhaps they shouldn't have done this. The broker was operating on a percentage of only one or two per cent of the value of the goods he handled. By allowing me generous terms, he was cutting his profits and increasing his risks. But if his gamble paid off, his volume of business and his profits would increase.

A fellow named Mr. Hooper, who was the manager at Donald H. Bain Limited, was the first to give me credit. He retired and I got to know his successor, Ritchie Brown, and his brother, Jim Brown, the Sales Manager. Once, when I was sitting having a drink with Ritchie, he brought out a personal file which showed that Canada

Safeway and all the big outfits were paying cash -- I was the only one who was getting ninety days.

The demand for nuts was enormous. I had to convert myself almost overnight from a small, local retailer and wholesaler into a sizeable processor and packager. Getting a supply of nuts at a low price was the key to the transformation. Once Donald H. Bain Limited had trusted me for that first carload of peanuts and I had paid up, I was in a position to ask for two carloads on credit, and then three. It was like those loans from my coffee shop that I used to give Tommy Bowden, the bookmaker. The principle was similar -- prove you can pay and ask for more next time.

Sometimes, in the months that followed, I was able to get a bank loan and pay cash for several carloads of peanuts, which kept the fellows at Donald H. Bain Limited happy. But, for much of the time, they went on giving me ninety days. From a nickel-and-dime merchant and coffee-shop owner, I transformed myself within a year into a businessman grossing hundreds of thousands of dollars.

The rising market for nuts was the escalator that carried me to a higher level. But it was my friends at Donald H. Bain Limited who boosted me on their shoulders so that I could reach the bottom step.

Riding the upward market

My next problem was organization. At the same time that I began buying peanuts by carload lots, I rented a two-storey building on lower Yates Street in Victoria and put in a processing plant. I couldn't afford high-cost equipment. For very little money I built from odd parts a system of machinery that was simple in principle, but complicated in detail. A girl operator would push a foot pedal, tripping a lever that released a measured quantity of peanuts into a cellophane bag, and a heat sealer would seal the bag as it ran along a belt.

An artist-cartoonist, who was working for the provincial government, drew up a well-designed sketch for our label, which we reproduced on the cellophane bags, and a design for a fancy, lithographed tin which Canadian Can Company manufactured for us. I put together a group of employees, associates and advisors, fifty-five in number. I already knew some of them as friends and fellow-members of clubs to which I belonged, and I knew what they could do because I had already worked with them.

Some of those employees and associates are still friends, and there are others whom I see from time to time. You can't forget the people whose work made you a business success. Wilf Hofstrand was my accountant then until his passing in 1985.

In Vancouver and the Fraser Valley we hired three ex-fliers from World War II, and equipped them with second-hand trucks to sell to stores in Vancouver. We did the same in Calgary, Edmonton, Regina and Saskatoon. From Winnipeg eastward we sold through brokers and wholesalers.

Within a year we grew to be Canada's biggest nut company. Some might dispute the claim, but it really isn't worth arguing about. Anyway, we had one million dollars a year in gross sales, which was a large sum for 1946.

We arranged with Woolworth's, Hudson Bay Company, Eaton's and other big stores in the West to put on counter and window displays of nuts.

And still the supply fell short of the demand. Len Keyworth, our Canadian Sales Manager, took a trip to Calgary one time and phoned me to say, "I've made three calls and I've sold one hundred and twenty thousand dollars' worth of cashews. Do you think we can produce any more, or should I come home?"

In fact we had more orders than we could handle. We had to cut back on each order until we could increase production.

But the boom in the sale of nuts was likely to be a short-lived event. It was linked to the scarcity of sugar and candy, which created a demand for something else to munch. When sugar came back in quantity, there would be drastic changes in demand.

The war had now ended. I had to make plans to protect myself against the slump in demand that was certain to come.

One defence against sudden disastrous change is to diversify -- to get into different lines of business so that, if one leg collapses, you will have other legs to stand on. I started doing this within a few weeks.

Both the nut business and the baker's and candy-maker's wholesale business looked prosperous, but they were not as profitable as you might have thought from the sales figures.

I could never have retired on the strength of the nut business and the specialty wholesale business. A comfortable semi-retirement was my eventual goal.

Furthermore, I was not yet properly protected against the decline in the market for nuts, which was sure to come as soon as substantial amounts of sugar became available.

The future of our bakery and candy-maker's business was uncertain. Retail and wholesale firms and food-processing firms were growing bigger, and they were joining together. A trend towards centralization and vertical integration was already beginning, meaning that big chain merchandisers owned production and marketing facilities, all the way from the farmer's field and the factory down to the retail store.

I could expand and consolidate, add some new merchandise, or sell out. When the market changes, you must change with it or go ahead of it. If you do not shift your balance and direction, you will fail and be wiped out.

Through the business-friendship network, I found one answer. Mr. Harris, the Manager of the National Grocery Company in Seattle, came up with a useful idea.

"Why don't you go into the peanut-butter business?" he asked. "We're putting in a new peanut-butter plant, and we're throwing out the old machinery. We'll give it to you at a good price."

"How much would that be?"

"You can have all the machinery on the floor for one thousand dollars," he said. "We just want to get rid of it."

It must have cost many thousands of dollars when it was new. It was a gift. I loaded it on trailers and had it carried by Black Ball Ferry to Victoria.

The Yates Street Building had been big enough to hold the nut business and the specialty wholesale business. We stayed there for about a year. Now we needed more space, so we took a larger two-storey building at 1626 Store Street, and installed the peanut-butter factory, along with the other two businesses.

This was the start of Kersey's Peanut Butter which, in most areas in western Canada, outsold all other brands on the market. One of the reasons for this was that we were using an old-style stone mill, which produced a product superior to anything that could be manufactured by new equipment on a modern assembly line. Also the product was pure, with no additives except salt.

Peanut butter

" Our child's demands on life are few.
Complaints, at nine, he does not utter.
He only asks his daily bread
Of life be smeared with peanut butter."   - Betty Isler

Peanuts, which are native to South America, were first introduced to India, then to the U.S.A. which, at this time of writing, are the largest commercial producers. States such as Alabama and Georgia are good peanut-growing regions.

The nuts are planted in rows of small hills, with six to eight inches between the hills and about thirty to thirty-six inches between rows. They take five months of warm weather and need an average of twenty-two to twenty-four inches of rainfall to grow. The spreading type of plant grows one-and-a-half to two feet high, with branches lying close to the ground. After pollination the flower withers and a stalk-like structure is thrust from the base of the flower into the soil, where the peanut develops and ripens. The quality of the crop is dependent on the soil. At harvest the entire plant, except the deeper roots, is removed and dried for four to six weeks.

There are many types of peanuts, also called Goobers -- Virginia is a fairly large nut, from a plant which has smaller-size runners; the Spanish peanut from Texas is a small round nut. Spanish peanuts have the most oil content, about forty per cent. Moisture content is also important.

Before being shipped the peanuts are dried and the outer shell is removed by feeding the nuts through rollers which crush them; high-suction air sucks the broken shell away while the nuts are travelling along a conveyor belt. The green peanut is left with only its brown skin on. The nuts are packed, approximately one hundred pounds to a sack, and shipped in railway cars which hold approximately sixty thousand pounds of peanuts. Depending on the time of year and age of the peanuts, they are usually fumigated on board the railway car; this prevents infestations and mould from running all through the green nuts making them unsaleable. When the carloads of nuts arrive at the processing plant, they are placed in storage.

Initially the nuts are roasted in a gas-fired drum until they start to change colour, and then are dumped into cooling trays. After cooling they are moved by air suction to the third floor of the plant where they start the process of being turned into peanut butter by the time the main floor level is reached. Travelling down through the system the nuts go through a blancher, which is a revolving scrubber that removes the brown skins and breaks the peanuts in half; the skins are sucked away by a vacuum. At one end of the peanut is a small piece called the heart (scientific term is the hypocotyl) which, if left in, would make the finished product very bitter; these are separated from the nuts by a shaker. The nuts then go into a grinder which can be set to fine or coarse for two different types of product. At one time the only ingredient added during the grinding process was salt; today sugar and a material called "Fix" are added to stabilize the peanut butter, so that oil separation is slowed down, and to homogenize it. From the grinder the finished product goes into a weighing and filling machine, which is all automatic, and then onto a conveyor belt for capping and labelling. The finished product is then put into cartons ready for shipping.

At one time in Canada there was more peanut butter sold than cheese. It contains no cholesterol and, pound for pound, is richer in protein. It has more proteins, minerals and vitamins than beef liver, and more food energy than sugar.

Some studies claim that peanut butter is not fattening. The Bordens Review of Nutrition Research says: eat all you want and stay thin; chubby people just lack Luxusconsumption, meaning excess. Luxusconsumption is a theory that excess food causes an increase in general metabolism or rate of burning up energy. The Luxusconsumption mechanism keeps the weight of these people normal because the excess food is soon used up.

Travelling peanut-butter man

In addition to our outside salesmen, I made regular sales trips through the B.C. Interior and into Alberta.

The small independent grocery stores and bakeries still controlled most of the retail market in those days. They had not yet been overwhelmed by the chain grocery stores, with their vertical integration and centralized purchasing policies. The proprietors were glad to see you, and they seldom failed to place an order.

I didn't like being away too long, and I didn't like driving, so I moved rapidly through the territory and I often took along a driver friend for company. Sometimes it was Bob Shanks, who took leave from his motorcycle shop to accompany me.

One time we heard loud voices as we entered a newly-established store in Castlegar, B.C. The proprietor and his wife had been arguing. He broke off the battle and lurched out to meet us, radiating a strong smell of alcohol.

"I'll take twenty-five cases," he ordered.

"You'll never get paid for it," his wife shrieked.

"I want to show you my new cold storage locker," he said, nudging us through a doorway towards the locker and away from his wife's reproachful voice.

So he ushered us into the cold room and, while we loitered among the beef carcasses, he disappeared. The door shut behind us and he locked us in. We shouted and hollered, but nobody answered.

So Bob said, "We better sit down because, if we move around, we'll use up all the oxygen in here."

"Yeah," I tell him,"and if we sit down we are going to freeze."

So we're getting panicky, and we finally took a side of beef off the steel hook to use it to make a hole through the outside wall, because we figure that there's an outside tile wall here, and maybe we can break through.

We just started to chip at the wall with the meat hook when he came back and let us out. This was supposed to be one of his jokes. We didn't see the humour in it.

I went on this Interior trip maybe once a month. Mostly I was detailing orders, which means that I would take the orders and the wholesaler would deliver them.

Sometimes we would travel and work around the clock. One night I was coming into Princeton, B.C., about two a.m. and I saw a light in a store owned by a Mr. Andrew. He was in there working on his books, so I called in and got an order. He said, "I've never had a salesman call on me this late."

We left there and drove down the highway; we swerved off the road to miss a deer, and ended up running over a spike and getting a flat tire. In those days the roads were so bad that you got flat tires quite often and our spare was already in use. It was three a.m. We found a service station with a house beside it, and we knocked on the door and got the proprietor out of bed. He was pleased to get up and help us out, and fixed the tire for two dollars. No problem -- so we gave him five dollars.

Usually we would get up at five a.m. to call on the bakeries, and about eight a.m. we would call on the retail stores. We were trying desperately to keep to a schedule, so we would try to move on by noon. On one trip we left Princeton in a rush, heading for Keremos, B.C., and were so absorbed that we forgot to check out of the hotel; we had to drive all the way back.

Then there was Tom King, the storekeeper. He was a Member of Parliament for Golden, B.C., who wouldn't buy any brand of peanut butter except Kersey's. Also there was Mr. Copozzi, of the grocery store and wine-making people of Kelowna, who bought peanut butter in twenty-five-pound tins -- fifty or one hundred of those large tins at one time for sale to thrifty people with big families.

Going on those sales trips was like living through a gentle, rustic, situation comedy, in which you met the same cast of characters in each episode, but there was always a surprise waiting around the corner. And there usually was a happy ending.

The peanut-butter mystery

"Sorry," said the U.S. Customs man. "You can't bring that peanut butter through."

"But I've been bringing it through for years," I said.

He shrugged and stared past me at another car that was approaching the custom-house. He was already losing interest in my problem.

Bob Shanks and I looked at each other in dismay. I had forty cases of peanut butter in the car, for samples and replacements. I was taking it through the United States, via Spokane, for one simple reason -- at that time there was no winter road through the mountains on the Canadian side from Grand Forks to Trail.

Usually I could cover the territory between the coast and Edmonton in two weeks, but this bureaucratic reversal at the custom-house near Grand Forks could spoil my timetable.

It was six p.m. on Friday; the U.S. border closed at seven p.m. If we were stuck on the Canadian side of the border now, our schedule would be disrupted. It was necessary to reach Edmonton on a Sunday night, and work from Edmonton back to B.C.

"Look, the United States is just a stretch of highway to me," I told the Customs man. "I only want to travel through so I can get to another part of Canada. I've done the same thing many times. Why don't you let me through?"

"Sorry," he said.

I got his boss on the phone, but he wouldn't change the decision. So we drove back to a house near the border, where we talked to an old lady, about eighty years of age, by the name of MacGregor.

"Do you mind if I leave forty cases of peanut butter on your porch for about a week?" I asked.

"Sure," she agreed. "That would be all right."

So we got through the border and reached Edmonton on schedule, and worked our way back to Grand Forks a week later. Strangely enough, we couldn't find the house where we had left the peanut butter. Wasn't it one hundred yards from the custom-house, on the right? Of course it was. And yet it wasn't. There was no sign of any house.

Could both of us be suffering from the same delusion? Or was somebody playing a weird trick?

So we drove to a garage about a mile up the road, and I said to this guy, "You'll think it's odd, but I left forty cases of peanut butter at a house, and I can't find the house."

"That was my mother's house," the garage man said. "We've been going to move that house for years to another site, and we finally got around to moving it. I have your peanut butter in the back of the garage."

Peanut butter takes to the air

"You're wasting a lot of time on your sales trips," Bill Sylvester said. "Why don't you travel by air?"

It was an interesting idea, and Bill Sylvester had a record of making ideas pay off in cash. He had shared a nine-dollar-a-month room with me in the 1930's. He prospered in his drive-yourself car rental business, and moved from that into charter flying, forming B.C. Airlines.

"Come with me and see how you like it," Bill offered.

Next day I was looking down on a panorama of green islands, mountains and sea, and watching the trees slide past the cabin window as we slanted in for a landing on a distant inlet.

Bill carried his charter passengers and did his company's personnel and public relations work, and I sold peanut butter in camps and coastal towns. Bill was one of the best professional pilots in Canada. Flying had become as natural to him as walking. He kept his float plane near his home base at Cadboro Bay in Victoria and, when he wasn't flying up and down the coast, he would commute each day to his base in Vancouver.

One time, when he was carrying out a logger on a charter from a camp on an inlet up the coast, in a sixty-five-horsepower, two-seater Luscombe float plane, a strong wind caught the aircraft as it was turning for take-off, and flipped it upside down. Bill and the logger struggled free and took refuge on the upturned floats for six, freezing daylight hours. When dusk came and a boat appeared in the distance, Bill dug out his waterproof matches and started burning letters and other papers that he had in his pocket, to make a beacon. He soon ran out of papers, but he always carried a lot of money in a big fat wallet, and finally he started burning money. He burned a lot before the small signal fire caught the eye of a person in a boat, and they were rescued.

Hundreds of miles from anywhere on the B.C. coast were lakes where we fished off the float of the aircraft, and caught a rainbow trout or a Dolly Varden with almost every cast. If the engine had failed to start, or if we had been unable to lift off high enough to clear the trees, I doubt that anyone would have found us in these wild places.

Often we would be grounded by bad weather in Tofino, on the west coast of Vancouver Island, and I would run over to the Catholic school in a boat and sell peanut butter to Father Kearney.

The waiter who served breakfast in the hotel in Tofino was also the barber and the undertaker. They had few visitors in those days and they always gave us a big, friendly welcome.

Up at the head of Knight Inlet we sometimes met a couple of old fellows who hadn't seen anyone for a couple of months. On every visit -- it seems to me in memory -- they wanted us to stay overnight and go fishing after dark for oolachons. We fished these with bare hands in the river and created much excitement. I regret now that we never found the time to stay.

I enjoyed those coastal journeys, and I felt comfortable in the air, so I became persuaded that Bill was right about the usefulness of an aircraft in my business. In 1950 I learned to fly, and a sales trip to Powell River, which previously was a four-day trip by boat, would take me one day by aircraft. Not only did I save time and money, but I started myself on an interesting career. I did not realize this until later, when I was out of the peanut-butter business.

For the time being, I worked to make the business grow.

Advertising

Over the years we used many different kinds of advertising; some paid off very well. In the depression restaurant days, one would buy a whole page of the Daily Colonist's Sunday publication. As we rarely had any money to pay for this, we would go to most of our suppliers, such as the bakery and coffee people, and sell them an advertisement on this page. It would be printed around our menu and write-up. There would be enough ads to pay the entire cost, and we would get a full-page ad for free; the ad usually included our picture and a small write-up.

In 1946 we had a different type of youngster than we have today. As a promotion of our peanut-butter and nut products, we would arrange with many stores, such as Eaton's and Woolworth's, to put large displays of our products in their windows, along with bicycles and other items. These items were offered as prizes for the boy or girl who could save the most Kersey's Peanut Butter labels by a certain closing date. This promotion produced a large volume of business. The children would go to the grocery store and pick up cases of Kersey's Peanut Butter, and go door-to-door selling it and asking if they could keep the labels. The number of contest entries was in the thousands.

One of our greatest ventures was to give free admission to the first Saturday game of the Victoria Professional Baseball Club to those who had a Kersey's Peanut Butter label. This would really fill up the bleachers of the park, which we had purchased for the event. The Daily Colonist published a story of the famous twenty-three-inning, tied Victoria Athletics ball game, at which we had admitted two thousand six hundred youngsters who each had a label. In our latter years we tried the same ideas with professional hockey and other contests, but to no avail; only a handful of youngsters would come. The world had changed; no youngster was bothering to go to a hockey game with a label, as his father would pay for his admission.

As manufacturers do today, we set up displays in major grocery stores and had girls demonstrating and giving out samples, and, when possible, putting a jar of Kersey's Peanut Butter in the customer's shopping basket.

A radio station programme called "Six for One" was one of the most successful quiz-type shows which gave cash prizes to lucky listeners. On one of these shows we advertised that Kersey's Peanut Butter didn't contain cholesterol. The Provincial Health Department stopped us; they said it was unfair advertising, as no competitor's peanut butter contained cholesterol either.

The case of the delayed cashews

"If you don't help me, I'm going to lose forty thousand dollars, and I can't afford it," I told my lawyer.

"Let's start at the beginning," he suggested.

"I ordered eighty thousand dollars' worth of cashews from Birks & Crawford, the Canada Safeway brokers, to be paid for on delivery," I told him. "These cashews were shipped out of India. That was away back last year."

"These nuts should have reached here in six weeks, but the ship that carried them ran aground. The shipowners refloated the vessel and transferred the cargo to another carrier."

"Now the cashews have arrived. It took them eight months to get here. In the meantime the price of cashews has dropped down to only half what it was, but the brokers want the eighty thousand dollars we contracted to pay. That leaves me forty thousand dollars in the hole."

"You mean they're still edible after being dunked in the sea?"

"Sure they are. If they had been peanuts, they would have spoiled. But they are green cashews sealed in four-gallon metal containers. They'll last for years."

"Let's see your contract with the broker," the lawyer said, and I waited in suspense while he studied it.

Legal quarrels are an ever-present risk for a businessman. You may escape them if you are lucky, but a small, rising entrepreneur had better be prepared to stand and fight, if he wants to survive.

My firm had just started to expand. Capital was scarce and spread quite thin. I was as weak as a crab that has grown out of its shell.

"You were crazy to sign this kind of contract," the lawyer said. "It doesn't say anything about the delivery date. All the brokers promised was that the shipment would leave port on May 18. If it left on time, you'll have to pay."

"I guess I'm sunk," I said.

"Wait a minute," he said. "I'm going to send a cable to the port authorities in India and find out what day the ship really did leave. You might still have a chance."

Two days later he called me with some good news. The ship had left on May 19 -- one day late. Technically the contract had been broken. The lawyer wrote to Birks & Crawford and said we were not accepting the cashews. The big firm could afford the loss, but it would have had a drastic effect on our business; we were saved.

Canada Customs

Being in the type of business I operated meant dealing with Canada Customs a great deal. When you are young and unaccustomed to bureaucracy, someone usually makes it most difficult to always adjust to their rule book. I was always polite and honest, which is a great help, but the red tape and delays make one very intolerant, especially when you are dealing with perishable products.

I considered Mr. Yardley, the Chief Collector (and boss), to be a friend, as I knew his family personally. He operated according to the book, no matter what the consequence. I had so many hassles with Customs, even Mr. Yardley doubted my sincerity. At one time he had myself and the company thoroughly investigated, with a warrant to search all records and close our business down, if necessary.

Our imports from the United States were considerable; each and every order required Canada Customs' forms to be filled out by the American supplier and signed in triplicate. One time the supplier from Washington, U.S.A., put down King County, instead of the state, and Customs refused to clear the shipment until the corrected papers were received. This usually meant a delay of a week, with the goods being held on the dock in Victoria. Sometimes these goods were not only perishable but also essential to carry on business. In a case like this, Customs had an arrangement where you could pay double duty and then apply for a refund when the proper papers arrived, but this also took a long time. The Customs' documents and procedures were fairly complicated; it usually worked out better to use a customs broker, which we always did.

When you paid the duty, etc., on a shipment, the regulations said it had to be by cash or a certified cheque. Hardly anyone doing very much business with Customs ever gave a certified cheque; an ordinary cheque was sufficient. We had been paying by regular cheque for years when, one day, Bill Huxtable, a Customs man, phoned me to advise that the previous day's shipment was being held because the cheque was not certified, and there would be a twelve-dollar penalty. I suggested to Bill that I would pick up the cheque and have it certified at the previous days's date by a friend in the bank, which my friend did, and I returned the now-certified cheque to Customs. This really blew the lid off, after Mr. Yardley phoned the bank manager. My friend was called up on the carpet and had to practically perjure himself by saying he must have forgotten to advance the bank certifying machine to the current date.

In another incident, I was too naive to know that, if one wanted to be dishonest with Customs, one way was to purchase something from the U.S.A., for example, valued at one hundred dollars, and ask the supplier to make out the Customs' M.A. forms for a much smaller amount, say sixty dollars. This way you would only pay duty on sixty dollars. I had ordered a small heat-sealing machine from Pittsburg, U.S.A., which cost about three hundred and fifty dollars. When the Customs' papers arrived by mail, they enclosed the regular invoices at three hundred and fifty dollars and the Customs' invoices at two hundred and fifty dollars.

I took both sets of papers to our broker, showing him the error, and, for reasons beyond me, he cleared them at the two-hundred-and-fifty-dollar cost; however, he did attach the three-hundred-and-fifty-dollar invoices to the papers. I was unable to get this equipment for some weeks and had to post an extra bond. Mr. Yardley then asked Ottawa to investigate our operation.

We had fifty-three employees, with an office staff of three girls and one man. Monday morning on my arrival at eight a.m. to start work, a two-hundred-pound Mafia-type gentleman was waiting at the front door of the plant. He introduced himself as Mr. Lawson of the Special Investigation Department of Canada Customs. He advised me he had a warrant to temporarily close our operation; however, if I wished to co-operate, we could leave our business in operation. I asked what he required, and he said he wanted to look over all our records, of which there were hundreds. At first I said I would call my lawyer, which he said was OK. However, on second thought, our operation was one hundred per cent above-board, so I said go ahead, and asked him to tell me what he wanted to see. He cleaned out my office files and desk, and then spent eight hours a day in our main office, talking to the staff and checking the records. After one week he advised me he had finished and would report back.

Three weeks later he phoned me, and said he was staying at the Dominion Hotel and could I have dinner with him at six p.m., which I did. On my arrival for dinner, he informed me that he had lived next door to my aunt on Princess Avenue, and he had known me since a small boy. I spent one of the most interesting evenings hearing his story of being with Customs in the rum-running, prohibition days, and chasing murderers and thugs all over the Strait of Georgia. They used a fast speed-boat to chase the rum runners, board their boats with loaded revolvers and capture them. Some of these rum runners were pretty tough customers, and he had a hand in capturing the most famous one of all on the most wanted criminal list, Siwash Baker.

After dinner he asked me to his room to explain the past three weeks. He told me that, first, he flew to Pittsburgh to visit the Heat Sealer Company, and found that we had done everything properly. From Pittsburgh he went to Seattle. Mr. Lawson said the gentleman who headed the National Grocers in Seattle spelled his surname Harras in such a way that there may be some collusion, as we were a big account of the National Grocers. He arrived in Seattle to find what a reputable man Gus Harras was and, after a discussion with him and other brokers in Seattle with whom we did business, he came back to Victoria.

The department Mr. Lawson was with had powers much greater than those of the collector in Victoria. After taking me from the hotel to the Customs' office, he showed me, in confidence, the letter he had written to the minister in Ottawa. In it he suggested that the collector should be sure before he asked for such a detailed audit, as our operation was absolutely honourable and it is considered a black mark to treat citizens this way. We received an apology from the minister.

The man in the middle

Getting to know a large number of people and listening to what they said was one of my main secrets of business success.

Through the clubs and friendship networks to which I belonged, I already knew a number of bakers, candy-makers and restaurant owners. Now, in the nut business, I began to make a number of friends among brokers and wholesalers in Vancouver and Seattle. They all seemed anxious to help. From them I picked up early reports of market trends. Some of the fancy foodstuffs and food ingredients that had been in short supply during the war were becoming more plentiful, but flavours, glucose, jams and nuts were too slow in reaching bakers, candy-makers and restaurant proprietors. From my friends in the local food trades, I learned that there was a place for a specialized, wholesale business that would supply them quickly and cheaply with some of the materials they wanted. From my new friends among the brokers, I found out how to get these materials at reasonable prices by purchasing them in bulk at the right time.

By creating a specialty wholesale firm, I put some more of my rented warehouse space to profitable use, and I gave myself another leg to stand on when the price of nuts took its inevitable downturn. If I hadn't started a wholesale firm, somebody else would have done it. But I got there first. I knew from the talk on the friendship network that demand and discontent were building up. The time was right to move.

There is always somebody, a wholesaler or a broker, who is stuck with a load of some commodity that he can't sell immediately, and, if he has it on his hands for long, he loses money. He is working at only two per cent, and he has to move the goods fast.

Sometimes, I would either buy the goods for re-sale later, or sell them immediately by long-distance telephone. We would make maybe five per cent profit, for which we would only have to merchandize the stuff through our warehouse.

Sometimes a bureaucratic quirk was preventing a broker from selling his goods, and, if you could solve the puzzle, you could make some money. For example, people at the broker's firm of Goebel Pratt in Seattle told me about a management decision that was preventing General Foods in the U.S.A. from supplying dried coconut in quantity to their branches in Canada. It had something to do with the relationships between the U.S.A. and the Canadian branches of the firm, and the fact that rules are made in the head offices of these corporations, which are big private bureaucracies.

I found out that I was allowed to buy carload lots of coconut in Seattle for re-sale in Canada. So a girl employee I knew at Goebel Pratt Brokerage Firm in Seattle would let me use a telephone in their office, and I would phone to Dad's Cookies and sell them a carload of coconut, which they could not buy from General Foods' salesmen in Vancouver. I kept doing this until General Foods awakened to the fact that the bureaucratic regulation was losing money for the company. Then they untangled their corporate red tape and started selling coconut directly to their own customers in Canada.

I sold walnuts and all kinds of commodities by long-distance phone out of the broker's office in Seattle, phoning to Winnipeg, Calgary, Vancouver and other places, and shipped them direct from Seattle.

The bakery and candy-makers' wholesale supply business was centred in B.C. I built it up rapidly through personal contacts with people in the trade who were mildly frustrated because they couldn't get the stuff quickly or reasonably enough.

People in these trades have to make a number of educated guesses about what people will want to eat tomorrow. Their business depends a great deal on the accuracy of these guesses, and, if they make a mistake, they must move fast to correct it.

We would bring in fifty-five-pound cases of shelled walnuts. The ordinary wholesaler wouldn't get into these specialized lines, because it was a perishable item that sold in relatively small quantities, and he felt the profit wasn't work the risk. If Welch's Candy Company wanted a case of walnuts for making candy, we'd send it right up, because we had it on our shelves. The same order from another specialty wholesaler might take two or three days.

We would buy thirty or forty barrels of ginger from China through a broker, and sell them to candy firms. I managed to deal with the Canada Starch Agency and the Love's Flavor Agency for western Canada. We would get glucose from Canada Starch in four-hundred-and-fifty-pound barrels, and the flavours in quart sizes.

We had one hundred pails of assorted jams and dozens of quarts of flavours in our warehouse, ready to send out to bakeries. If Weston's or McGavin's Bakery gave our man an order for two pails of raspberry jam, a case of walnuts, a barrel of glucose, some baking powder, and three quarts of Love's vanilla, we would send it over the same day or the next morning. If someone said Vancouver was selling walnuts two cents cheaper, we met the price.

We would bid on the contract to supply peanuts in the shell to the professional baseball parks in Victoria and Vancouver, and we usually got the contract. At that time you could ship peanuts into Victoria at the same freight charge you paid to Vancouver. This made it easy for us to shave our bids lower than others.

Our competitors were bigger, unionized outfits. They weren't as productive as we were. We paid good wages, but we were a small company, and everybody worked hard, because they had a personal interest in the company's success.

Goodbye to the nut trade

"We have ten thousand dollars' worth of nuts we can't sell," said the man on the telephone. He was speaking for W.H. Malkin, wholesalers. I waited in silence for a few seconds to see what else he was going to say.

"We'd like you to take them back," he said.

"No, we can't take them back."

Sugar had been released from government control, and the bottom had dropped out of the nut busness. It didn't just taper off. It suddenly fell to ten per cent of its former volume -- just as I had feared. As candies came back to the market in quantity, people lost interest in nuts.

"Why not?" the Malkin's man wanted to know. "They're just cluttering up our warehouse."

"You ordered them, " I reminded him, but I knew I was talking to myself. He had hung up.

Two days later I heard that W.H. Malkin had put out a blanket order to all its branches in western Canada not to buy Kersey's Peanut Butter. They were hitting back at us. Then Malkins refused to pay us for the nuts which they had stored in their warehouse for many months. They still owed us for a quantity of peanut butter and for the nuts as well. They deducted the ten thousand dollars from their payments. We had sold these nuts when demand was brisk and nuts were in fairly short supply. Originally, we could have sold them easily to anybody, but, by now, these nuts were not saleable because of deterioration due to age.

As a manufacturer, anything you sell to a wholesaler or anyone else is on a guaranteed sale -- if they do not sell it, you will take it back. However, in Malkin's case, the nuts were bought many months before, and apparently got pushed around in their warehouse until they became unsaleable. We would have been happy to have them back earlier, when there was a market almost desperate to get merchandise.

I finally sued W.H. Malkin Company and collected my money through a settlement out of court. Malkin's peanut-butter boycott didn't work. The stores ordered Kersey's Peanut Butter regardless. We were so well established that the retailers and wholesalers couldn't afford not to have it.

But this was no time to pat myself on the back. I would have to move fast to keep up with the rapidly-changing, post-war market. Despite the slump in the sale of nuts, I still had a fairly-prosperous, small-scale, wholesale bakers' and candy-makers' supply business, and a high volume of sales for peanut butter. But both divisions of my business faced perilous changes. The wholesale business had worked well in times of widespread shortages and fluctuating supplies, when a small and fast-moving trader, working through a network of personal contacts, could line up materials and make special deals.

But now it was a new game. When sugar, jam, chocolate, flavouring compounds and other commodities became plentiful, the small operator would lose his edge. The big firms would move in, cut prices and grab his markets. To stay in the game, the small wholesaler would have to grow bigger and become better organized. It would take a lot of effort, and it could turn out to be a losing gamble.

The peanut-butter business faced a similar problem. But, in this case, I believed I could keep growing and outsmart the competition -- if I put all my energy into it. But, if I tried to save and enlarge the wholesale grocery business as well, I would be spreading myself too thin.

So I sold the wholesale grocery-and-nut business in 1946. The purchasers were aware of the difficulties they faced. They carried on a relatively properous trade for several years.

From that time onward, I concentrated on peanut butter. My hunch told me I had made the right choice.

Problems and opportunities

This was my lucky day. The offer I had received was so generous that I had to run through it again.

"Do you mean that I can have your chocolate quota?" I asked.

"Yes, all of it," said Francis Norton Senior, boss of the Northwestern Dairy.

It was wartime. Chocolate, cooking oil, glucose, sugar and candy, among other commodities, were scarce, unobtainable or rationed in small amounts.

"We make Revel Ice Cream Bars dipped in chocolate, as you know," Mr. Norton said. "But there are shortages of everything, including skilled labour. We don't dip the ice cream bars in chocolate anymore. It's just added work for us. Would you like to buy the chocolate?"

"Yes, I certainly would." Mr. Norton had a quota of two thousand pounds every three months. He sold it to me at what he had paid, with no mark-up.

The wartime shortages were challenging us to find coping mechanisms. The corn-derived glucose that we used to make our Carmelcrisp candy had disappeared. We found a substitute -- a new kind of glucose that an ingenious Vancouver manufacturer was making from potatoes. It was nowhere near as good as corn glucose, but it did the job.

Because of the scarcity of cooking oil, we were cooking peanuts in something called "Nujol", a mineral oil which is used in medicine. Nujol would burn at a low temperature, and gave the nuts a different taste, but people were hungry for all sorts of snacks and confections, so they bought those peanuts.

Hundreds of thousands of people were rattling around the country, a long way from their homes. They were often excited, restless and bored. They wanted entertainment; they wanted snacks to soothe their anxiety. In the case of nuts and candy, the demand was sharpened by shortages of materials. When someone says you can't have a particular food, you crave it all the more.

So we had a big demand for candy and nuts, but only a limited supply. We still had our quota of sugar from the exhibition. We melted the chocolate down and made it into a confection with sugar and peanuts. This stuff sold as fast as we could make it.

The wartime shortages, like the poverty and unemployment of the 1930's, gave businessmen both problems and opportunities. The challenge was good for our wits. It forced us to think and invent schemes and short-cuts.

If Francis Norton had been greedy, he could have squeezed me for a fat profit on the chocolate quota. But he didn't do business that way. He was a gentleman.

I ponder to this day as to why Mr. Norton was so kind to me. It was like him giving away gold. There must have been dozens of other businesses passed by.

Reaching my limit

"Sure, we're buying your peanut-butter company," said the man from Kraft, "but there's more to it than that. We're buying you as well."

"What do you mean?"

"We're offering you a five-year management contract, along with the purchase price for the company."

"You mean you'd keep me here on salary as manager?"

"You'd be working in Montreal."

This was bad news. Montreal was a different world.

"Couldn't I sell you the company without the management contract?"

"We need your knowledge of the business," the Kraft man said.

"Let me think about it."

Kraft was offering a good price, and it was a good time to sell. The increasing size and power of the chain grocery stores had begun to squeeze our business. Selling out had been at the back of my mind ever since I began to hurt from the chain stores' pressure.

Most of the big stores, like Safeway, are much more than retail stores. They are producers, manufacturers and wholesalers as well. So they favour their own products in the retail store.

If there is enough demand for your peanut butter, they will let it into the store. But they take their own line of peanut butter (which was "Beverly" at the time) and they display about six shelves of Beverly at eye level. Then they take your competing brand and stow it on the very bottom shelf, where a woman has to get on her hands and knees to reach it.

That was how the system worked in those days. Store managers had an incentive to favour their own brands. The manager got a percentage of every jar of Beverly sold. If he sold a jar of Kersey's, he got nothing.

I either had to grow bigger and stronger, or sell, and the time for that decision was fast approaching.

The Kraft offer was attractive, except for the move to Montreal. That spoiled it.

My skills as a trader, promoter and organizer, which I had developed over the years, were only part of the formula for success. A much more important part was the network of friends, helping one another, exchanging information, exchanging benefits.

True enough, I had extended my own network of friends to Vancouver, Seattle and other cities. But the centre of it was Victoria -- a warm, peaceful place a few miles away from the strawberry patch where I grew up. If I moved to Montreal, I would lose my home base.

Next week I phoned Kraft and turned down the offer. I had reached my limit, just as Father had reached his limit when he sold the bakery and moved to Keating.

I still wanted to make some more money, but I wanted to do it in my home town.

In 1953, I sold out to Derek Todd, the son of the founder of the Victoria-based firm of J.H. Todd and Company, the world's largest fish packers at that time. A few years later, Todd sold to Kelly Douglas, who eventually phased out Kersey's Peanut Butter.

I didn't make big money from peanut butter, but I made a comfortable profit. I learned to fly, and I gained some useful experience. I think I quit at exactly the right time.

Dirl products

After selling the peanut-butter business to the Todds, I decided to try a new venture -- non-perishable and no large investment necessary. In a rented basement on Douglas Street I started manufacturing hand cleaner, detergent soaps, cleaners and allied products. The products were very good as Harrison and Crosfields, our supplier of raw materials, gave us all the necessary help with proven scientific recipes.

I had sold the name "Kersey's" with the peanut-butter business, so I had to devise a new company name. It is difficult to register a trade mark in Canada, and so many names are already taken. After several names were turned down, I looked through my scrapbook and saw a horse's name -- Dirl; I bet on him in Mexico. Nobody had this name registered. I set up a company and went into production with one staff, myself. I not only manufactured the products, but I also delivered and collected payment for them.

After manufacturing for some months under the registered trade name "Dirl", I received a letter from Armour and Company's lawyers in Chicago, demanding that we immediately cease and desist using this name, as it conflicted with their "Dial" soap. Actually there was no similarity and we did have an approved Canadian registration, so we didn't get too excited. However, their letters became very demanding, threatening to take us to court. They also flew a lawyer out to Victoria to talk with us. After a lot of negotiations, they made several cash offers for us to change our name, which we didn't do; their threats eventually disappeared.

The operation proved to be quite successful. If I had put the same effort into Dirl as I did Kersey's Peanut Butter, it certainly would have been a national business today. But it was time for a change so, a couple of years after starting up, I sold the company to a local manufacturer.

Ralph was a gambling man

My friend Ralph Calladine had just as tough a time with his theatres during the depression as I had with my coffee shop.

According to some of the stories you hear, the depression was a boom time for the theatres. But it didn't seem to work that way for Ralph. He had to push hard to make a profit, with admission prices at ten and fifteen cents, and the theatres were often partly empty.

He ran vaudeville shows as well as movies. He was always alert for new gimmicks to bring in the audiences.

One fellow phoned from Port Angeles, offering to have himself frozen in a block of ice and released by breaking the ice in front of the audience. After being released from the ice, he would answer questions from the audience. This stunt had already been done successfully. (In the process of freezing the water around a thick protective suit, somehow a hole was left for the man to breathe.)

If Ralph would pay his fare from Port Angeles, the man said, he would do the stunt. All right, Ralph said, he would try it. So he featured the stunt in his advertisements.

They had the man frozen into a block of ice at the B. Wilson Company, and put him on display in the theatre lobby for the patrons to see on entering. At the end of the first act, they transported him in the block of ice to the stage. Then they cracked the ice and set him free. But the man was unconscious. They wheeled him away in an ambulance. The theatre was a sell out, but all patrons had to be given refunds.

Luckily the man recovered, but Ralph had to refund the money. It turned out that the man had never done the stunt before. He had his first try at Ralph's expense.

Ralph was a gambler, but also a likeable person, a man of his word and a gentleman. I met him through playing bridge. He could play for one dollar the whole evening and have a wonderful time, or he could gamble heavily and win or lose a lot of money. One night he won eight thousand dollars in a game on Yates Street -- a large sum for a small town like Victoria. He was nervous about being robbed on the way home, but he reached there safely.

Just before the 1939-45 War, Odeon Theatres wanted to get into Victoria, so the chain made Ralph an offer for his leases. I realize now that Odeon foresaw a boom in theatre-going. The boom was caused by some of the factors that had touched off the big demand for nuts -- the wartime economic revival, widespread anxiety and the uprooting of thousands of people from their homes.

Odeon knew that theatres would bring in big money, just as I realized dimly that there would be money in nuts and candy. Odeon bought Ralph's leases for a rumoured five hundred thousand dollars, which put him on easy street.

Ralph would have gambled all his money away, but his wife gave him an allowance of about twenty-five thousand dollars a year to gamble.

One time, when he and I were in Las Vegas, I was putting down one dollar at a time and he was betting one thousand dollars. He ran out of money. Then he and I drove to Los Angeles.

"I'll go to the bank and get a couple of thousand, and we'll go to Reno."

He introduced himself to a bank manager, who telephoned to Ralph's bank in Victoria, and soon came up with the two thousand dollars.

So we barrelled up to Reno and got in a crap game. Ralph won five thousand dollars, while I bet one dollar at a time and broke even.

We walked over to another casino, and soon Ralph had lost every cent.

We went into a bank in Reno, and this time the manager turned down his request for money, pleading problems in guaranteeing identification. But Ralph went to the bank on the other corner, and soon had one thousand dollars more.

After an hour he was broke again. That was how he lived.

He was quite knowledgeable about horse racing too. Sometimes he won a lot of money at the races, and sometimes he lost.

In the long run, he lost money. He died a few years ago, and I was the executor of his estate. It had shrunk to about one-quarter of the amount that the Odeon had paid him.

That was the difference between Ralph and me. I was much more timid. If I gambled, I wanted to make the odds as good as possible. So he lost a great deal of money, and I kept most of mine and made it grow. But maybe he had more fun.

The Kinsmen Club

Nearly all young people in my time, and older ones, belonged to a service club, also to most other clubs and organizations. These organizations were a way to raise funds for the poor and less fortunate, and for many other causes.

You knew practically everyone in the city. One night I attended what I thought was going to be the Travellers' supper meeting in the Douglas hotel. I arrived at six-fifteen, sat down, was welcomed and knew most of the people there. I had soup and part of my main course when I discovered this was the local photographers' group dinner. I finally got up and, just a little late, found the A.T.C. meeting in another part of the hotel.

Through the 1930's and the 1940's the Kinsmen Club was my second family and my school of world knowledge. The club gave you the feeling that you were an independent, useful member of the larger community.

This sense of combined independence and team membership helped me with my losing encounters with wartime bureaucracy in the army and the shipyard. The bureaucracy was a gigantic, non-human monster -- a paralyzing set of rules. It seemed oppressive, wasteful and incompetent.

In the Kinsmen Club you were a person, co-operating with other individual humans. Yet you had to do a lot of work. They gave you responsibility from the start. Nobody over the age of forty could hold office. When you joined the club in your twenties, you would go through various offices from secretary-treasurer and bulletin editor to president, and, when you served in those offices, you did a lot of community work.

These jobs also gave you practice in learning public speaking. I was on the speakers' committee at twenty-two or twenty-three years of age. You could call up just about anybody, no matter how eminent or celebrated, and ask him to speak. I called up Premier Duff Pattulo once, and he agreed to appear. I picked him up at his home, brought him to the meeting, and introduced and thanked him. Some weeks later he invited me to his home for a chat.

The club met at the Empress Hotel every other Thursday night. During the 1930's dinner was one dollar and twenty-five cents per plate.

One meeting time our guest speaker became ill at the last minute. I noticed the name of Stephen Leacock in the hotel register. I assumed it was the famous humourist, so I telephoned and recruited him as a speaker. When he got to the club I discovered that he was a different Stephen Leacock -- a professor of psychology from Saskatchewan. So I hastily revised my introduction, and he gave us an interesting talk on child psychology.

We were always holding money-raising drives for the heart fund, cancer fund or community chest. This meant hours and hours of work each week. If we had a programme going, every member turned up. You never heard of absenteeism in those days.

During the 1939 to 1945 War the Kinsmen Club gave members an outlet for their sense of duty and their sense of guilt for what they were missing. We raised money for the Milk for Britain Fund. During the 1942 Kinsmen convention in Vancouver, Bob Shanks and I put a calf in a crate, took it across in the C.P.R. boat, and wheeled it up Granville Street with the Kinsmen national band playing. We took the calf to the Hotel Vancouver and parked it in the lobby, without asking permission. This stunt raised thousands for the Milk Fund, and stirred angry complaints from the hotel management. In ways like this, I used up most of my spare energy during the wartime years.

I must agree that today's welfare state is better than the way it was in my day, when the poor were looked after by other citizens and friends. One thing we have lost, though, is the impact on our personality and emotions. In some way it made us understand life better when, for example, at Christmas we took the money and foods we had collected to a very poor family to brighten their Christmas. It touched us to see their gratitude and happiness that someone did care.

Corporal F. S. Farrar

I was introduced to Ted Farrar of the R.C.M.P. by my brother's mother-in-law. He proved to be one of the most interesting people in my generation. The R.C.M.P. patrolled the northern waters of Canada aboard the famous ship "St. Roch", now on display in Vancouver. Ted Farrar was the first person ever to circumnavigate the continent of North America through the Northwest Passage. Unfortunately Ted died at an early age and was writing a book on the North at the time of his death. It was later finished by another person and is in our library, but unfortunately many hair-raising stories died with Ted.

During the Second World War, as a member of the Victoria Kinsmen Club, I asked him to give a talk on the Far North at the Victoria High School auditorium, on 15 March 1943. He also gave talks at Christ Church Cathedral. These events were packed; admission was thirty-five cents, which helped to swell the thousands of dollars for the Kinsmen Milk for Britain Fund.

R.C.M.P. officers took a four-year stint in the North, without leave until they returned home. To the best of my memory, Ted took four of these tours of duty, totalling sixteen years of service.

There usually was a crew of seven on this small ship, and it was pretty confining for such a long period. Occasionally, one of the crew would be lost to illness as there were no medical personnel aboard. When a crew member got sick during the winter, it was necessary to tie him down on deck so he wouldn't get washed overboard in the rough seas.

When winter set in the North, the ship would get completely frozen in the ice and remain stationary until the next thaw. When the thaw arrived, it was necessary to blast the ice away from the sides of the ship, without blowing it up. Ted became the expert at this, by boring a hole in the ice, taking a stick of dynamite and putting a fuse and blasting cap on it. He would light the fuse and shove the stick down the hole. They would then wait for the explosion, which usually was very successful. On the odd occasion the stick of dynamite with its lit fuse would come back through the hole, and a few exciting minutes passed while he rammed it back down, hoping it would stay.

In places the crew would catch trout weighing up to fifty pounds. One day while the ship was frozen in the ice, Ted thought the end had come. A fish bone lodged in his throat and would not move. After two days it started to swell in his throat. The crew got the dog sled and drove many miles to a Hudson Bay post; they brought back a nurse who fed Ted orange segments, followed by warm mustard water. The fish bone dislodged and his life was saved.

On their patrols by dog-sled, the R.C.M.P. usually took along some Eskimos. The Eskimo would build an igloo for the overnight stay. In the terribly cold climate, it was necessary inside the igloo to sleep naked in a sleeping bag; otherwise, if clothes were kept on, ice would form under arms, etc. At night the dogs would have to be staked apart, otherwise they would destroy one another.

Also, because of the temperature, the guns had to be left outside on top of the igloo; they could not be taken from inside to outside as they then would not fire. One night Ted was awakened by a polar bear who was attacking the dogs. His job was to get up and get dressed, rush outside, grab his gun and shoot the intruder.

Ted told me he couldn't agree with some of the police work -- to stop the Eskimos from shooting and killing their old parents who could no longer move around. It was necessary for survival for Eskimos to move about the country and, when a parent became unable to do this, they had no alternative. It was a difficult task for the police to try and change this custom by arresting and charging people.

The gallant little St. Roch required over two years to make the voyage through the Northwest Passage, covering ten thousand miles from Vancouver, B.C. to Halifax, N.S. It was an experience which included topping waves hundreds of feet high, living with the Eskimos and using the magnetic pole as an outhouse.

The following articles are from the Victoria Daily Colonist:

28 March 1950:

When the St. Roch arrives at Halifax early in June, Sgt. F.S. Farrar will be the first man to have sailed completely around the continent. He served aboard the famous Arctic ship for ten years under Inspector Henry Larsen.

The RCMP Arctic patrol ship St. Roch, only vessel ever to navigate the Northwest Passage from west to east, and also the only craft to have sailed the famed top-of-the-continent route in both directions, will soon have another "first" to add to her impressive record.

She is scheduled to sail from Esquimalt April 6 for Halifax, but this time she will go via the Panama Canal, and thus become the first ship ever to sail completely around the North American continent.

The voyage will involve several other "firsts", for the first time an ice-box has been installed in the hold of the St. Roch, awnings are aboard to be rigged in the southern waters, tropical clothing will be worn by her crew instead of parkas, and for the first time she will be under the command of someone other than Inspector Henry Larsen, veteran Arctic skipper. Inspector K.W.M. Hall is now her captain.

One of her crew, Sgt. F.S. Farrar, will have the distinction of being the only man to have sailed completely around the continent, for he is the lone member of the present crew of 14 members of the RCMP marine division who was aboard the ship when she went from Vancouver to Halifax, via the Arctic, from 1940-1942, returning in 1944.

Sgt. Farrar, who served for 10 years on the St. Roch, has just come from RCMP headquarters at Ottawa to serve as third mate of the 105-foot ship. He will record the voyage on motion picture film for the force.

Built at Burrard, North Vancouver, in 1928, the 300 horsepower, diesel-driven St. Roch will stop at San Francisco, San Diego, Acapulco, Mexico, Balboa, Canal Zone, Havana, Cuba, and Norfolk, Va., en route to Halifax.

Inspector Hall is allowing two months for the journey, but expects to do it in less with favorable weather.

The Southern voyage has made it necessary to add two water tanks, each of 500 gallons, in addition to the ice-box.

When the ship is in the Arctic, she can get ice from loose flows and the great northern pack. Water is obtained from the pack where it lies in hollow "pans". Though salt water ice, the water in these pans is fresh.

There have been a few changes in accommodation on the RCMP vessel -- most notable likely being that to the bunk in the captain's cabin. Originally it ran fore-and-aft, but was less than six feet long. Inspector Hall took one look at it and had it made athwartships -- and seven feet long, because the new commander of the St. Roch is six foot one in his stocking feet.

June 1950: *Ship makes round-continent-trip history*

By its safe arrival at Halifax, the 105-foot St. Roch became the first vessel ever to semi-circle the North American continent. St. Roch, a RCMP supply ship, started its great adventure in 1944, when it left Halifax for the Pacific Ocean via the fabulous Northwest Passage, under the charge of former Victorian, H.C. Larsen, Inspector of the RCMP, who is now stationed in Ottawa.

After an adventurous voyage, St. Roch arrived at Victoria, having circumnavigated all the perils of the polar waters with its crew of 15 men. The St. Roch left Victoria this year to complete the less adventurous journey, from Victoria to Halifax via the Panama Canal.

Of the crew which braved the Northwest Passage only one remained to complete the second leg of the journey. He was Sergeant Ted Farrar, a Liverpool-born member of the RCMP. He now holds the distinction of being the first man to encircle the North American continent by sea.

Commenting on the polar bears of the Arctic and the veiled senoritas of the tropics, Sergeant Farrar found the second part of the journey not up to the standard of the first in the quality of excitement.

Professional baseball

In 1948 a group of Victorians gathered together and arranged for a professional baseball franchise in Victoria. Actually my feelings were that Victoria, at that time, was too small to support such a team financially.

The team had many different managers, players and directors over a short period of time. In 1953 we had Ted Norbert as a manager; he proved that we had a winning ball club. In the Western International League our team was always near the top, giving us really good baseball.

We were a farm team of the New York Yankees. Some world figures developed their skills in Victoria, most notably Gil McDougal who became a hero in professional baseball. There were many others.

Some of the players would provide other entertainment also. Len Kasparovetch from Hawaii would occasionally don a grass skirt and paraphenalia, and do a Hula Dance in the infield for the patrons. Balassi would serenade with a guitar and a horse, and the six-foot twin White brothers would play piano and write songs about the team.

The pro ball games were played at the park on North Park Street. Slim Hunt, the City of Victoria groundsman, took as much interest in keeping these grounds as he would his own home.

Baseball started in April each year, and it was nearly always too cold for patrons to sit out in the open.

The ball club installed the most modern lighting for the park. One night, though, the fog kept rolling in; we would lose sight of the outfield and, eventually, of the pitcher. Finally the patrons had to be given a rain check for another night.

As far as I can remember, the directors of the ball club were:

Bill Straith	Lawyer and M.L.A.
Johnny Johnson	Evans Coleman Cement
Francis Norton	Northwestern Dairy
Em Neeley	Owner, Douglas Hotel
Eric Cox	Controller for Bill Dunbar
Ed Mallek	Famous Clothier
Morris Kersey	Kersey's Peanut Butter

Of these directors, only Ed Mallek and I were middle age (forty); all the others seemed to be pretty old, but had been very successful in their businesses. Personally, I felt that, as far as being directors of a professional ball club, they were either not interested enough or didn't understand the problems. Anything Ed Mallek or I brought up at a meeting was quickly defeated.

The club was operating at a terrific loss and was always overdrawn at the bank. All the directors, at one time or another, were individually signing bank guarantees. One time, when the bank called on the directors, I was alarmed to find out that each and every one of us who had signed a bank guarantee was responsible for the entire debt, meaning, if some guarantors didn't pay, the others were required to pick up this portion. In my business life, this was the first and last time I ever signed such a form.

A gentleman from Duncan and his wife, who were ardent supporters of the baseball club, had been left a huge fortune by some relative in England. Reg Patterson, the manager, sold him many thousands of dollars of shares; their value was lost pretty rapidly.

At one particular directors' meeting, it was decided by a majority vote, with Mallek and myself voting against it, to hire "Cupe" Barrett. Barrett was notorious throughout all the upper levels of professional baseball in America. He had been fired from all the good teams for his personal behaviour, and came to us with a reputation that would not recommend him for any position. Mallek and I were outnumbered and he was hired on a long contract. He lasted a very short time, and it cost the club an arm and a leg to get rid of his contract. As a result of this, I resigned, along with Bill Mallek. The club was soon bankrupt, which was the end of professional baseball in Victoria.

Victoria, like all cities, had its so-called characters. One of these was Joe North, who always wore a bowler hat and, almost always, was drunk. He attended most ball games and was an absolute nuisance, but nobody seemed to want to ban him from coming to the games. Not even the police could handle him; they would often take him home from the ball park to sober up.

Joe was always able to produce the finest "raspberry" with his mouth, spitting over everyone near him. At one particular game, Joe was sitting in front of me, and had really spit over a few patrons who couldn't get far enough away from him. The police were asked to remove him, but to no avail. A fellow sitting beside me suggested that he and I take him out. The fellow got him around the neck and I took his feet. We carried him out; all the patrons stood and gave us a thunderous round of applause. He was not allowed back in the park again.

During his life, Joe would be at every sporting or public event, taking up a collection for the poor with his hat. His collections were good, but how much went to charity nobody will ever know.

"Life is too short to be little." - Disraeli

Fred McGregor - *" My favourite quotation is the sentence above. It has helped me through many a painful experience. Often we allow ourselves to be upset by things we should despise and forget. Perhaps some man we helped has proved ungrateful; some woman we believed to be a friend has spoken ill of us; some reward we thought we deserved has been denied us. We feel disappointments so strongly that we can no longer work or sleep. But isn't that absurd? Here we are on this earth, with only a few more decades to live, and we lose many irreplaceable hours brooding over grievances that, in a year's time, will be forgotten by us and by everybody. No, let us devote our life to worthwhile actions and feelings, to great thoughts, real affections and enduring undertakings. For life is too short to be little."*

Promise Yourself

To be strong, that nothing can disturb your peace of mind.
To talk health, happiness and prosperity to every person you meet.
To make all your friends feel that there is something in them.
To look on the sunny side of everything and
make your optimism come true.
To think only of the best, to work only for the best,
and to expect only the best.
To be just as enthusiastic about the success of others,
as you are about your own.
To forget the mistakes of the past and press on
to the great achievements of the future.
To wear a cheerful countenance at all times and have a smile
for every living creature you meet.
To give as much time to the improvement of yourself
that you have no time to criticize others.
To be too large for worry, too noble for anger, too strong for fear, and
too happy to permit the presence of trouble.
To think well of yourself and to proclaim this fact to the world --
not in loud words but in great deeds.
To live in the faith that the whole world is on your side
so long as you are true to the best that is in you.

- Fred McGregor

My father's bakery truck for bread delivery
Alpha Street, Victoria, Canada
circa 1918.

Keating School
Mrs. Parberry, Principal
circa 1922.

*Third home of the Kersey family
Veyaness Road, Keating
circa 1922.*

*Strawberry patch
Stelly's Cross Road, Keating
circa 1919.*

*First home of the Kersey family at
Keating, Stelly's Cross Road
circa 1919.*

Morris Kersey's coffee shop circa 1935.

A
DELICIOUS
LUNCH
AWAITS YOU

LUNCH WITH
US EVERY DAY

WE GIVE YOU 18 SPECIALS TO CHOOSE
FROM DAILY

Soup. Hot Roast Spring Chicken with Dressing, Vegetables, Potatoes and Gravy. Bread and Butter. Blueberry, Apple or Raisin Pie. Tea. Coffee. Milk **30c**

Soup. Hot Roast Beef with Vegetables, Potatoes and Gravy. Bread and Butter. Blueberry, Apple or Raisin Pie. Tea. Coffee. Milk **30c**

Soup. Grilled Spring Salmon Trout with Egg Sauce, Vegetables, Potatoes. Bread and Butter. Blueberry, Apple or Raisin Pie. Tea. Coffee. Milk **30c**

Choice of Soup or Dessert. Macaroni and Cheese. Bread and Butter. Stewed Plums. Tea. Coffee. Milk **25c**

Soup. Poached Egg on Grilled Ham and Spinach with Toast. Tea. Coffee. Milk **25c**

Fried Ham and Sweet Potatoes with Corn. Bread and Butter. Tea. Coffee. Milk **25c**

Toasted Devilled Egg Sandwich. Blackberry, Apple or Raisin Pie. Tea. Coffee. Milk **20c**

Choice of Soup or Dessert. Cold Roast Beef Sandwich. Stewed Plums. Tea. Coffee. Milk **20c**

Choice of Soup or Dessert. Minced Steak on Toast. Stewed Plums. Tea. Coffee. Milk **20c**

Fresh Salmon Sandwich. Blackberry, Apple or Raisin Pie. Tea. Coffee. Milk **20c**

Choice of Soup or Dessert. Toasted Cheese and Bacon Sandwich. Stewed Plums. Tea. Coffee. Milk **20c**

Salmon Sandwich. Fresh Pear, Blueberry, Apple or Raisin Pie. Tea. Coffee. Milk **20c**

PIE Apple, Raisin or Blueberry for **5c**

Morris Kersey Coffee Shop

644 FORT STREET   PHONE G 0133

Morris Kersey's coffee shop (Carmel Crisp)
644 Fort Street, Victoria, Canada
circa 1936.

Staff photo from the Kersey peanut butter plant
1626 Store Street, Victoria, Canada
circa 1946.

Unloading peanuts
1626 Store Street, Victoria, Canada
circa 1947.

One of the Kersey delivery trucks in front of the Royal Theatre
Victoria, Canada
circa 1946.

Part 4: <u>*1954 - PRESENT*</u>

"In every man there is something wherein I may learn of him, and in that I am his pupil."   - Emerson

<u>*Yes, there is a free lunch*</u>

People often say, "There's no free lunch," or "You can't get something for nothing."

But this item of folk wisdom is not strictly true. I know you can get something for nothing, because I did it. In fact, I made hundreds of thousands of dollars without investing any money of my own.

Not long after I sold the peanut-butter business, a good friend of mine, who was a salesman with Texaco Canada, came to me and said, "You ought to build service stations."

"I operated a service station for a while, but that was years ago," I said. "I hadn't thought of getting back into that business."

"You don't have to operate a service station," he said. "Our company wants to get into the Vancouver Island market, and the company's policy is to rent its service station buildings, not to own them."

"All you do," he said, "is get the site, put up a building and rent it to Texaco. We'll give you a non-cancellable lease for twenty years. It will pay you between four and six per cent on the investment, but you don't have to raise any money of your own."

"We'll get you the mortgage money, and you can go ahead and use the money to buy the site and put up the building. It's no gamble; we'll guarantee the rent."

I talked to my bank manager about the proposal. He didn't like it, and he tried to discourage me from going ahead. The way he assessed the deal was that there had to be something wrong with it. It was too good to be true. Luckily I didn't take his advice. There was nothing wrong. It was just that Texaco didn't want to sink its money into that much real estate. Safeway Stores did the same thing -- advanced the money to people who built store buidings, and then rented them back.

I built seven service stations this way. I never put any money into them; I just took the rent and paid off the mortgage. I sold five service stations a few years after I built them, and realized a tiny profit on the money that Texaco had advanced.

The Provincial Highways Department expropriated one of the service stations at the corner of Burnside Road, to make room for the widening of the Trans-Canada Highway.

In 1988 I sold the last station, located at Sooke and Kelly Roads, in what is now Victoria's Western Communities. Let me give you a few figures. The Sooke Road station cost nineteen thousand dollars for the land and buildings. I got a twenty-one thousand dollar mortgage, so I had a couple of thousand dollars to spare. The twenty-five-year mortgage was paid off with rental income, and in 1988 the property's value was nearly ten times its cost.

I suppose Texaco chose me on my friend's recommendation, because the company saw me as a reliable person, who could be trusted not to get into a mess and mismanage the property. But there wasn't much management involved; the deal ran itself.

Today (in 1988) it is much easier to construct a service sation, as the money is so easy to get, even without security, and even Texaco and other oil companies are anxious to develop new sites. All you have to do is the ground work, and right in our own area there are many sites available that only need a proposal to be presented, and it could be accepted. They make a great pension if you are fortunate enough to live for another twenty-five or thirty years. In the thirty years I had the Sooke and Kelly Roads property, I received net rentals totalling over one hundred and fifty thousand dollars, and sold the station to Payless for one hundred and seventy-five thousand dollars. Out of this income and sale, totalling over three hundred and twenty-five thousand dollars, all I had to pay was the original cost of the land -- nineteen thousand dollars -- plus mortgage and income taxes.

There are many more, easier opportunities today, but being too old or not needing a pension, I look around and wonder why some of our younger people, who could be interested, wouldn't stop long enough from playing around to work on such ideas.

Airport Gift Shop

In 1964, the government decided to replace the poky little buildings of Victoria International Airport with a new terminal building, and tenders were called for the construction, also for a private contractor to run a coffee shop. I was the only bidder for the coffee shop, and won the concession by offering to pay six per cent of gross income for the coffee shop or a minimum of one thousand eight hundred dollars a year. It was a tiny operation. A large number of the customers were employees of the airport, Air Canada and Canada Customs.

We got started in 1965. I kept on working part time as a flying instructor, hired a girl to work in the coffee shop while I was busy flying, and watched the business grow. At the start, the gross receipts were less than thirty thousand dollars a year. There was about enough profit to pay for my toast and coffee.

By the 1980's the size of the terminal had been progressively expanding to cope with the increasing number of passengers, and we had added a gift shop.

In 1977, I decided to sell the restaurant and keep only the gift shop.

This was a time of greater prosperity and more lenient unemployment insurance rules. In one girl's case I had refused to sign her separation certificate, which she needed for her unemployment insurance claim. This brought on an official hearing, like a trial, in which I had to explain why I would not sign the certificate.

"She's a good worker; we don't want to lose her. We'll keep her," I said.

"Never mind," the government man said. "It's a free country. She has the right to quit if she wants."

I had to sign her document to enable her to get unemployment insurance benefits.

We hired a new girl to replace her and, within three months, she started losing interest, so I gave her a kindly-uncle talk and a small raise in pay. Then she disappeared.

Her case was just a re-run of a number of others. The first dozen or so times I accepted it as part of the game, but I was beginning to get tired and angry. Was it worth going on? I had serious doubts.

There were other irritations. Inflation was moving steadily upwards but, when we increased our price of coffee to fifteen cents, a number of people who worked at the airport took it as a personal affront. They began bringing their own coffee pots to the office and conspicuously boycotting the coffee shop. When we dared to raise the price of a hamburger to sixty-five cents, along with most other restaurants in town, one fellow got so angry that he lodged a complaint with the Ministry of Transport, and there was an investigation.

At the news that one more waitress had left without notice, all these annoyances -- flighty waitresses, government investigations of the price of a hamburger -- pooled into a mass of resentment that triggered a decision.

"All right, I'll advertise for another waitress," I told the manager, and I said to myself, "I'll advertise the coffee shop for sale."

The next day, by lucky coincidence, a fellow named Richard Impett appeared at the airport to see his boss off on a journey.

"You can have the restaurant for fifty thousand dollars, and I'll keep the gift-shop portion," I told him. "You can take over right away and pay five thousand dollars a month out of the profits at six per cent on the balance. Are you interested?"

"I sure am," he said. He called me that night and said, "I'll take it."

That was in 1977. He has been there ever since as a full partner, because the lease was in both our names. We have never had a written agreemant. He ran the restaurant, paid his percentage, and I ran the gift shop and paid my percentage. He paid me in full in less than one year.

Before Richard Impett came along, I had offered the same deal to several others. They wanted time to think it over, and they asked me to sign documents, contracts and guarantees. But Impett trusted me. It's wonderful to think that there are still people with whom you can do business on trust. I don't recommend that everybody try the trust system; there may be some people around who can't be trusted. But it worked for us.

I ran the gift shop from 1977-1986, moving around the airport lobby to enlarge it three different times. I also put in a duty-free liquor outlet. The gift shop was not the greatest money maker, but it always made a good profit, in spite of the high gross rental percentage we paid to the government -- twenty-five per cent gross on liquor and fifteen and three-tenths per cent on other items. It was a pleasure to operate and had less than one per cent of the restaurant problems.

In 1986, it was time for a change. I had worked for Totem Travel, along with my other business, for over fifteen years, so today I am marking time and promoting sales in a small way for Totem Travel.

"Somewhere I suppose I have enemies but they do not openly declare themselves, so I cannot make amends for wrongs I may have done. I am the most fortunate of men, since I have not lacked love, friends, accomplishments, laughter or health. There has only been a terrible balancing - where are we at this appointed time and place in relation to all that has gone before. We have too many personal toys and apparently not enough time to use them properly. We are surfeited with all manner of luxuries. Our engagement calendar is as full or as empty as we wish it to be. Most of the friends I held dear are still mine to enjoy, even if our reunions are sometimes infrequent."

- Earnest Gann

Part 5: <u>FLYING</u>

*"To soar with the birds
And reach for the clouds,
Leaving the world's care --
That is feeling close to God,
As you fly alone in the air."*

- Ursula Thomas (SKY PILOT April 2001)

Flying has a long history in Victoria. In 1927 Nick Carter became the first president of the Victoria Aero Club, which was renamed the Victoria Flying Club after the war, in 1946. Some of the founding members were D.W. Hanbury, Stewart MacLeod, R.H.B. Kerr, N. Yarrow, Sidney Pickles, L.S. Duke and H.M. McGiverin. Most of them were quite a bit older than I was. However, as a young person, I was very interested in flying and would watch the activity at the Lansdowne Field, which is now the site of Lansdowne Junior High School. Maurice McGregor, of my age group, did quite a lot of flying from Lansdowne.

A Victoria-Seattle commercial service was started with a Ford Tri-Motor. However, unfortunately, in 1928 the plane was lost with fourteen passengers en route to Seattle.

After the Second World War, thousands of wartime pilots, would-be pilots and youngsters were eager to get into the air. The Victoria Flying Club licensed many local pilots, too numerous to mention.

Bill Sylvester opened an air charter business, flying under the name of Victoria Flying Services, where many more Victoria boys and girls learned to fly. (Seventeen-year-old Phyllis Drysdale became the youngest licensed woman pilot in all Canada in the late 1940's.) I worked for Bill part time as a flying instructor, which is a pleasant and rewarding line of work. Our students needed no motivation, were very keen to learn their skills and seldom gave any trouble; they all aspired to become air-line captains.

My thoughts of a flying career almost stopped while I was visiting in Los Angeles. Jack Knock was a flight instructor in Los Angeles in the early thirties; he looked after Wallace Beery's aeroplane, as well as many others. I volunteered for a flight with him, and spent close to one hour doing aerobatics over Hollywood and area. Being in an open cockpit, upside down and all ways, had me so frightened and upset that it took me many years to get over it. Later when I became a flight instructor, I always remembered how terrified I was and tried to relate this to my students, especially when giving spins in an aircraft, which was mandatory in those days.

In the 1960's many young fellows learned to fly, as it was within their reach financially; today it is very costly to obtain a transport licence or even a private licence. Teaching flying in those days, we had a line-up of students waiting. One after the other, they were usually given a thirty-minute lesson. In a few weeks, after the pupil showed he was capable, he had his first solo flight -- at about eight hours total time. He was then on his own, taking a check ride every four or five hours of solo. After approximately forty hours total time, dual and solo, he could obtain a private licence. From there he could take a commercial and transport licence. We hardly had time to get to know the pupil before he finished completing his course. To this day it is nice to fly on a commercial airline and know that the captain was one of these students.

Some of the things you remember -- the first Piper Apache Twins when doing a simulated engine-out and shutting one engine down. On this model it would be difficult to get the engine started again, so you would be forced to return to the airport and land with one engine, causing some excitement.

You always remember your first spin with an instructor, and your first solo spin. In a spin you shut the engine down to idle and hold the control stick right back, bringing the nose up until the aircraft stalls, meaning it no longer has any lift and quits flying. The engine, being heavy, drops the aeroplane straight down; by pushing the rudder control, you put the plane into a spin, which is quite a sensation. It is not a dangerous procedure, or damaging to the aircraft structure, and, with a modern aeroplane, it is quite easy to bring it out of a spin.

I also did a very small amount of float, charter business, but this is much harder -- usually fighting weather and other elements, transporting loggers in and out of camps, telephone installers to the various islands, and land purchasers looking over B.C. from the air.

One of my charter-flying customers included the now-deceased, movie-star Jimmy Rogers. I took him to a Gulf Island which was for sale; however, he didn't buy it.

One gentleman from Germany wanted to look around most of the coastline of Vancouver Island. I flew him, along with his friend and his daughter, who did most of the translating. To my knowledge, he did not make any purchases, but he gave me a one hundred-dollar tip and sent a thank-you letter from Germany.

Another customer, a photographer, would photograph farms and houses on both sides of roads all over Vancouver Island. After developing the pictures, he would call on the people living on these farms to sell the aerial pictures. His business seemed quite profitable; he told me he had nearly ninety-five-per-cent sales of all pictures taken.

At one time Dick Moore, of Moore and Whittington Lumber Company, asked to be flown over a tug towing a boom of logs. They would be located somewhere in the Strait of Georgia. The idea was to land the float plane alongside the boom as it was being towed. My passenger would jump out of the aeroplane and walk over the boom to check the quality of the logs. He would then call in and make a bid for it. It was a different way to purchase timber.

On Friday nights I would fly loggers out of an interior lake to Nanaimo or some place for the weekend. They would go to the beer parlour and spend their money. On Monday morning they would fly back to the camp.

The cook in this camp made the best doughnuts you ever tasted. In fact all cook houses served the finest food; otherwise the loggers would not stay. One customer, Don Ross, an insurance adjuster, would always arrange our flight schedule to arrive at a camp ten minutes before lunch. In those days the dining rooms had cups with no handles, but they offered about three different roasts or steaks and massive amounts of vegetables, etc. The rule was "no talking at meal time"; the room was silent by request.

Tofino, on the west coast of Vancouver Island, was often so foggy and the weather so poor that you would be grounded. At the small hotel where we stayed, the operator was the clerk, barber, chef and undertaker -- quite a combination.

One time we had an emergency call to pick up a lady on Saturna Island; she had a miscarriage or something. She was in an unconscious state, with no room in the aircraft for anyone other than the two of us. After picking her up I flew her to Ladysmith Hospital. She recovered and sent a thank-you note to the company along with her payment.

Over the years many things happened to us, but, as I was only flying charters in my spare time, I did not encounter the things many pilots did.

A chap I had only met casually, Ralph Edwards, homesteaded in Lonesome Lake, many miles from Bella Coola on our mainland coast. The man was very short and stocky, and did the impossible -- living in the wilderness with a daily struggle for survival. Here he raised a family, and made all his own equipment and power plant. He eventually came to Vancouver to purchase an aeroplane, and he taught himself to fly. His book, "Crusoe of Lonesome Lake", was published in 1957, and is possibly the most unusual, true-life story of survival that I have ever read.

One evening a man came into the Flying Services about six p.m., two hours before sundown. He was wearing only pants, shoes and a T-shirt, and was carrying a small brown bag; he was loaded to the gills. He wanted to go to Port Angeles, so he prepaid the fare. While we were taxiing for take-off, he opened the brown bag which contained three bottles of beer. He offered me one, which I refused. During the fifteen-minute trip from Victoria to Port Angeles the three beers were consumed. About every two minutes he would slap me hard across the back and say, "Look behind and see if my wife is following me."

When we arrived in Port Angeles I got out ahead of him and asked the Customs man if he would allow this fellow entry in his condition. The Customs man said it was OK and apparently drove him into town. Early the next morning the R.C.M.P. phoned the airline office requesting to know his destination; his wife was looking for him. Two days later the fellow phoned to be picked up. However, there was a policy on this -- anyone who is on a bender would be broke, so never pick him up; leave it to someone else.

I spent a short time as B.C. Airlines representative in Victoria; this was after Bill Sylvester sold his company to Maurice MacGregor and Associates.

B.C. Airlines had an interesting array of old-time pilots. Bill Waddington, who later became Captain of the Mars water bomber, is a story unto himself in flying experiences. We never mention to Bill the story about his youth when he was flying a new Cessna 180 on floats near Vancouver. He was following too close to Johnny Boak who was piloting a Beaver. Bill actually hit the tail end of the Beaver and flipped the 180, nose-diving it into the water from a thousand feet or more. Bill was submerged to quite a depth, but escaped; he ended up with two broken legs. A fishing boat picked him up. He was soon healed and flying again.

Tommy Walsh was Chief Engineer for B.C. Airlines and had some interesting events to recall after the Second World War. On one flight, while they were coming across the Atlantic with a load of military personnel, the Whip Radio Antenna they used in those days broke loose and was lashing the fuselage of the aircraft. It had to be removed; otherwise it could tear up the skin of the plane. Tommy volunteered to have a rope tied around him and climb out the door to remove the antenna, which he did. This would make the average person's blood run cold, but he just took it in stride.

Another time, on a famous Seabee, the wing float on one side came off during landing. To get the plane airborne again, it was necessary for Tommy to hang on outside the aeroplane, to the remaining wing float on the other side, until they got off the water; then he clambered aboard.

A contractor who was flying, under the influence, over Patricia Bay Airport in a Cessna 210, gave the tower quite a problem. The tower cleared all other aeroplanes from the area and finally got the drunk on final approach to the runway. The tower operator cleared him to land and said, "Wheels down and locked."

The pilot said, " Buddy, you take care of the tower and I'll look after the aeroplane." After landing he was picked up by the R.C.M.P. At his court hearing sometime later, the tape of the landing was played and the pilot sat there with a red face. He was only suspended from flying for about thirty days.

Canada's Centennial

The following is a short story written in 1967:

On July 1, 1967, Canada will celebrate one hundred years of confederation. In this foundation of nationhood, that we are rightfully proud of, aviation played a great part. In 1867 there were approximately three million people in Canada, but, with this small population, we were second to none in the development and pioneering of flying.

In 1928, Victoria, British Columbia, Canada, held the honour of having the first scheduled air service in Canada -- from Victoria to Seattle, Washington, U.S.A., using a tri-motor Ford.

Again today, because of the good, year-round, weather conditions, we are being similarly honoured by having in our skies, almost daily, a rare vintage aircraft -- the Avro 504K, a forerunner of today's transporters. This biplane is training to participate in the Golden Centennial Aerobatic Display, formed to commemorate the fiftieth anniversary of military flying in Canada, and is scheduled to appear in most Canadian cities this summer. It was manufactured in 1913 and flown by the Royal Flying Corps and the Royal Naval Air Service in Britain early in the First World War, being the trainer in British service at that time.

Two jet pilots are putting it through its paces. For the air shows the pilots will wear thermal underwear and authentic copies of flying gear from that era; these are presently being made and include riding boots, blue breeches and jackets, leather helmets, goggles and long white scarves -- plus, in 1967, a parachute.

The Canadian Air Board received sixty-two Avros from the British government in 1919. In 1924 the first R.C.A.F. pilots received their basic training on these planes.

The specifications are: all-wood frame of Sitka spruce covered with a doped linen, thirty-six foot wing span, twenty-nine feet five inches long, ten feet five inches high, empty weight of one thousand two hundred and thirty pounds, carrying load of six hundred pounds, cruising speed of eighty-five miles per hour, range of two hundred and fifty miles, and ceiling of sixteen thousand feet. The engine is a one-hundred-and-ten-horsepower LeRhone and is designed so that all nine cylinders circumnavigate the crank shaft clockwise when running. The engine is lubricated by Castor Oil, which has a one-way trip through the cylinders to the outside of the fuselage and crew. The spark plugs also have a one-way-trip life expectancy, being of the common tractor type; they are used and replaced with new ones about every two hours. There are no brakes or throttle. The pilot presses a button on the control column to slow down; this shorts the magnetos and cuts the electric power to the engine. It is easy to turn right but difficult to turn left because of the torque produced by the entire engine turning. The only instruments are an altimeter and airspeed and r.p.m. gauges. The plane has a tail skid and also a front skid which is used for drag-wire bracing and nose-over protection for the wooden propeller.

Martin Mars Flying Boats

There were only four Martin Mars aircraft, the largest flying boats ever built, other than Howard Hughes' Spruce Goose. These four aircraft, trade named after the Roman God of War, bore the individual names Marshall, Philippines, Marianas and Hawaii, after the Pacific islands.

They had four Curtis Wright radial engines of two thousand four hundred horsepower each, a wing span of over two hundred feet, and a tail as high as a five-storey building.

In 1959 these aircraft were purchased by The Flying Tankers Limited, a group of B.C. forest companies, and converted to use as fire fighters. They proved to be most satisfactory as water bombers.

Today there are still two aircraft in operation. One was lost in 1961 near Nanaimo while fighting a fire. The other was damaged beyond repair in 1962, when it was on the ground at Victoria International Airport; Typhoon Frieda, with winds up to ninety miles per hour, tossed it across the airport like a balloon.

Bill Waddington became Captain of the Mars Bombers after leaving B.C. Airlines.

Hugh Thomas

Hugh Thomas is one of the characters of aviation. He is ten years my senior and still so motivated he has engineered a new design of aircraft that we all hope will fly in the next couple of years (1990), at which time he will be pushing ninety.

Hugh was born in Colorado. His father was a Canadian geologist. His family moved back to Canada in 1903, to Vancouver where Hugh attended King Edward High School and became interested in aviation.

In 1919 Hugh went to Texas during the oil boom, where he joined a firm which serviced oil rigs. His boss was a World War I pilot, and owned an aeroplane; he was instrumental in convincing Hugh that he should learn to fly.

Hugh moved to Los Angeles in 1921, and soloed in a "Canuck" JN 40. Afterwards he owned his own "Canuck", powered by a one-hundred-and-fifty-horsepower Hispano 5U12A engine. At that time Hugh was working for the Packard Automobile agent.

In 1922, Hugh went on his own, building custom automobile bodies for movie stars.

In 1929 Hugh and a friend owned a machine shop and engaged in subcontract work for the Douglas Aircraft Company. He designed an eight-cylinder, one-hundred-and-sixty-horsepower radial engine, an almost unheard of engine of which he still has photos.

Hugh completed a course in aeronautical engineering in 1932.

Hugh returned to Canada in 1936, and went to work with Coates Limited at Vancouver Airport. He owned and flew a Ryan monoplane, sister aircraft to Lindberg's "Spirit of St. Louis".

In January 1940 Hugh went to Brisbane Aviation Company Limited, as chief engineer and instructor at their school for aircraft technicians and engineers. Brisbane became a subcontractor for Boeing Aircraft in 1941-1942; Hugh was the firm's chief inspector.

During the war Hugh spent three months in Los Angeles with Sperry Gyroscope Company, obtaining a certificate that licensed him to overhaul their equipment.

In 1948 Hugh joined B.C. Airlines, the company Bill Sylvester formed.

In 1951 Hugh was employed by the B.C. Government as chief engineer, aircraft maintenance; here he remained until his so-called retirement.

Hugh has owned many aircraft -- a D.H. Tiger Moth 82C on floats, a Fairchild FC2W2 which he sold to Bill Sylvester, a Stagger Wing Beech on floats, a Piper Clipper on floats, a Seabee, and a Stinson L5. In 1940, Hugh did some aeroplane swapping and other things to procure Hudson Island and two adjacent islands. They are located in the vicinity of Thetis Island, which is only a few miles east of Chemainus on Vancouver Island. Hudson Island is an "Island Paradise". On this small island Hugh, along with many flying enthusiasts, built a small grass airstrip between the trees. Overall, it is two thousand one hundred feet long; however, only about half is really usable. Over the years there have been some very interesting landings. It is really only for pilots who have experience landing on small airstrips. Hugh has shared the island with nearly all flyers, and it has been a hidden playground, with birds, oysters and warm water for swimming.

There are few people in Canada or America who have the aeronautical knowledge and can apply it as Hugh does. If there is a Hall of Fame, Hugh should be there.

Pacific Ocean to Atlantic Ocean and return in a Cessna 170

Living here in the Pacific North West (Victoria, B.C.) it had always been my desire to fly a small aircraft from the Pacific to the Atlantic. I was fortunate enough to have been in a position to purchase a nearly-new Cessna 170, which I later sold and purchased a Cessna 180.

Flying is a very economical way to see the country. In 1958, piloting a 170 single-engine Cessna, I flew my friend Dick to see his daughter in New York, and took along another friend, Lorne, a successful local lumberman who had recently received his Private Pilot's Licence. On this particular cross-country trip, Dick, a non-flyer and a retired wholesale fruit executive, sat in the back seat and did all the bookkeeping of headings, expenses, etc.

We had a very simple financial arrangement. We each put up a starter amount of fifty dollars, which Dick put into one of his pockets. From this total of one hundred and fifty dollars, Dick paid all the expenses for food, lodging, taxis, entertainment, etc. When the pocket emptied, we would all replenish it. This sure simplified the bookkeeping. Although I might sometimes have lobster for dinner while the others had a hamburger each, over the trip it all balanced out. Our expenses were often offset through the kindness of others. It seems to be the law of the land in a pilot's world that, practically everywhere you land, a welcome hand is held out to you by a local pilot -- a car is loaned to you and you really get the V.I.P. treatment.

On a trip of any length, you are almost certain to run into inclement weather, which necessitates changing your direct course or landing and sitting out the storm. Unless you have an I.F.R. (Instrument Flight Rules) rating and the aeroplane is so equipped, it is generally impossible to go directly from A to B, unless the weather is perfect. This is nearly always the problem, summer or winter, over the Cascade Mountains and any direct route going east.

On July 8th in the late afternoon we left Patricia Bay Airport (Victoria), in below V.F.R. minimums, to go to Bellingham, Washington, to clear American Customs, and then down to Portland, Oregon, a route I knew very well. We landed at Troutedale, just east of Portland Airport. After refueling and checking the weather, we learned that conditions were not too bad up the Columbia River so we flew east, landing at dusk in Dalles, Oregon, to overnight. I must say that here, as was our experience everywhere when we landed, the "red carpet" was rolled out -- only the most courteous people must be in aviation!

The Dalles Airport operator loaned us a car to drive to the city, and friend Dick, not being a pilot, volunteered to do the driving, but this was a first and last arrangement. You may consider flying hazardous, but your life could be at stake with Dick at the controls of an automobile on a busy highway. There was a stop sign on the side road leading from the airport onto the main highway. Dick not only didn't see the stop sign, he didn't see the arterial highway, and the next thing we knew we had completely crossed it at right angles. After proceeding along the freeway the wrong way and then the wrong way on a one-way street, Lorne and I couldn't stand any more of these close calls, and I do mean close -- what with us going one way on a one-way road and a double-trailer truck going the other way, whishing by us within an eighth of an inch. Lorne took over the driving chores. Generally speaking, Dick's driving is quite good, but this chain of circumstances had us somewhat upset; however, the above comments about him are somewhat unjust.

The next morning we drove to the Dalles Airport at five a.m., which was before any of the personnel arrived, other than the night range operator. We checked the weather forecast, filed a flight plan to Burley, Idaho, and left a little gasoline money for our friend who so graciously loaned us the car, regretting he was not around so we could thank him personally.

One does not expect such inclement weather, practically from coast to coast, in July. Due to continuously poor weather conditions on the entire trip coming and going, it was impossible to cover very much territory on any one day. Much of our time was spent sitting around airports, which fortunately proved most interesting, meeting fellow pilots and hearing their stories. However, it also made us realize the necessity of an I.F.R. rating; we could have saved ourselves many waiting hours.

We spent the night in Burley and were away early the next morning, soon passing over Bear Lake, which is quite a sight and fairly rugged, but nothing in the U.S.A. could be as rugged as our Canadian Rockies.

We landed at Rock Springs, Wyoming, for lunch and refueling, and were driven into town, courtesy of an airport half-ton pick-up. After returning to the airport we began to wonder if a fully-loaded Cessna 170 could get airborne at Burley's altitude of six thousand seven hundred and fifty-two feet, with no wind and an air temperature of one hundred and five degrees. The longest runway is about six thousand seven hundred feet. After a discussion with some of the local boys, we decided that we could get the plane airborne. The Cessna manual shows that use of flaps at this altitude and temperature would require more runway than if we didn't use them, so, without flaps, we started our takeoff and used approximately half the runway before the tail decided to come up on its own accord. At three-quarters of the runway length we became airborne and practically staggered out of the valley surrounding the airport, on our way to Denver, Colorado.

Before reaching Denver, it was necessary to go "on top". Finally the weather deteriorated to the point that Denver was reporting below V.F.R., so we changed course to Cheyenne, Wyoming, which was V.F.R., and landed.

We were quite impressed with the Cheyenne escort system. When a Cessna calls the tower, it is monitored by the Cessna dealer, and a Jeep, bearing a large sign saying "Follow me", comes out to the runway to route you to their hangar; similarly, a Piper product would have a Piper Jeep escort.

After refueling the aircraft and ourselves, we left for North Platte, Nebraska, where again we were driven into town and to a good hotel.

That night I witnessed something I had never seen before -- a thunder and lightning storm that lit up the country for miles around. To us it was like a blind man seeing for the first time. Somewhat alarming, but we were assured by the locals that we would live through it.

Following a good night's rest, we set out for Lincoln, Nebraska, crossing the Mississippi on the way to Quincy, Illinois, about two minutes ahead of what looked like a giant thunderstorm. I witnessed my first tornado twisting to our north. It would have been the end of us if we had been caught in it. We called the Quincy, Illinois, tower and were advised that our aircraft was fast enough to outrun the tornado; if necessary, we would go south down the Mississippi River. However, they said they would assist us if we wished to land at Quincy. Before we could get the aeroplane hangared, we nearly lost it in the gale-force winds. About six men volunteered to come out and hold the aircraft, and moved it into a hangar as the disturbance skirted us.

We rented a U-Drive in Quincy and ended up in the poorest motel on our entire trip. This was unfortunate, as we found out later that there are plenty of good motels in Quincy. However, the hotel where we dined and watched the Friday-night fights made up for any discomfort. Even Dick, who is a grandfather, appreciated the girls who served us. Not only was there good food, but there was also a piano and a lady pianist, who led all the patrons in singing the old songs.

The next morning we flew to Springfield, Illinois. From there the weather forced us to land in Indianapolis for a delay of some hours. Finally, we decided to head north north east, as poor weather had closed all the other routes, and eventually refueled in Findlay, Ohio. From there we moved on to Cleveland to spend the night.

We were quite taken with Cleveland's waterfront airport, which we were told is on reclaimed water frontage. We could almost step out of the plane into our hotel. We paid a one dollar landing fee, which was most reasonable considering that we were right down town. The very kind attendant, who was closing for the night, drove us to the Statler Hotel.

The next day we started for New York, stopping en route at Penn Field. The very helpful weather office warned us about the mountainous area. To us the Allegheny Range could hardly even be called hills in comparison to the Pacific North West, but we realized that they have taken their toll. In British Columbia our mountains are anywhere up to twelve thousand feet high and are snow-covered all year round. One can fly over at ten thousand feet and, as far as the eye can see in any direction, there are snow-capped mountains. For those who may wonder about the vastness of Canada's Province of British Columbia, it is larger than the States of California, Oregon and Washington combined, and three times the size of Texas. But all mountain areas should be respected and we did appreciate the advice.

At Penn Airport we met some very interesting people; we were taken out for coffee and given a detailed routing to New York. We were advised to go to Flushing Field rather than to La Guardia Airport.

On leaving Penn Field we flew in some rather rough air over the hills, but shortly thereafter we could see New York in the distance. Arriving by air in New York is an unforgettable sight, with the Empire State and Chrysler Buildings peering into the sky, the George Washington and Brooklyn Bridges down below, and the Hudson River winding along its way. During our entire trip this was the only area in which I felt uncomfortable with a single-motor aeroplane, with visibility less than three miles in a light rain, and wondering where to go if we lost an engine.

We landed at Flushing Field, paid one dollar and were given every courtesy by "Speed", the operator. We tied the aircraft down and asked to use the phone to call a cab. We were quite amused and educated by the device that locks the telephone so one cannot dial. It is a small cylinder lock which fits into the circular dialing hole of the number one on the phone; Speed carries the key to unlock this before the phone can be used.

Almost immediately we were initiated to the New York cab driver's dialect, peculiar apparently only to New York. We were entertained with continuous jokes while cutting in and out of traffic driving to the recommended (by the cab driver) Manhattan Hotel. One really has to see, hear and drive with a taxi driver here to truly appreciate the experience; no words can explain it. In fact our cashier Dick had quite a lapse in responsibility -- he was so taken with the jokes that he left the driver a five-dollar tip. This experience will be imprinted in our memories forever.

The Manhattan Hotel was quite respectable and not too bad in price considering its location near Times Square. However, we felt it a little ridiculous, in the middle of the hot summer, to refuse patrons admission to the coffee shop for breakfast if they weren't wearing a tie.

From our Sunday arrival to our Tuesday departure it rained most of the time in the New York area. We wasted the one-dollar charge to go to the top of the Empire State Building as we could not even see out the windows. From there we moved on to tour the R.C.A. Building, the Bowery, the Stock Exchange, the United Nations Building, and to Grand Central Station for a subway ride to Coney Island. We were very taken with the Eastman Kodak photo on the wall of Grand Central Station. Its size must be somewhere about twenty feet long by six feet high; it appears to be an actual colour photo which has been enlarged. The scene of horses stopped on a mountain pass looks so real; one looks in amazement and cannot believe it is only a picture. Tremendous credit is due to the men behind the scenes at Eastman Kodak.

Our thirteen-cent subway ride to Coney Island was quite an experience. It is certainly the answer to traffic problems, as I imagine the underground travels around sixty miles per hour, whereas on the highway we would have difficulty maintaining any reasonable speed. You see all types and personalities aboard, including plumbers, office workers and stockbrokers. On our return, which was a late run, there was only one couple aboard, other than ourselves. During the entire trip the fellow made love to the girl, doing everything but undressing her. I suppose, in a busy town like New York, where there are no parking places, a fellow has to take advantage of any opportunity to do his courting.

Coney Island on a Sunday sure awakens you to how the other half of the world lives. It develops a picture in your mind of the songs of New York and the Boardwalk which you've heard since childhood.

Much to our surprise, as there was an apparent shortage of show tickets, upon asking at our hotel information and ticket office, we were offered tickets to any play in town. Naturally we purchased tickets for "My Fair Lady".

After we paid for and received the tickets, the ticket clerk said," You don't want to see 'My Fair Lady'. I can let you have tickets for the 'Music Man'."

After some discussion we were convinced to change our tickets and found them to be a few dollars cheaper. However, we later realized that we should have stayed with our first choice. The "Music Man" was pretty slow to start, but finished not too badly. The beautiful girls in the audience attracted us more than the show did, especially a most attractive brunette, who was suitably escorted. If we had missed some of the show, we would not have been too disappointed!

A friend at home had been kind enough to arrange for guest cards for us at the New York Yacht Club. Lorne telephoned from our hotel to the yacht club, asked if our guest cards were there, and was advised by the party answering the telephone that the cards were at the desk. At the same time he cordially invited us to make full use of the club facilities. We called a taxi, asking to be dropped off at the New York Yacht Club. Upon arrival at our destination the driver pointed, and instructed us to go in the door and upstairs to the front desk. Lorne introduced himself to the desk attendant and asked for our courtesy cards, while I stood back a few yards waiting. After quite some time and searching, we were advised there were no guest cards for us. Lorne immediately asked who he had been talking to just ten minutes before on the telephone. The desk clerk had no idea and mentioned that he was on duty at that time. Finally, after everyone was becoming a little short-tempered, I asked if this was the New York Yacht Club. We quickly realized that our cab driver had left us at the Harvard Club, which is practically next door to our destination.

Our next objective was to purchase some clothes for our wives. We decided to phone a close friend in Ottawa, Canada, who was a buyer of ladies' garments, for advice on where to shop in New York. I was given the name of a young lady in Saks Fifth Avenue. We taxied over and introduced ourselves; we were welcomed and shown around the store. Lorne pulled out sizes given to him by his wife and daughter, and purchased several dresses, shoes, etc. I purchased a dress. Everything was gift-wrapped, and we were out of the store in fifteen or twenty minutes. Incidentally, everything fitted perfectly -- so, ladies, it can be done in short order!

Over the years the famous Waldorf Astoria Hotel has often been in the news, and it was a place that I thought we shouldn't miss seeing. Dressed in sport coats and slacks we taxied to the front door, looked the lobby over, as well as the other main parts of the hotel, and decided to have lunch in the Piccadilly Room. It wasn't too large and had only about a dozen patrons eating at that time. Upon entering we were escorted by the head waiter to a table. There were another four waiters standing around looking for something to do, but this didn't help us over the course of our meal. To put it mildly, the service was deplorable. After ordering we received only part of our vegetables. There was no butter and, when we asked for some, a plate of it was practically dropped on the table. We could not get any attention for the rest of our meal. Finally, when we were unable to get coffee served, we decided that the welcome mat was not out for us, or for anybody else. Not for one moment did we think that any other customer would have been treated any differently, if they had neglected to tip the head waiter as they entered, which I understand is customary.

Rather than cause a disturbance, we proceeded to leave. The four waiters surrounded our table immediately and literally took it apart looking for a tip. Dick went to the cashier's desk and paid the exorbitant cheque. As he opened the lobby door to leave, the head waiter grabbed him by the shoulder and said, "Sir, you forgot the waiter." Dick quickly replied, "You forgot the service."

This is a sad situation which, undoubtedly, is out of hand. I suppose we tourists are partly at fault for leaving tips when service is poor, and at times giving the head waiter a bribe for a certain table. We all know that, in spots like Las Vegas, the only way to get a good table is to pay the head waiter in advance. This is done every day by most of us.

During the two and a half days of rain we looked over quite a few spots in New York. Some day I would like to return for a long stay, as I think it is one of the most interesting cities I have ever visited. However, this was not the time, as it looked by the weather that, if we didn't get out on the Tuesday, we would be there until we ran out of money. Visibility was about two miles in light rain.

We telephoned "Speed" at Flushing Field. He suggested that we could get out of New York by taking off to the north, make a climbing, three-hundred-and-sixty-degree turn to three thousand feet and, after approximately ten minutes, let down until we could see the Hudson River and follow it to Albany, where the weather would be much better.

We then checked out of our hotel. Dick, our cashier, mistakenly gave the number of the room next to the ours, and almost paid Jack Dempsey's account; unknown to us he had been our neighbour.

We called a taxi. By now we were getting a little more used to these rides, but this cab driver was the prize of them all. He had never heard of Flushing Field and, after studying the map and driving for one and a half hours, landed us at La Guardia. With the aid of our insistant questioning every mile from there on, we finally arrived at Flushing Field, after a total time of two hours. Meanwhile, the weather continued to deteriorate.

En route on this long taxi ride our driver drove fifty miles per hour in a thirty-miles-per-hour zone, using the extreme left lane. Suddenly, a siren roared and a patrol car with flashing red light was behind us in our lane. The siren kept on for some minutes, as our driver could not get over to the right-hand lane because of the traffic. Finally we were able to pull over. The cabbie made a dash for the glove compartment to get his glasses; his driver's licence was restricted to him wearing them. In fact, I don't think he had much vision without them. It turned out that the policemen couldn't care less about our speeding; they just wanted to get past us. In the process they hollered some pretty good language at us. With the way the New Yorkers drive, it may be better if you can't see too well!

We took off from Flushing Field and, following Speed's advice, we had no problem. Flying at a low level we missed the traffic at Kennedy and La Guardia Airports. We refuelled at Albany and set out for Ottawa, Canada.

Flying on a trip like this, with a flight plan and covering so much territory, I found it difficult, when giving a position report, to remember what town we had left or where we were going to without first making reference to the map. You sometimes wonder when you ask your passengers and they also cannot recall the name of the town from which we departed!

Pronunciation of some town names also makes reporting difficult, e.g., North Platte (Kings Plate is a well-advertised rye whisky in Canada), Cheyenne ("Shyanny"), Indianapolis ("Indiaplis"), and Poughkeepsee ("Powe Keepy"). From Albany I intentionally bypassed Schenectady, because I couldn't pronounce it, and went via Burlington to Montreal and on to Ottawa.

During our flight from Montreal to Ottawa, visibility was down to one or two miles in heavy rain. We had a very unusual experience flying at about one thousand feet, skirting a thunderstorm. Co-pilot Lorne was looking at a map when, suddenly, a load of hailstones hit across the aircraft like somebody had taken a shovel full of gravel and let us have it across the windshield. There was no warning, and there was just the one sudden violent attack. Lorne, not being prepared or looking, nearly evacuated the plane. However, the storm did no damage.

We arrived at Ottawa, were cleared through Customs by a most courteous officer, hangared the aeroplane and took a cab to the hotel. We spent the evening visiting some friends, had a few snifters and not much sleep.

The next morning we couldn't fly the northern route to Winnipeg; the only weather open was to Toronto. En route, for the first time in my life, I fell asleep at the controls. However, the co-pilot was wide awake. I awoke suddenly, thinking I had heard the engine miss a beat, which gives one quite a start.

We landed at Toronto Island and were amazed to see students learning to fly in winds of thirty to thirty-five miles per hour. We gassed up, ate and left for London, Ontario.

Upon arrival, by accepting the advice of our taxi driver, we had the poorest food ever and were dumped at a smelly motel, with the airport located three miles on one side of the city and this motel three miles the other side. We should have learned by now not to pay any attention to recommendations from cab drivers; very few work out.

We left London, Ontario, the next morning under clear skies, the first on the entire trip. However, it only lasted a short while.

We landed at Detroit City Airport and cleared Customs. I cannot say enough about the courtesy and efficiency of the tower controllers at Detroit. We called in when we were five miles east at four thousand feet. After we were cleared to the circuit, the controller cleared us to land from downwind, ahead of a DC3 on final, with seven or eight aircraft of all sizes and types in the pattern. There was no confusion. These boys are sure on their toes and are a credit to aviation. Once on the runway we were given complete and detailed taxi instructions to Customs.

At Detroit City, like so many other airports today, there is virtually nowhere to go if you lose an engine after take-off. You keep your fingers crossed until you get a little altitude and distance out.

Next stop was Niles City for lunch and fuel. Here again, as most everywhere, we were loaned a car to go down town, where we had a wonderful lunch at the coffee shop recommended by the airport operator. We sure knew we hit the right restaurant. It was full of customers, and will continue in business as long as they serve such good food. The girl behind the counter interested us in her accomplishments as general cashier, counter waitress and telephone operator. The telephone had a thirty or forty-foot extension; this girl packed the phone all around the counter area talking on the phone, taking cash and serving customers simultaneously.

As we left Niles City the weather was back to our usual three-mile visibility and light rain, so we took a course across the bottom of Lake Michigan and over Chicago to Aurora, where we would head north to Minneapolis. We had planned on stopping over in Chicago but it was below V.F.R. limits, so instead we flew over top, descended to one thousand feet over Aurora, and turned to a new heading for Rockford, Illinois.

We drifted off course and, in very poor visibility, found ourselves over Janesville where we landed. A short while later we decided to go back to Rockford, where we were forced down in the middle of the afternoon. In a very short time conditions were below I.F.R. minimums.

The accommodation in Rockford was excellent. The restaurant "Jacks or Better" is a credit to the food purveyors.

Early next morning Butler Aviation checked our aircraft over and changed the oil, but the airport was socked in until about two p.m., when we took off. At about five or six hundred feet we headed for Minneapolis where the weather was C.A.V.U. This is not too bad a terrain for low V.F.R. flying, but we had neglected to check our map for TV towers. After all the kindness we had been given here, we felt that the weather boys or local operators slipped up in not warning strangers about the local TV tower, especially in this kind of weather. It gave us quite a scare, suddenly looming up about fifty feet to our starboard side and several hundred feet above us. We must have been within a few feet of the guy wires.

After we passed La Crosse, the weather cleared considerably. We finally landed at Fleming Field, Minneapolis, in a forty-mile-per-hour cross wind that kicked us around a little.

From Minneapolis we flew to Fargo, North Dakota, and were amazed at the amount of water lying around, especially since it was summertime. It appeared that half of Minnesota was under water, along with Illinois and other states. One operator told us that it had rained steadily for three months, and it certainly looked like it from the air.

On the subject of airports, Fargo is possibly the most modern and well-appointed place we had been in. It would serve as a model airport for any community.

The next overnight stop, after leaving Fargo, was Bismarck, where we met a chap with a 172; he had been forced to return to Fargo by the weather.

Next morning the weather cleared a little and we started for Miles City. After about ten minutes, it literally bucketed rain all the way to our destination. This was the eleventh straight day of rain in July. En route we located the Yellowstone River, and followed it to Miles City in poor visibility. The clean and newly-pressed trousers I had on were so soaked with rain when I ran from the aeroplane to the airport waiting-room that I might as well have jumped into a barrel of water; my clothes had to be wrung out.

After a few hours the weather cleared enough for us to proceed to Billings, Montana, and then to Livingston, Montana. The weather was good, except for numerous thunderstorms which we were able to skirt, but we almost lost our back-seat passenger who had had enough rough air for one day.

We refuelled at Bozeman, Montana, and headed for Helena and the Missoula Pass on the way to Spokane. The radio range boys certainly looked after us, especially in this area; they called us every ten minutes or so for a position report and our heading, etc. Sometimes pilots do not realize the tremendous, costly network of installations and personnel placed at our service by the government.

Our next stop was at Cour de Lane, Idaho, where we spent the night.

We started fairly early the next morning for home, but could not get past Ellenburg, Washington, as the mountain passes were socked in. After we had a few interesting hours' discussion with the range operator, weather conditions broke up enough to allow us to depart. We climbed to ten thousand feet over Snoqualmie Pass, and one and one-half hours later we were clearing Customs at our home airport at Patricia Bay (Victoria Airport).

We logged approximately seventy hours on the trip, and my total expenses, other than gasoline costs which my two passengers looked after, were one hundred and fifty-five dollars. This included everything -- entertainment, food, lodgings, taxis, etc.

In conclusion, I must say that had I any idea of writing a story about this trip, I would have obtained the names of some of the operators and all the kind people we met.

A trip of this kind has uncounted value in navigation and flying experience. There is no doubt that it is much easier to tune in an Omni A.D.F. and have less stops en route, but, on our entire trip, the Omni was of little value due to the necessity of our flying at such low altitudes. It will be a sorry day if and when our L.F. ranges disappear.

In addition to a most interesting trip to Florida and the Bahama Islands in a single-engine Cessna 180, other trips I've flown include Alaska, several to California, and most other U.S. points. I also ferried a Commanche aeroplane from Hamilton, Ontario, to Vancouver, B.C.

Trans-continental holiday
(Victoria B.C. to the Bahamas and back)

Few aircraft are utilized to the extent they should be. Take a look around your airport and see how many of your flying acquaintances have taken a cross-country trip of five or six hundred or five or six thousand miles. Yet this kind of trip works out much more reasonably than using an automobile, and it includes not only the fun of flying, and meeting some of the most wonderful personalities in aviation, but also an education in geography you can get no other way.

I have made a couple of trips from the Pacific to the Atlantic, the latest from Victoria, B.C., Canada, to Grand Bahamas in a Cessna 182 which is equipped for I.F.R., but you can cross the continent in a J3 Cub without radio if you so wish, and have a lot of fun doing it.

Victoria, located on Vancouver Island approximately one hundred miles NNW of Seattle, is the capital of the Province of British Columbia. Our province is larger than the States of Washington, Oregon and California combined, and its rugged and mountainous terrain is equalled in only few parts of the world. We have beautiful valleys and lakes, and a varying climate ranging from ninety degrees Fahrenheit above to ninety degrees Fahrenheit below zero, depending on the season and how far north one goes.

On my last trip from coast to coast in the 182 I took along two flying enthusiasts, one an I.F.R. man. We left Victoria on October 7th and cleared American Customs at Bellingham, Washington. As the Denver area was in the throes of a large low-pressure area with snow and zero visibility we found it necessary to go via southern California. After stopping for fuel at Melford, Oregon, we climbed to sixteen thousand feet going south over the Siskiyou Range. This gave us an opportunity to use our Scott oxygen console, and we found the disposable mask arrangement quite comfortable; it allows conversation while wearing it.

We arrived after dark over Bakersfield, California, in a blowing dust situation that necessitated a V.F.R.- I.F.R. approach. This was the first time we had seen the High-Intensity Flasher Lights. Bakersfield Tower asked us to advise them when we wished to have the lights turned off because they could be pretty bothersome on final if left on.

Sunday the weather office advised that conditions going east were poor for V.F.R., but we decided to fly east towards Palmdale and take a look. We found the ceiling at three thousand scattered with visibility three miles, and this condition rapidly improved to a higher broken condition with good visibility. The en-route weather reports were rather disconcerting. We listened to "Warning to light aircraft, severe turbulence at six thousand five hundred feet on Victor Airway 137 from Gorman to Palmdale" -- our present position. The air was certainly not smooth, but light or moderate turbulence would have been a more accurate term. Since our understanding of severe turbulence is that it would be nearly impossible to fly, even at reduced speed, without structural damage to the aircraft, we would suggest that the terminology be changed to something not quite so alarming.

Weather for V.F.R. deteriorated considerably near Needles, so we decided to land and wait it out, but since we could not stir any life at Needles we took off for Blythe, a short run of about seventy-two miles, in rough air at a low altitude. We crossed the Colorado River and fueled at Blythe for our next stop, Tucson, Arizona, where we stayed overnight.

Rontel

Tucson has a great setup. The airport Rontel is just a few hundred feet from your tie-down, and brand-spanking-new accommodations cost only nine dollars for the three of us. The operator was most helpful and the adjoining restaurant serves good food.

The weatherman said there was a large cold front from California to Texas with strong winds. A group from Beech Aircraft on their way to a meeting in San Diego -- I believe in a Travel Air -- had come in from El Paso, and told us it was too turbulent for them, so they had set down at Tucson for the night. Another fellow traveller in a Cessna 172 with his wife and two children said they were en route to Houston, Texas, when forced down at Tucson. We were quite amused by his co-pilot wife, as she told how she diapered the two babies in rough air by hanging them upside down by their feet in the back seat.

Local Acquaintance

Joe Howroyd, travelling with us, is a sort of wheeler dealer and the Mr. Aviation of our area. He'll do anything to help flying, usually at a cost to himself. Anyway, he was grounded last winter in a snow storm in New Mexico while ferrying a Cessna 150 from Wichita to Victoria, and met a chap from Tucson named Haynes Burrus who was also grounded, so, while we were waiting out the weather, Joe phoned him. Haynes came out and took us over to show his prodigy -- a 1952 Ford half-ton pick-up that he was converting to a small diesel trailer, complete with air conditioning, for camping and fishing in Canada. In a hangar adjoining, he showed us a Beech Bonanza conversion to a twin, to be called a Cavalier, that he will be test flying. It differs somewhat from the Super V as the tail design has been changed to a conventional one, and at this time was being tested by the F.A.A. for certification. It is quite an eye opener to see the severity of the tests necessary for certification -- turning the aircraft upside down and sand bagging the wings with enough weight to break them off, putting winches on it, stressing and straining it, literally trying to pull it apart. My feelings were that I would prefer to test fly a model that had not been put through these paces.

War Stories

Haynes had lived through a battle for life in the rugged terrain of our province. He had left Alaska in a DC3 with twenty-three passengers en route to Seattle. While over British Columbia they began to lose the range leg, and finally were flying at ninety degrees towards it with it still fading, and finally lost it. After close to six and a half hours out of Alaska and at eighteen thousand feet, no range leg, no oxygen, almost out of fuel, and with some radio antennae snapped off by ice, it looked pretty hopeless. By flying ninety degrees towards the range leg for such a long period, they should have been far out over the Pacific Ocean, but he said he could feel terrain turbulence. Finally they picked up a faint signal on the remaining radio, and eventually identified it as Dog Creek in British Columbia, a small strip in the middle of nowhere. They landed with the aid of lights from a jeep, as an alert was out for the overdue DC3.

What had happened was that the winds close to the mountains were blowing up to one hundred and sixty knots that night, and actually they were flying backwards.

Haynes told us that the next day, after refueling and flying to Seattle, he was still so shaken that he neglected to clear Customs, and the airline was assessed one thousand dollars per passenger, a total of twenty-three thousand dollars, to be held as security until they could be rounded up and cleared. A year and a half later they rounded up the last person and had their deposit returned.

Turbulence

On Monday we left Tucson for El Paso, Texas, and started to get some of the severe turbulence we had heard about on the radio the day before. We slowed down until our airspeed was indicating about eighty knots and at Cochise Head (eight thousand one hundred and nine feet high) one bump lifted everything on board to the ceiling -- the only real severe shakeup we were to get in our eight thousand miles of travel, but we were not overly concerned about structural damage to our plane at this speed.

We passed over the Continental Divide and before long landed in El Paso, fueled both aircraft and ourselves, and were on our way east again. Terrain here is level desert type with numerous dry lakes and not much civilization. We crossed the Pecos River and could see roads, literally hundreds of them, dead-ending at oil wells. Not until we approached Abilene could we see any green, and now oil wells were all mixed in with green fields and farming.

After a short stop in Abilene we took off with lowering ceiling and rain. We were catching up with the front and flew at three hundred and four hundred feet with five and six miles' visibility, but finally TV towers and obstructions were too much for us, and we landed at Eastland, Texas, in heavy rain to stay the night. We phoned for a taxi and had the good luck of having Don Pierce drive out for us in his Karmann Ghia. We put the 182 in the hangar alongside Don's Cessna 210, and the three of us plus baggage climbed into Don's little car, along with his young son. Don operates the Eastland Hotel where we had good accommodations.

Oil Wells

Flying over Texas it looks like everyone owns an oil well -- literally hundreds of thousands of pumps, pumping away only a few feet apart. But each well, by law, can pump only about thirty barrels per day, which is worth one hundred dollars, and the farmer owning the land would get about one-eighth of that for his lease. You can have only so many wells on your acreage, so unless you leased out a very large piece of property you would not necessarily be a millionaire.

We left early the next morning but the ceiling was still less than five hundred feet so we were forced down again, after dodging TV and radio towers, at Weatherford. Perhaps the best way to miss them is to fly down the middle of the highway, but who knows what might be coming the other way?

We walked around in mud up to our ankles in the pouring rain, examining a Cessna 170 Tricycle Conversion and a Stits home-built with a sign on the side of the fuselage "Experimental - Amateur Built". Then we walked downtown to eat and taxied back in a couple of hours when the ceiling raised enough to take off for Fort Worth.

Fort Worth

We would like to have stayed at Fort Worth as the next day was the annual Plane Auction -- everything from a Piper Cub to a DC3. We looked into the closed office of the Cross Country News as Miss Toni Page was away. This is quite a paper, worth looking over, especially for the jokes.

We headed out of Fort Worth still in the front, but towards Longview we could get up to one thousand feet, and the ceiling gradually went up until we had passed ahead of the front and were in good weather. This part of Texas is rolling, with cattle in the fields, though you wonder how there is space to grow grass among the solid mass of oil wells. We passed over Lake Cherokee, which looks like a long narrow marsh, and began to think it was about time we got out of Texas; it sure seems to never end.

With the Jepaid we used, it's not easy to distinguish the state borders, but soon the Mississippi came into sight winding its way, with the river barges we have heard so much about, and we saw below us green trees and flat farming-type country. We crossed Lake Maurepas and then over Lake Ponchatrain, with the longest bridge in the world, and on into New Orleans.

We had heard on a TV programme about education that over seventy-five thousand people in New Orleans cannot read or write. Maybe so, but educated or not, these people are your friends and the welcome mat is waiting.

We spent several hours in the French Quarter and then picked up a bus for our return to the motel. While the bus was waiting to leave, a very old gentleman got on, asked the driver if he would like a cup of coffee, jumped off and brought one aboard, which the driver slowly consumed en route. That's New Orleans. Nobody appears to be in a rush, everyone is extra friendly and has plenty of time to talk to you, and their speech is music to your ears.

We left New Orleans on Wednesday morning with a sure promise to ourselves to return, and headed for St. Petersburg. As we passed Pensacola, flying on the Victor Airway at the correct height, we were surrounded by training aircraft, a lot of them -- Beech Mentors doing acrobatics. This gives one quite a shaking when you see them all around you doing loops and rolls.

We stopped at Tallahassee for fuel. The boys drove us about a mile to the beautiful terminal, and asked us to phone them to be picked up after we had eaten. The food here was *par excellence*.

Suwannee River

Out of Tallahassee we soon passed over the Suwannee River, and we all sang Stephen Foster's fine old melody slightly off key. The weather was closing down, and, to avoid thunderstorms, we flew a slightly zigzag course in the rain at five hundred feet along the west shoreline of Florida. We were unable to receive any Omni stations, even though the terrain looks pretty level and line of sight should be OK at this low altitude. This gave us a close look at some of the Florida subdivisions we had seen advertised. The ones we noticed seemed to be hacked out of the swamps and looked as if they would be underwater at high tide. We saw no road, and wondered about water and power.

When we arrived at St. Petersburg the weather was quite a lot better, and to our embarrassment we approached the wrong runway. On realizing it, we asked the St. Petersburg tower for permission for a pull up. The tower apparently did not have us in sight, and asked if we were approaching the correct airport. We were, but what happened was that our calculations were miscalculated. We finally made it without upsetting the tower as they were not too busy at the time, and tied down for the night.

The manager of the Chief Motel in St. Petersburg, which is just a few minutes from the airport, picked us up with their courtesy car. This is a first-class motel with a swimming pool and a courtesy car to take you to the airport.

Palm Beach

Next morning on the way to West Palm Beach we climbed on top of a broken condition for a smooth flight. At Palm Beach we cleared Customs for the flight to West End, Bahamas. After lunch we filed a flight plan for 7500 and proceeded on our way in weather which was practically C.A.V.U., except for an odd thunderstorm which we skirted. We saw two boats about halfway across. If you lost an engine over this sixty-two miles, you should be able to call on Emergency and almost get picked up before you glided to water. We had life jackets, but because of the sharks a life raft is probably the ideal set-up.

West End

We closed our flight plan while still airborne, as we were told it could cost up to twelve dollars to close it by phone once you were on the ground. We called West End tower on 119.1 on the Mark 2 Omnigator. We found it difficult to understand the tower operator's broad English. He gave us runway 35 but we deciphered it as 25, which we could not line up on our compass. Finally we realized it was 35, landed, and for the first time felt the heat which was about ninety degrees Fahrenheit. We were told to report to Customs, who told us that, since October 12th was an island holiday -- Discovery Day or something like that -- there would be a small charge. After we signed many documents and gave three copies of the one we received in West Palm Beach, the fee was eleven dollars and twenty cents. Customs then asked the Captain to report to the tower, where I signed another few documents and paid one dollar and fifty cents for landing fee. All this brought back memories of many articles warning flyers to be careful what day they arrive in the Bahamas, as there are many holidays.

The hostess welcomed us at the hotel and handed each of us a glass of Planter's Punch, mostly rum and crushed ice. In a matter of minutes we were in the swimming pool, the second largest in the world, which has salt water pumped in from the ocean. We also swam in the ocean, and I would say the beach outclasses Waikiki in Honolulu. In the evening we were invited to a cocktail party put on by the hotel, where they served deep-fried conches with sauce, worth a special trip to the

Bahamas.

After dinner we took an evening walk and looked over sixteen acres of land with waterfront priced about eight hundred dollars per acre, and felt that if you lived long enough it sure would be worth much more. We stopped in at the cocktail lounge, and the hotel organist came over and asked if we would like him to play a Canadian number; we Canadians must have something in our lingo to spot us. He played a few songs for us, including the "Maple Leaf Forever", and we retired for the evening.

Grand Bahama Hotel

The Grand Bahama Hotel, situated on two thousand acres, was built by English capital in 1949.   After an unsuccessful operation it was closed for some time, until a Dallas insurance group purchased it and spent about two million dollars on it, and then sold it to the Jack Tar interests. There are three hundred and twenty rooms but during our off-season visit there were only forty guests, so we were given nearly individual attention.

In the liquor store, which I visited next morning before breakfast, they have a large refrigerator full of liquor and you may sample all you like, which goes pretty good before breakfast if you do not have to fly. Imported Scotch, which sells for six or seven dollars in our part of Canada, and is also well watered by the B.C. Government before selling it, is three dollars and fifty cents in the Bahamas. If you want to become an alcoholic, this is the spot.

Heading Home

Friday morning we departed for the airport, which belongs to the hotel and is on their property. The departure fee was two dollars, and the hotel mailed home to us membership cards in the Bahamas Flying Club, which allow you to land and take off without charge. We filed a flight plan for West Palm Beach and cleared Customs there with most courteous officers, and proceeded to St. Petersburg for the weekend. We had a very interesting talk there with Mr. Piper, who is indeed the "Grand Old Man of Aviation".

Our I.F.R. man feels that when you are holidaying you should really loaf, and on Sunday he had us up at four A.M. instead of the usual six A.M., so that by getting up a couple of hours earlier we would have two more hours to loaf! We flew to Montgomery, Alabama, and then due west, arriving at El Paso by nightfall, with the sun setting behind the mountains -- a sight too beautiful for words. El Paso has three runways in use and we had quite a problem taxiing after touch down. The night was clear and very cold, and we would have liked to go across the Mexican border, but were too sleepy after our early rise.

Next morning we got a free ride from our motel to the airport, but on our way out the young chauffeur mentioned that he had just taken a four-star general out to the airport, and the general hadn't even given him a dime tip. This shamed us into giving him a dollar, which was still pretty reasonable transportation. From El Paso we went to Thermal, California. Many a night on our local TV weather forecast we have heard Thermal given as the hottest spot in the U.S.A., so we wished to take a look at it. The temperature that day was one hundred degrees Fahrenheit. We refueled, and since there was no coffee shop we stopped off at Palm Desert Airport near Palm Springs for lunch. The grass runway on this field is as good or better than our lawns. We had to fly through the sprinkler system while landing. Everything is here -- swimmimg pool, motel, dining room and cocktail lounge, and the food is excellent.

We took off from Palm Desert, headed for Palmdale on Victor Airway 137. While heading out we found ourselves southwest of the airway, in fact quite a bit off course, and finally took a bearing on Oceanside to find ourselves beside a small prohibited area. We noticed several jets below us and it seemed to take longer than it should to get out of the area, but nobody shot a missile at us. Maybe they picked us up on radar and realized it was some Sunday flyers, but if we had received a citation we would certainly have deserved it.

We called in at Madera, California, for fuel, and then followed Victor Airway 23 to Victoria International Airport to clear Canadian Customs at home.

The two days returning from Florida to Victoria were absolutely C.A.V.U. with tail winds all the way, except for fifty minutes on top from Dunsmuir, California, to Eugene, Oregon.

A trip like this gives one an idea of the reasonable cost of flying. None of us could have taken such a trip by car or by the citizen's airline. Other than gas and oil, we spent in eleven days approximately one hundred dollars each, and we had a lot of fun. You can't beat that!

Part 6: *TRAVEL*

Life's thrills of travel

If you are fortunate enough to have health and stability to work, and save as most people did in my day, it usually reaps great rewards. Younger people just look at you today and wonder how you can have such a beautiful home, travel the world and have all the good things in life. They never stop to realize how much easier it is today to be able to enjoy their latter years in luxury. All it takes is very long hours, hard work and doing without. However, there are some unfortunate people, due to poor health or some inherent reason, who cannot compete, but the greater percentage can. Happiness, with or without money, is another pursuit. However, I was fortunate to have found happiness and was in a position to do a lot of travelling.

Q.E. II

The Q.E. II is England's pride and joy. Her vital statistics are gross tonnage of sixty-seven thousand, length of nine hundred and sixty-three feet, and maximum speed of twenty-eight and a half knots. Captain Doug Ridley, a world-famous career man, was in charge; he is now retired.

She appears to carry with her the old English class distinction; I feel that the accommodations and food are a lot different depending upon which class you travel in. We were in Cabin 2041, a very large stateroom, about twice the size of the average cruise ship stateroom; I suppose this was about middle class or better. Each class has its own dining room; ours was quite small, but not crowded, and offered superb food and service.

However, the English don't have quite the same standards as the Americans -- the ship was a little on the tacky side with dirty ashtrays, dust, broken-down ping-pong tables, and an uninviting swimming pool. If you wanted a deck chair, it had to be paid for separately.

Entertainment on board was very good, especially Reg Varney who is best known here as an actor on the show "On the Buses". He was a very interesting and entertaining gentleman.

We travelled from Southampton to Norway and return, and certainly saw a part of the world that looked like home. The Norwegians are the most friendly people, and are all so rugged and healthy.

Going up the Geiranger Fjord is like travelling the west coast of British Columbia. When we arrived at Hellesylit, the end of the fjord, we couldn't figure out how they would turn the ship around. In fact, I didn't think they could. However, they dropped the anchor in the correct spot, and the ship gradually drifted through one hundred and eighty degrees, turning with the prevailing wind.

Trondheim, the Bergen Fish Market, and the flowers made us feel that we must return someday.

Cruising by ship

We have sailed on board many ships, in many different parts of the world. Some of the ships we have cruised on are the Royal Princess, Island Princess, Nordic Princess, Noordam, Odessa, Q.E. II, and we have been on twelve cruises with the Royal Viking Line.

The Royal Viking Line is in a class by itself, and so is its price. I do not know how they select their entertainment, but every night there is always an unbelievable stage production, with costumes and talent you can't even find in Las Vegas or Paris. At most ports of call they have local talent come aboard and perform a show illustrating their culture.

Their chefs are the finest; every day and every night there is the regular dining room menu or a smorgasboard. Festivities, such as the Norwegian Grand Buffet offered at midday on the Norway / Sweden cruise, were feasts to behold. From the *Skald* (this is an on-board daily newsletter which is sent to each cabin), it says:

PREPARATION OF THE NORWEGIAN BUFFET:
There are many such nights complimenting all countries, and we especially liked the Italian Buffet.

THE GALLEY CREW GIVES YOU ITS BEST:
Every cook knows that the time it takes to prepare a good meal far surpasses the time it takes to consume it. Apply this to our Norwegian Grand Buffet and you'll realize that the hour you spend admiring and devouring the feast was preceded by days of preparation. Yes, days. Some of the items on the buffet tables take two working days to prepare, and the planning begins even earlier. To help you better appreciate the Norwegian Grand Buffet (if you don't already), here is a behind-the-scenes look at its preparation:

In the Hot Galley
First of all, the chef de cuisine draws up the menu at least four days in advance. Then, in the hot galley, broiling and cooking of the meat begin 48 hours prior to the buffet, in order to make the most efficient use of limited oven space. An average quantity of meat includes two legs of beef, seven or eight turkeys, two venison saddles and eight roasts of beef. A normal day for the hot-galley workers is 10 hours, putting out the buffet stretches it to 14 or 15. The hot-galley cooks also are responsible for some of the colder items at the buffet -- the ice and butter sculptures. Three of each are prepared. The ice sculptures are begun with a chain saw, then carved with special hand chisels. A single ice sculpture takes two hours -- provided the carver is experienced. The butter sculptures are made with a special blend of butter and margarine. These, too, are carved by hand, not molded.

In the Cold Galley
In the cold galley, preparation begins at 2:00 the afternoon before the buffet,

with cooks working into the early hours of the following morning. The cooks begin with approximately 100 pounds of salad, 50 to 60 pounds of fruit, 350 pounds of seafood and 250 pounds of meat. (Divide that by 655 passenger and, well, we won't get into the math!) Shelling the lobster is the most time-consuming task, and lobster is the most popular food item at the buffet.

Unlike many shoreside operations, the galley on the Royal Viking Sky does not have a lot of space. It becomes a problem to prepare all the platters and fit them all into the refrigerator. "But," says Pantry Chef Josef Prem, "we make the best possible show with a minimum of space." Sometimes, rough seas can make preparation treacherous -- one good pitch or roll can destroy a show piece. Seven cooks and one first cook in the cold galley work 16 to 18 hours per day for the two days involved in preparing the Norwegian Grand Buffet.

In the Bake Shop

In the bake shop, four people are responsible for all that delicious, fattening fluff. Their creations will use up to 100 pounds of sugar, 60 quarts of whipping cream, 30 pounds of icing, 10 pounds of chocolate and 20 pounds of vanilla cream for this buffet alone.

The pastry cooks start two full days ahead of time making the sponge cakes and certain pastries which have to be filled. Most time-consuming are the petit fours, which are made by hand, and the kransekake or Norwegian wedding cake. The Grand Pastry Buffet includes 20 different kinds of pastry and 15 cakes. Some cannot be made until the morning of the buffet so the most difficult task is to have everything ready when it's time to set up.

The bake shop is used 24 hours a day -- by the pastry cooks during the day and the bread bakers at night. The Royal Viking Sky's two full-time bakers average nine working hours per day and work 13 on the buffet. In addition to their regular daily output of rolls, breads and breakfast pastries, they bake 1,500 rolls, 66 pounds each of dark and white bread and 88 pounds of whole-wheat bread for the buffet.

The Finished Product

The Norwegian Grand Buffet, which will be served from 12:30 p.m. to 1:30 p.m. in the Trondheim Lounge, is the culmination of hours of work by the galley staff, and the result certainly is one in which to take pride. "It's hard work, but the galley enjoys preparing the buffet, " says Chef de Cuisine Fritz Mariacher. "It gives us the opportunity to demonstrate our skills."

Flying the Concorde

When the Air France Concorde was in its early years, my wife Iris and I flew from Paris to New York in three hours and fifteen minutes. The crews are dedicated professionals and the passengers are treated like royalty. As Concorde says: *It's as close to the heavens as most of us can get -- at least in this life.*

Few of us have the opportunity of being supersonic passengers, flying fifty-five thousand feet above the earth faster than the speed of sound, aboard the most impressive passenger aircraft of these times. Breaking the sound barrier in the ninety-eight seat Concorde is not a shattering experience, and reaching Mach 1 (which corresponds to the speed of sound) one merely feels a slight nudge. The Concorde's cruising speed is approximately one thousand three hundred and fifty miles per hour (Mach 2), which is faster than the speed of a rifle bullet. Concorde has a wingspan of eighty-four feet, an overall length of two hundred and four feet, and a height of thirty-nine feet. Maximum take-off weight is four hundred and seven thousand, eight hundred and fifty-five pounds. Concorde's range is three thousand five hundred nautical miles, with a cruising altitude of fifty to sixty thousand feet.

To pilot the Concorde is a privilege granted to a very few skilled and dedicated airmen. There are fewer than one hundred pilots and flight engineers for the fleet. They are all professionals and have reached a coveted status after years of experience.

At five p.m. the announcement to board was given. From the Concorde brochure, I quote: *Every flight is an occasion. An experience to savour. A chance to reflect on man's ingenuity, on the sophisticated engineering and breathtaking technology, that can take you soaring high, into the dark blue of a limitless sky. In speed, in comfort, in peerless style.*

The food and wines were exceptionel. Wines are selected by an expert committee of connoisseurs. The food consisted of canapes, including caviar and lobster, and many courses of all classic foods, including desserts. Most of this was wasted on us as, at our age, one cannot handle all the liquor and goodies provided.

In June 1988 we flew the British Airways Concorde from London to Washington, D.C., in three hours and thirty minutes. On our earlier trip from Paris to New York, our one-way fare was about three thousand U.S. dollars; this included a hotel in Paris, all meals, wine and spending money, and a chauffeur-driven Rolls Royce for transportation. On the London to Washington trip, the one-way fare had increased to five thousand one hundred U.S. dollars per person, and all the extras had gone.

We boarded from a beautiful lounge in Heathrow Airport and, of course, the lounge had all the liquor, snacks, etc., suitable for a royal party. I filled my pockets with chocolate bars of special design and size made by Cadbury's, some cigars and other goodies which we didn't eat until we arrived home.

Washington, D.C.

Washington is a most interesting place to visit. I was quite taken with the Old Town trolley tours. You can purchase an all-day-and-evening reboarding pass for about ten dollars U.S. The motor-driven streetcar, which has a conductor, covers practically all the places of interest in a large area. It travels a distance of about twenty or thirty miles on a return trip. One of these trolleys runs past your hotel every thirty minutes; you can get on and off as often as you wish to look around, and then catch the next trolley. The conductor-guide has been extensively trained and gives you a steady narration, which includes many jokes.

The taxi cabs do not have meters, but it seemed that the fare was always just under five dollars, no matter what the distance was. I was taken with the arrangement at Dulles Airport where the taxis do have meters. When you request a taxi, an attendant in charge calls one to come forward. The attendant then gives you a Washington flyer on which he writes your cab number; our number was 626. He then gives you all the current rates and tells you what fare to expect when you reach your destination. This certainly must save a lot of problems. If you do have any trouble, the flyer has a phone number to call for assistance.

After visiting this city, it makes the U.S. news on TV much more interesting when we see all the places we visited, including the White House, Lincoln Monument, Kennedy Center, and the Ford Theater where Lincoln was assassinated. The highlight to us was, of course, the Smithsonian Institute Museum, especially the Air and Space Museum which houses Lindberg's plane. This is a place we would like to revisit because there is so much to see.

We flew from Washington, via New York and Toronto, to Victoria, where our cat was waiting for his dinner.

Virgin Islands

We visited the island of St. Thomas in 1977. It is one of the most attractive places we have ever been to. The island is thirteen miles long and three miles across at its widest point. It has a built-up commercial area, but the beaches are out of this world. Vehicles travel on the left-hand side of the road, at a thirty-five-mile-an-hour speed limit in the country and twenty miles per hour in the towns.

We took a taxi to Megans Bay Beach. There are few spots in the world to match this bay. The water is warm and crystal clear -- even when swimming out a distance, to a depth of maybe fifty to one hundred feet, it is so clear you can see the bottom.

There is a variety of locally-made goods and crafts, and a perfume factory. At one time it was a rendezvous used for molasses and rum storage; these facilities have since become stores.

You don't have to travel too far to reach the Virgin Islands. These historic patches of tropical sun are one thousand four hundred and seventy-four miles southeast of New York, and one thousand two hundred miles south of Miami. Jet service gets you there in a hurry.

The Virgin Islands are part of the curving Antilles chain that separates the Caribbean from the Atlantic Ocean. Clustered together in sparkling seas, the one hundred or so islands, islets and cays, that make up the British and American Virgin Islands, are among the most beautiful geographic areas in the world, blest with powdery beaches and sun-drenched weather.

The islands lie in the path of soft tradewinds blowing directly from Portugal. This perhaps accounts for the fact that "Santa Cruz" was among the first lands to be sighted by Columbus on his second voyage westward. He then sailed northeast, passing St. Thomas, St. John and Tortola, and called them collectively, Las Virgenes.

After that excitement the islands went back to sleep for more than a hundred and fifty years. They awoke to find the flag of Denmark planted on St. Thomas, the French tricolour on St. Croix, and the Union Jack flapping over Tortola (where it still flies). In addition, the Arawak Indian population had disappeared. Denmark later claimed St. John, bought St. Croix and built the Danish West Indies into thriving sugar cane and trading islands.

Slaves were imported as early as 1763 to work the growing number of sugar plantations. The islands were also used as a base for the reshipment of slaves to other areas. After the abolition of slavery in 1848, planters began to abandon their estates, and the population and economy dwindled.

Threatened by German expansion during World War I, the U.S. bought the Danish West Indies on March 31, 1917. Even then the islands were expensive real estate -- almost three hundred dollars per acre. In 1931 the islands were administered by the U.S. Navy. Then the Department of the Interior took over.

However, a locally-elected legislature has operated since 1852. The U.S. Virgin Islands are now governed by an elected fifteen-member legislature and a governor. Though citizens of the U.S., residents have no vote in national elections.

Islanders represent many nationalities and backgrounds, with the majority being of African descent. Since 1960 the islands' population has more than doubled. Guesstimates put the figure at thirty-seven thousand five hundred on St. Croix, forty-five thousand seven hundred on St. Thomas, and two thousand three hundred on St. John.

Many Virgin Islands' plants bear provocative names -- "Catch and Keep" is a thorny vine that sticks to everything, the trunk of the "Monkey Don't Climb" tree bristles with thorns, "Jump Up and Kiss Me" has a beguiling scarlet blossom, the "Sensitive Plant" closes its leaves at night and at the slightest whisper of a touch, and the "Nothing Nut" is so named because it is good for nothing. Others are Pink Shower, Crown of Thorns, Jembi Cutlass, Clashie Melashie, Eye Bright, and Cock-a -locka.

Cruising the Caribbean

In 1981, we flew to New Orleans from Victoria, and took a seven-day cruise on the Russian ship Odessa. She was built in 1974, and has a gross tonnage of fourteen thousand pounds, is four hundred and forty-seven feet long, and has a capacity of five hundred and forty passengers. The ship was clean and we had a good cabin and good food, but it was nothing like the American standards. The musical entertainment was very loud. The ship no longer operates out of the United States, apparently due to political reasons.

For some reason we always think of the Russians as a different-looking people, but, for sure, the bevy of girls who met us upon boarding could all enter any of the world's beauty contests. They had limited English, but were very polite, courteous and efficient. Russian language lessons were offered to the passengers. However, at first glance, it looks impossible -- for example, "Good morning" is "Do broie utro", and "Thank you" is "Spasi bo".

We cruised to the Cayman Islands, Jamaica, and to Playa del Carmen in

Mexico. I feel that the Cayman Islands are one of the last greatest resorts in the world. The people like you and it is a country of the past, with beautiful beaches. It is a restful place and not too large. No doubt it will be like today's Waikiki in a few years.

A friend to whom I gave some flying instructions in Victoria, Dr. Godfrey Paul, has built a lovely hotel on the water. He is really in on the ground floor of development.

We drove a few miles from the major settlement to a post office called "Hell", and mailed a letter to Victoria just to have the "Hell" cancellation on the stamp.

On our cruise we also visited Jamaica, whose proud motto is "Out of many, one people". Of the nation's two million people, about ninety-five per cent are of African or Afro-European descent. Therefore, most of the faces one sees are black. In the minority are groups whose ancestors came from Britain, the Middle East, India, China, Portugal, Germany, South America, and other islands of the West Indies. Over countless years there has been intermarriage, so there are many faces and many shades of colour -- from black to tan to white.

In general, the use of the word "native" is perfectly proper as you are, of course, a native of the country in which you were born. However, you might pardonably get uptight if, historically in your country, the term has always been used derogatively to mean uncivilized and primitive. For this reason, Jamaicans of whatever racial descent, regard themselves as Jamaicans, and love to be called Jamaicans, not natives.

Our ship continued on to Playa del Carmen, Mexico, which is located about twenty-five miles southwest of the Island of Cozumel (Land of the Swallows). This is one of the strangest and most fascinating of the lost Mayan cities, with its Temples of the Descending God, the Temple of Fiscoes, and Xel-Ha Lagoon, a natural aquarium sacred to the ancient Mayas and which offers good swimming.

Chichen Itza is the most impressive of all the ancient Mayan cities. Its great temple is the Mayan calendar, with each step representing a day of the year. There is also the Sacred Ball Court, where the Mayas played an intricate game in which the losers were put to death.

Lima, Peru

We have been more than fortunate to have travelled all over the world, mostly in luxury. In writing about it, I suppose one remembers the negative side, but the positive outranks it many times over. However, it seems that in a lot warmer climates there is more political unrest and more poverty; it is difficult to adjust to these conditions when we have come from such a free society with almost everything. It does one a lot of good to see how these countries survive when faced with so many problems. I would never suggest that Canadian travellers pass these countries by, as long as they avoid most of the unrest. However, they should not expect to do and speak as they would at home.

We flew from Los Angeles to Lima, Peru, with Varig Airlines. This is a long flight, landing in the middle of the night. The first things you see are the poverty and unrest. Reading the complimentary guide to Peru makes you a little nervous.

The following is quoted from the Lima paper:

WATCH YOUR WALLET - Pickpockets and thieves, especially in Lima and Cuzco, are everywhere, enterprising, and of all ages. Do not wear good jewelry of any kind or carry passports, tickets or other documents while outside your hotel. If you wear a watch, be sure it is well covered by your shirt sleeve. Shoulder bags, camera cases and knapsacks are easily slit open from below or behind. Keep purses and packages in your lap when resting, not in a chair or on the floor beside you. Do not deal with any individual calling your hotel room, or approaching you in the hotel lobby or in the street saying he represents a travel agency, guide service or specialty shop. The only thing he represents is his own interests. If your passport is stolen, contact your consulate.

DRUGS - Peru has a strict and comprehensive law forbidding all possession of, use of and dealing in drugs, including marijuana and cocaine. Violators are not deported, but are tried under Peruvian law. Foreign offenders are usually dealt with as international traffickers with sentences ranging from fifteen years to life. The entire legal process from arrest to sentencing can take nine months to two years. There is no bail. Your consulate can provide moral support and little else.

We stayed at the Sheraton Hotel one night and at the Crillon Hotel the next night. As in many foreign countries, there were guards on every floor in the hotel. The guard is there to see that no one enters your room and, when you come up in the elevator to your room, he unlocks your door. You wonder how trustworthy he may be, as most of them are huge men and are not dressed in uniform.

Our Royal Viking ship was a day late getting to Lima, which necessitated us staying an extra night. We had intended to fly up to Cuzco, capital of the Inca empire, to visit Machu Picchu, which is called "the archeological capital of America". However, due to much political unrest, we passed it up, with some regrets.

Buenos Aires, Argentina

Though, today, Buenos Aires is the eighth largest city in the world and Argentina's capital, for the first two hundred and seventy years after it was founded, the city was of little importance. In its early days, as a simple outpost for Spain, Buenos Aires survived by smuggling, and there was no hint of its future potential. In 1853 Buenos Aires had less than ninety thousand inhabitants.

The European clamour for cheap food in the second half of the nineteenth century convinced Argentina to make use of its grasslands. Thus, the area of the pampas surrounding Buenos Aires came to life. Today, the pampas is a highly-important agricultural area, and its stress on raising livestock is well known throughout the world. Agriculture and livestock production provide about eighty per cent of the cattle and thirty per cent of the sheep reared in the country.

The transformation of the pampas was probably the most important thing ever to happen to Buenos Aires. The country's new riches flowed out to Europe through this city. Fulfilling its needs made the port grow from a relatively insignificant city to one of the greatest in the world.

The core of Argentina's massive capital has a population of about three million three hundred and twenty-three thousand, though close to nine million people live in Greater Buenos Aires, which includes the surrounding districts. Like any great metropolis, the streets buzz with the noise and activity of its people. It's a great city to walk around in, with over one hundred and fifty parks, large and small, adding colour to the scene. Some streets are lined with jacaranda trees, which blossom for ten days about mid-November, and beautifully-lit fountains sparkle on the plazas at night.

The heart of the city, both now and in colonial times, is the Plaza de Mayo. Here you'll find the historic Cabildo, the town hall, where the movement for independence from Spain was first planned, and the cathedral where San Martin, the great liberator of South America, is buried.

Argentina has the second highest standard of living in Latin America, and its cultural life is highly renowned. North of the Plaza de Mayo is the shopping, theatre and commercial area of the city, with the traditional shopping centre, Calle Florida. This fashionable downtown district, which offers some sophisticated shops, is reserved for pedestrians only. For blocks you can walk along a beautiful boulevard of flowers. It is difficult to imagine that you are in a city. Even the monuments are surrounded by flowers. A hired man chases away all the pigeons with a broom.

Avenida Corrientes is considered to be the entertainment centre of Buenos Aires, with a street full of theatres, reasonably-priced restaurants, cafes and nightlife. Nearby is Calle Lavelle, also closed off to traffic from six p.m. until midnight, where more restaurants and numerous cinemas can be found. Every night is New Year's Eve, with zany and noisy music, dancing and entertainment. (The locals mix their wine with soda water if they want to survive the next morning.)

For the more adventuresome, the picturesque old port district, known as the Boca, has its own distinctive life. Situated where the Riachuelo flows into the Plata, it was here that Pedro de Mendoza founded the first Buenos Aires. Cobble-stoned streets wind in and out among gaily-painted houses. One of the side streets has been sealed off to form a theatre, the Camimito. The huge Avellaneda Bridge gives a splendid view of the port. The main attractions of the Boca, however, are the many Italian restaurants, cafes, and the fun-filled, sometimes rowdy, nightlife.

Inflation is so rapid that, when using a taxi, it is necessary to multiply the meter reading by the month's magic number. As in so many other South American countries, the value of the peso varies almost hourly with the U.S. dollar.

There seems to be no racial discrimination because of the multiracial combination. There are three major groups -- Indians, mulatoes and whites -- plus the countless European Indian and black combinations. Author Roy Nash wrote, "The Brazilians are the most color blind people in the world. They are color blind to the point where they can look a man in the face and see nothing but a man."

Valparaiso, Chile

A very long, narrow country on the west coast of South America, Chile extends from just north of Arica to the almost literal end of the world at Tierra del Fuego. Within this narrow strip of land, a wide variety of cultures has existed, ranging from the very sophisticated Incas to the primitive Alacalufes, whose cooking style gave Tierra del Fuego its name -- Land of Fire.

Excavations in Chile have revealed complete, organized villages of an unrecorded pre-Inca civilization in the north of Chile. Later, the Incas extended their civilization as far south as central Chile. The other native Chileans -- the Chango, the Araucanians, the Onas, the Alacalufes and the Yaghans -- were all less-advanced cultures.

Before the Spanish invasion in the early sixteenth century, Chile had almost no contact with the western world. When Spanish forces began pushing their way south from Peru, forcing the Araucanian Indians further and further south, they met fierce opposition. The Spanish invasion brought the rule of the vice-royalty in Lima, Peru, over the Chilean colony, which became merely a farming colony, subject to numerous raids by English and French pirates.

On September 18, 1810, the Criollos (Chileans of Spanish descent) declared their independence and formed their first Junta de Gobierno. Fighting continued until 1818, when the Chilean army under San Martin, the Argentine general, and Bernardo O'Higgins, Chile's national hero, won the final victory.

Today Chile is a developing country. Production of copper accounts for about fifty-five per cent of the country's foreign exchange income, and its reserves of two hundred million tons of copper insure the importance of this metal in the economy for years to come. Industry, agriculture and business are also on the rise as the friendly and industrious people of Chile strive to make their country a better place to live and an exciting place to visit.

The most important of Chile's ports, Valparaiso, is about four hundred and thirty years old, and has witnessed much of the important history of Chile and South America. Capital of the Fifth Province, the port is situated on a picturesque bay surrounded by numerous hills, all inhabited and each with its own unique personality. It is the centre of one of Chile's richest and most attractive zones.

We took a taxi from Valparaiso docks and went along the beachfront for about six miles to Vena de Mar, a city of approximately one hundred and eighty-five thousand, set amidst a forest. It is the city most favoured by well-to-do Chileans and foreigners. Vena de Mar is a flurry of activity. You can take a horse-drawn carriage along the avenue to the marina. There are palm trees, chalets and castles. An inlet of the sea lies crossed by narrow bridges. There are six separate beaches, and the water is frigid. This city is a contrast to Valparaiso, which is a myriad of bars, underground taverns, sailors' hangouts, tattered houses and shacks. In 1906 it was devastated by an earthquake which claimed the city's former face; only the old colonial town, built around the small church La Matriz, remained.

We went into one of the most modern gambling casinos I have ever seen. It was on a par with Las Vegas or Monte Carlo. As in Monte Carlo, it is necessary to wear formal dress in the evening before you are allowed to enter and gamble.

In Chile, as in Italy and France, children begin drinking wine with water at a very early age. As they grow older, the water is gradually eliminated, bringing about a virtual immunity to the alcoholic content of the wine. It has been said that the last tourist who tried to drink wine, glass for glass, with a Chilean woke up under the table complaining about the noise from his wristwatch.

A journey through the Strait of Magellan

Here we entered one of the stormiest, wettest areas on earth, where more than sixteen feet of rain fall each year in some places. Seven days a year are tempestuous; twenty-five are stormy; ninety-three are squally; and the sun only shines through a blanket of mist and cloud an average of fifty-one days a year. This is an area where all four seasons can occur in a single day.

Our inland journey began northward of fifty degrees south latitude where, from the Gulf of Trinidad, we turned eastward and then south into the Canal of Sarmiento. Here we began our journey through the fragmentary geography of islands, gulfs and channels, past fjords and glaciers, toward the Strait of Magellan and the continental land's end.

Sailing down Canal Sarmiento, we observed Isla Esperanza on our right. To the east, glaciers flow from an elevation of seven thousand five hundred feet in the Mt. Balmaceda National Park. These glaciers represent the southern end of the Patagonian Ice Cap. In the waterways, we hoped to see dolphins, sea lions and black-necked swans.

Canal Sarmiento feeds into Paso Farquhar, a narrow twisting passageway, at the end of which we turned eastward, north of Newton island, and then sailed south past the eastern coast of the island and entered Estrecho (Strait) Collingwood. To our left and inland toward Puerto Natales, caves, which were inhabited by man an estimated ten thousand years ago, had been found.

At the end of Estrecho Collingwood, we turned west and entered Canal Smyth. Once into Canal Smyth, we could see Mt. Burney on our port side. Mt. Burney, at five thousand seven hundred and forty feet, is one of the highest mountains in the area.

We then sailed through Guia Narrows, another narrow Patagonian passageway, and continued our southerly course. The maze of islands around us is formed from the tops of submerged mountains, separated by torturous fjord-like channels which, in earlier times, provided a veritable topographical hysteria for exploring sailors.

Passing Isla Manuel Rodriguez on our right, we entered Gray Channel. Ahead of us we could see the five-thousand-one-hundred-and-ninety-eight-foot Seno Glacier. The glacier was on our left as we passed the Fairway Lighthouse, manned by five Chilean volunteers. Once south of the lighthouse, we began the portside turn past Cape Tamar. It was here that we officially entered the Strait of Magellan.

Upon our entry into the strait, we proceeded on a southeasterly course down to

Cabo Froward, the southernmost tip of continental South America. More than halfway down to Cabo Froward, we rounded the northern side of Isla Carlos. Here we entered the Passage of Crooked Reach, the narrowest point of the Strait of Magellan (one and one-tenth miles wide), and continued on to Punta Arenas. To our left was Mt. Tres Picos, rising three thousand six hundred and ninety-seven feet above sea level. North of here, the Chilean government had developed and was energetically working a number of rich coal mines.

Starting as a penal colony in 1849, Punta Arenas thrived because of its location on the trade route. Many a windjammer put in here on her rough journey around Cape Horn to the south. After the opening of the Panama Canal in 1914, the city had to settle for a quieter existence. Today, with nearly eighty thousand residents, the city serves as the commercial centre for the area's cattle and sheep ranchers, and for an oil industry to the east, that now supplies almost one-third of Chile's petroleum needs.

Almost fifteen hundred nautical miles from Valparaiso and fourteen hundred nautical miles from Buenos Aires, Punta Arenas is located at fifty-two degrees south latitude, which is the same latitude in the northern hemisphere as London, Amsterdam and Berlin. July is the coldest month in Punta Arenas, but still this is relatively mild if one considers only the temperature, which averages thirty-six degrees Fahrenheit (two and two-tenths degrees Celsius). What makes this area so inhospitable is the wind. Punta Arenas is within a large southern area of intense meteorological depressions. Very strong winds batter the houses, eliminate the possibility of substantial tree life, parch the ground, and, at times, whip up the sea to frightening heights.

South of here, South America becomes a scattered Andean mosaic of islands which reaches down toward the Antarctic Peninsula, leaving a gap of only five hundred miles, called the Drake Passage. Taking the brunt of fierce winds and erosive current is Cape Horn, the final rocky statement of South America.

It seemed to me that whoever first brought the beautiful yellow broom to our area (Victoria, B.C.) must have dropped off a lot of seed in Punta Arenas. We travelled for quite a few miles by taxi and the yellow broom was everywhere.

Sailing from Punta Arenas, we were scheduled to cruise within one-half mile of Isla Magdalena, a one-time, penguin breeding stronghold, where as many as twenty-five thousand pairs of Magellanic penguins could be found. Reportedly, there are few, if any, of these migratory birds to be found on the island today. In the same area there are numerous playful dolphins, and along the island's shoreline one can usually spot sea lions.

Rio de Janeiro, Brazil

In November 1981, after cruising around South America, we arrived in Rio aboard the Royal Viking Sky.

As beautiful a city as this is, we had a skirmish both on arrival and on flying out of Rio. It seems that so many of these countries have a lot of political strife and problems; in fact, all of South America seems that way. I suppose one should overlook this and see only the beauty of the area; however, it is difficult, unless you are travelling by yourself. You are open to all things, from petty larceny to robbery, or are frightened to really go out and see the town.

We disembarked from the ship on a rainy, misty day, and cleared Customs in a partially-wired enclosure. The baggage handler, wearing a large identification card, took our luggage to a taxi outside the enclosure. Of course, the language barrier made transactions difficult, and it turned out that the baggage man was also the taxi man. The driver took off his white jacket and identification, and got into a Volkswagon van. A male friend was sitting in front. We were going to the Sheraton Hotel, a distance of approximately six miles. Before we left the ship, the passengers were advised about local costs; it was suggested that we pay not more than six dollars American for a taxi ride to any hotel. We entered the van and, after we had driven for a few minutes, the driver's friend said he wanted forty dollars American, which I refused to pay. I said I would pay when we got to the hotel. With this, the driver turned down a side street and suggested we pay or get out. If you can imagine getting out in a poverty-stricken area with four bags -- I soon gave him the forty dollars. Even then we didn't feel sure he would take us to the hotel; however, he did. In talking with the hotel personnel we were advised that you never take a taxi this way. The procedure is to phone the hotel, then they send a taxi and the fare is put on your bill.

Rio simply has everything, from beaches to mountains, enhanced by a beautiful climate. The most famous sight is Sugar Loaf Mountain, with its statue of Christ the Redeemer, perched at a height of two thousand three hundred feet. The statue is over one hundred feet tall and weighs over seven tons.

The major sport in Rio seems to be suntanning. There are sixteen beaches, the most popular being the Copacabana, famous for its beautiful women.

Inflation is almost out of control. If you cash a travel cheque at ten a.m., you may not get nearly the same amount of money (cruzairos) as you would get a few hours later in the day, when the rate may change.

A lot of the larger South American cities have enormous jewellery stores with outside salesmen. These salesmen fly from port to port, meeting the ships. It is strange to arrive aboard ship in a new port city and, as you disembark down the gangway, the same jewellery salesman is on the dock, approaching you as he has in every other port.

Some salesmen also book passage on a cruise ship and mix with the passengers. You may be having a cocktail with a man or woman, only to find out they are salespeople who will eventually endeavour to sell you a diamond or other jewellery. The Royal Viking Line has always attempted to avoid selling passage to these individuals. However, the jewellery companies are constantly developing new strategies by which to get on board. The Royal Viking Line issues a notice to you in your stateroom advising that various salesmen manage to book passage and are unknown to them.

We flew from Rio to Los Angeles via Varig Airlines. This seems to be one of the leading companies in flying -- terrific service and clean aeroplanes. We were fortunate enough to be travelling First Class, so we had a pretty good sleep during the fifteen-hour flight.

At the Rio airport, we were in the First Class Lounge, along with about a dozen people, watching television and having coffee, waiting for departure time. One of the passengers was Mrs. Kissinger. All of a sudden, watching the TV news, we saw demonstrators, police and others in what appeared to be a riot. A police wagon pulled up, and several policemen picked up Henry Kissinger and pushed him bodily into the wagon. About fifteen minutes later, he arrived at the airport lounge but didn't appear to be too upset. In fact, his wife was more disturbed by watching it on TV. We felt quite disturbed ourselves to be travelling on the same aircraft, and were much relieved after it was airborne. Some hours later, about four a.m., the Kissingers got off in Lima, Peru, where they were met by forty or fifty armed soldiers. It was nice to see the end of them.

The following is from an Associated Press news story in Brazil:

Brasilia, Brazil - Former U.S. Secretary of State Henry Kissinger fled the University of Brasilia in a police paddy wagon Wednesday after 400 student protestors besieged an administration building where he was lecturing on international relations.

Kissinger and about 300 other people were hustled away after the demonstrators, screaming anti-U.S. slogans, burned an American flag, lobbed eggs, tomatoes and rocks at the building and barricaded the doors for two hours.

Many foreign diplomats assigned to the Brazilian capital attended the morning talk, including the deputy chief of the United States Embassy, George High.

Kissinger's speech on international relations was at times drowned out by the students who shouted," Kissinger go home", "We need food" , and other protests against the U.S. and Brazilian governments.

Police with riot gear broke through the student cordon and rescued the dignitaries, forming a human cordon around Kissinger as he emerged from the building.

"I'm not going in there," Kissinger said as he saw the police vehicle and shouting demonstrators, but police forced him to enter and the paddy wagon left.

No injuries were reported as police ordered the protestors to disperse and the rest of the audience departed. Earlier, a federal congressman, Pinheiro Machado, negotiated with students and was able to guarantee the safe departure of seven ambassadors -- from Japan, Israel, Finland, Iraq, India, Argentina and Chile.

The student protest came during a country-wide strike by professors at federally-run universities, including the Brasilia University where the walkout was partially observed.

"The rector didn't have money to hire professors for a translation course, but he spends $15,000 to bring to the university an imperialist agent who killed more than a million people," read one banner prepared for the protests. Another read, "Money for teachers, not assassins."

Kissinger is on a week-long visit to Brazil for a series of lectures sponsored by the university.

South Africa

We flew from London to Johannesburg with one stop at Nairobi, Kenya. This would possibly be our longest flight as to hours in the air, relative to other areas we have visited -- approximately seventeen hours.

It is hard to understand all the problems of South Africa, a country jammed between two oceans, the Atlantic and the Indian. When travelling throughout the country, one sees little evidence of all the difficulties you read about, and there is no feeling of being on edge, like we felt in South America and many other countries.

There certainly are injustices in the country, but how to change them is another story. The level of literacy within the non-white population goes all the way from uneducated to educated. The racially-divided society (apartheid) simply means separation physically, socially and politically of the blacks and coloured people from the white population. I would relate it to our native Indian problems here at home, and, if the Indians outnumbered us to the extent the non-whites do in South Africa -- four to one -- I wonder how we would handle it.

There are so many different tribes of black people, with some hating one another. Apparently, most of the fighting is between the non-white people themselves, but we witnessed none of this. We were served by non-white taxi drivers, waiters and waitresses who were all very pleasant and sociable. One hopes this country, somehow, someway, can settle its problems. I do not know many countries, other than ours, that are so beautiful and have such an ideal climate.

In 1924 a skull with human and ape-like characteristics was discovered in Africa. Anthropologists have generally agreed we humans originated in Africa more than a million years ago.

In 1985, when we visited, the cost of everything was very reasonable due to the dollar exchange. Our hotel, the Sandton Sun Hotel, was an elegant, beautiful five-star hotel, and cost only eighty-four dollars per night. In most other parts of the world, an equivalent hotel would be well over two hundred dollars per night.

South Africa is unique for its natural beauty. Its wilderness is vast, with endless beaches. The urban centres are modern.

Gold and diamonds are mined from the earth, like coal is in British Columbia. However, along with great wealth, there is much poverty.

Every country in the world has its own unwritten laws, and visitors should know and respect them, if they do not wish to appear boorish. The following are some of the social customs we found in South Africa:

* South African women are fairly reserved in public, especially in traditional male spheres. For example, ladies do not go into bars, either alone or even when accompanied by men. For them and their companions there are Ladies' Lounges.
* The man always does the inviting.
* Ladies are not seen in public in excessively scanty clothing, not even on the beach. Topless bathing is officially forbidden.

* Men should remember that it is not always correct to appear in casual clothes, i.e., without jacket and tie, no matter how hot it may be. Obviously, this does not apply on safaris or in game lodges.
* Correct dress is expected in good restaurants and private clubs, especially during the evening.
* It is not usual to look for a seat in a restaurant. One should wait until a member of the staff shows one to a table, even if this demands a little more time.
* It is usual to give a tip in hotels and restaurants, unless ten per cent has been included in the bill. The amount is left up to you and depends on the quality of service. Native chambermaids and other native hotel staff take their tips with both hands open, a traditional gesture of thanks.
*You should only photograph people if you feel they will not mind, or at least will not be bothered; this applies particularly to non-whites. If you are not sure, then ask politely. If there are language problems, your guide, or the use of sign language if you are alone, will help.
* Pornography and the exhibiting of naked bodies in any form are forbidden. Even if you hold other views, please respect theirs.

Blue Train

The world-famous Blue Train, a legend of unequalled luxury was officially named in 1946, and is regarded the world over as the epitome of luxury train travel. In 1972 two completely-new Blue Train sets were built. They are like five-star hotels. The train is hauled by two Class 6E 1 locomotives, and I feel sure the wheels are made of rubber.

We travelled for twenty-four hours, overnight, from Johannesburg to Cape Town, the legislative capital of the nation, which is a beautiful town and area. Our trip cost three hundred and forty-six dollars Canadian each, and our accommodation was superb with all the amenities -- shower, wine, and a porter on duty around the clock. The many courses of food were equivalent to those served in the best hotels.

We highly recommend this trip -- it adds to the seven wonders of the world.

Durban, South Africa

Durban is the busiest seaport in South Africa and overlooks the Indian Ocean. The harbour was once a lagoon used by hippos, pelicans and other birds. At one time a sand bar lay beneath the water at the entrance. Between 1845 and 1885 there were many shipwrecks. However, constant dredging and land reclamation make it an excellent harbour today.

There is a beautiful beach which stretches for twenty-eight miles, and includes North Beach, South Beach and Brighton Beach. The beaches are protected by shark nets. Up to the time we arrived, there were beaches for the non-whites and beaches for the whites; all of them are now open to everyone.

The following is a special recipe obtained from Hotel Manager Peter Einfield:

Elephant Stew

one elephant
salt and pepper to taste
brown gravy
two rabbits (optional)

Cut elephant into bite-sized pieces. This should take about two months. Cover with brown gravy. Cook over kerosene fire about four weeks at four hundred and sixty-five degrees. This will serve three thousand eight hundred people. If more are expected, add two rabbits. Do this only if necessary, as most people do not like to find hare in their stew.

Nosey-Be, Madagascar

Nosey-Be is one of the satellite islands of Madagascar. It is nineteen by twelve miles of volcanic island. At lower elevations, the weather is hot and humid. The island produces sugar, coffee, tobacco, oils for perfume, vanilla and black pepper, and also has a rum distillery.

It has a romantic history of sea-going migration, warfare, piracy and foreign colonialism. Very little English is spoken. The national language is Malagasy, but French is used also.

In most places where one travels U.S. dollars are accepted, but they are not accepted in Nosey-Be. At most of the local ports, the ship arranges to have a local bank open up a money-exchange on board the ship; when you leave, the bank converts your remaining rufiyaa back to U.S. dollars.

There are Comet butterflies, which have a wingspan of twenty centimetres, and colourful orchids growing wild.

It is also the home of the lemur, a cat-sized animal with big round eyes and monkey-like hands. Their appearance is much the way it was fifty million years ago; it is believed that they closely resemble the ancestors of man. They live in trees and feed on insects, fruit, bark, leaves, and even on small mammals. They are nocturnal; at dusk they feed and then are active all night. They never form large groups, and they sleep in holes in trees or nest in leaves and twigs.

Maldives

The following is taken from the Royal Viking Line brochure:

Over 1000 islands, atolls and reefs sit like jewels in the vastness of the Indian Ocean, existing to the beat of the great rhythm of the sea.
No great monuments testify to the egos of kings.
No powerful Maldivian army changed the history of the world.

But for all that, the Maldives exist as an example to the world of serenity, charm and the closest thing to PARADISE.

The archipelago is spread over an area of more than thirty-five thousand square miles. The total land area is only one hundred and fifteen square miles. Less than three hundred of the islands are inhabited and the total population is under one hundred and fifty thousand. The highest peak in the Maldives is only ten feet, and most of the islands (each of which covers a mere half square mile) rise but four or five feet above the level of the sea. The islands are grouped into twenty atolls, the most southern being abreast of the equator. Relief from the equatorial climate is a daily caressing of sea-breezes, and the seas are seldom other than calm.

The Maldives are very much a product of the sea. Islands have been known to appear and disappear. Somewhere in the mists of time, sailors, probably from south India or Ceylon (Sri Lanka), discovered the coral islands that are the Maldives and settled there, and were joined by further waves of immigrants through the Indian Ocean.

The original rule was by a succession of kings, until 1153 when a traveller from North Africa, Abdul Barakaath Yoosuf al Barbary, visited the islands. As the story goes, he banished a monster and converted the Maldives to Islam. Islam remains the official and predominant religion today, despite a Portuguese colonization from 1568 to 1573, and despite its being a British Protectorate in 1887. Independent since 1965, the Maldives boast a population of over one hundred and fifty thousand, spread over two hundred islands. The resident Malkivians are a mixture of people -- descendants of Arab traders and of black slaves imported from Africa. The language is related to that of Sri Lanka.

This island country, located in the Indian Ocean southeast of India and Sri Lanka, is popular with English tourists. It is not humid and has an average temperature of about eighty-eight degrees Fahrenheit (twenty-nine degrees Celsius). The water temperature averages eighty-four degrees Fahrenheit (twenty-seven degrees Celsius). The best time to visit is from November to April.

Fishing provides most of the jobs, with fresh fish being the chief export. The Malkivians also farm tropical fruits -- mangoes, bananas, coconuts and pineapples. Coral and coconut wood are the main materials used for constructing houses.

The local currency is the rufiyaa (Maldivian rupee); one rufiyaa equals one hundred larees. Notes are in denominations of Rf100, 50, 10, 5, 2, and1. Coins are in larees 50, 25, 10, 5, and 1. (Currency exchange rates are usually announced on board ship upon arrival.) Banks are open from nine a.m. to one p.m., Sunday through Thursday.

The capital city of the Maldives is Male. This island city of six square kilometres, and forty thousand people, can be explored by foot in a few hours. It is a place where traffic jams are no more than several bicycles and locals travelling abreast, where a skyscraper is not more than five stories tall, and where the number of available hotels can be counted on one hand.

Although, naturally, the chief attractions are watersports of the sun-surf-and-sand variety, there are many places to visit in Male, including Friday Mosque Hujuru Miski, built in 1656, which contains carved religious writings on the conversion of the Maldives to Islam; Minaret Munearu, from which the people are summoned to prayer; Medu Sivaarath, the tombstone of Abdul Barakaath Yoosuf al Barbary; Muleeage, the President's residence built in 1913; and Sultan Park, comprising the former Sultan's palace and the museum, formerly the Sultan's living quarters.

The tourist shops are located in the back lanes of the bazaar, behind the fish market. There are also "Singapore" bazaar shops in Chandani, Orchid, and Fareedhee Magu. Things to buy range from fresh fish and vegetables to tortoiseshell wares (which are not allowed in the U.S.A.). There are souvenirs of black coral and shells, as well as many varieties of handicrafts. Indian merchants own many of the shops as their familes have lived on the islands for more than three hundred years.

Driving around in a very, very old beaten-up taxi, we visited the outdoor market, which sits on the side of the road, where all the women sell their vegetables, fish, handicrafts, and weaving. One woman had a huge pile of very small shrimp that looked dried; the pile was approximately two feet in diameter and three feet high. With the prevalent standards of sanitation, it was difficult to try a sample.

The Royal Viking Sea hosted a beach party on a small island located about two miles from Male. Early in the morning, the crew transported to the beach, by tender, equipment, food, chairs, tables and a band of musicians. Ship tenders operated from ten-thirty a.m., transporting passengers to and from the little island. This was probably the grandest beach party I have ever seen. There were only a few small buildings on an island about two acres in size, nothing but glorious beaches, sand and warm water for swimming. The crew had set up a barbeque consisting of about seven pieces of equipment, so we had many choices for lunch -- from roast beef to Italian-style food, with all kinds of desserts and drinks with ice, both soft and hard. We had comfortable seats to sit on, and a five-piece band for music. It was a credit to the crew to have such a picnic set up.

Orient Express

In 1987, my wife Iris and I decided to travel from London, England, to Venice, Italy, on the famed Orient Express. We had travelled previously on the Blue Train in South Africa, and it is always difficult to make comparisons. However, the Blue Train, costing about one-fourth that of the Orient Express, is in a separate class, very much superior in all aspects. The Orient Express is certainly something I would not have missed, as I could not fault it as to service, food and area travelled, but it is the most overpriced travel I have ever experienced -- only those that have no respect or consideration for money would use it. From London to Venice, including the one and one-half hour ferry ride, takes approximately twenty-nine hours. The fare was two thousand seven hundred and sixty-three dollars and sixty-seven cents Canadian, or approximately one hundred dollars per hour for two people. The Concorde is in the same fare category, but at least you see and travel on one of the world's great wonders.

About eleven a.m. we left London from Victoria Station's Platform Eight on a British Pullman. All the cars have names -- Audrey, Cygnus, Ibis, Ione, Lucille -- and were each built in different years. Ours was Cygnus, a twenty-six-seat parlour car, outfitted with Australian-walnut panels, mirrors and old prints. Its construction commenced in 1938, but completion was deferred until 1951 due to the war. In 1951, during the Festival of Britain, it was reserved for use by royalty and visiting heads of state.

We boarded our car and waited one hour while they tried to locate an engine. During this time a light, three-course meal, with champagne, wine and tea, was served. After an engine was found, we were served afternoon tea en route to Folkestone.

We travelled through Kent, with its beautiful gardens and hop fields, where my parents lived before they came to Canada. We passed the White Cliffs of Dover, and our thoughts went to one of England's finest entertainers, Vera Lynn, who made this area famous in song to the troops in the 1939 - 1945 War. Without any doubt, Vera Lynn leaves her voice and songs until eternity for those veterans of the war. In 1980, when she was possibly in her seventies, she sang at the Royal Victoria Theatre to a packed house, who gave her close to a thirty-minute standing ovation -- one of the most intimate, beautiful evenings of a lifetime, and a feeling that cannot be translated unless you were part of that era.

From the White Cliffs of Dover, we went on to Folkestone to board the ferry for Boulogne, a one-and-a-half-hour ride. At Boulogne, where the Basilica of Notre Dame is visible on a hilltop, we boarded the Orient Express, which they call the Continental Train.

The Continental Train has seventeen carriages, including the bar car, which has a grand piano, and three restaurant cars -- our sleeping car was located behind these. Our double cabin was very small, about six feet by six feet, like in the trains of yesterday, with an upper and a lower bed, and a wash-basin cabinet with hot and cold water. The W.C.'s are located at both ends of the sleeping car. Ventilation may be increased by rolling down the window. All the cabins are finished in inlaid wood, very elegant, and not only look like the 1920's, but also are from that vintage.

It is a pretty bumpy ride. In order to go from our cabin to the dining car, it was necessary to walk through the bar car. Again the elegance of decor is hard to explain -- much inlaid woodwork, lamps and designs of the First World War. We were served a delicious meal, equal to any of the world's finest restaurants. It is a wonder how they can produce this from just a small kitchen, which you pass by on the way to dinner. After dinner we had to pass through the bar car again to get back to our cabin. This part of the train was really hitting the high tunes, crowded, smokey, and noisy; it was necessary to step over people to get past.

From the Orient Express brochure I quote:

Dress: You can never be overdressed on the Venice - Simplon - Orient Express. The historic decor of the train and its atmosphere encourage everyone to dress to suit the occasion. Dinner provides you with a marvellous opportunity to recreate the style and glamour of a bygone age. Our minimum requirements are a jacket and tie for gentlemen and an equivalent standard for ladies. During the daytime, casual but elegant clothes are the custom. Please do not wear jeans in the dining car. If you are travelling in Day Sector accommodation we realize it will not normally be possible for you to change for dinner. However, it would be appreciated if you could dress according to our minimum standards.

Before departure we had read the brochure and did take suitable clothing. However, to our amazement, while passing through the bar car after dinner, we saw one fellow in his bathing trunks sitting at the piano celebrating. It would have been great to join the party, but our constitutions were not up to it.

From Boulogne to Venice the train averaged a speed of seventy kilometres per hour, with a maximum of one hundred and forty kilometres per hour. Leaving Boulogne we crossed the river Somme. Arriving at Amiens, the diesel engine was exchanged for an electric locomotive. We passed through Chantilly, the centre of French horse racing, and then on to Paris.

The train departed Paris from the Gare de l'Est, which was built in 1855 and has been used for the Orient Express departures since 1883. We went through Troy, Belfort, and Basle, the walled city and Roman stronghold founded in 374 AD. (Until 1850 the night train from Paris used to whistle to get the city gate open.) Our next stop was Zurich, and then on to Bucks where the Swiss locomotives were exchanged for two Austrian ones.

We travelled through Liechtenstein, where we saw Vaduz Castle -- the home of Prince Franz Josef, and continued on through the Arlberg Pass on a single-track railway line. The train passed through the six-and-a-third-mile-long Arlberg Tunnel, which was built between 1880-1884, at an altitude of five thousand eight hundred and eighty-two feet. We continued on to St. Anton, a ski resort, and to Innsbruck, a medieval city. (This latter city hosted the Winter Olympics in 1964 and 1976.) Via the Brenner Pass, at a summit of four thousand five hundred and thirty-seven feet, we passed into Italy near Brennero, where Hitler and Mussolini met during the Second World War. This section of the railway was built in 1864.

The train's final destination was the Santa Lucia Station just outside Venice. From here we were to be transported to the Grand Hotel by boat. However, due to circumstances beyond the control of the Orient Express, when we were about one hundred miles from Venice, the Italian railway unions went on strike from seven p.m. until eleven p.m. The train came to a halt for several hours while discussions went on as to whether we could proceed. The decision was in the negative. Since we were supposed to have arrived in Venice at seven p.m., no arrangements had been made for dinner on the train, and we all wondered about eating. Somehow the crew arranged to go out where we had stopped and picked up eggs and other supplies. They prepared a very good supper to tide us over.

Finally the strike was over and we were on our way, arriving in the Venice railway station after midnight and in a light rain. There were hundreds of people and baggage crowded into the station. By the time our baggage was unloaded and inspected by Customs, it was after one a.m.

Since Venice is a series of canals and islands, to get anywhere you must use a water taxi. Before getting off the train we had paid two thousand five hundred and sixty francs in advance (in our case, twenty-six pounds Sterling) for transportation by boat to the Cavello Hotel, where we were going to stay. Along with twenty other people and the baggage, we boarded a twenty-foot, partially-open boat . The captain of the boat, the only crew member, was so far under the influence of alcohol that he could hardly stand up and could not lift our baggage without falling down. How he managed, in semi-darkness, to navigate the waterways for about a twenty-minute ride, I'll never know.

On arrival, in pouring rain, at the dock at St. Mark's Square, we ascended about thirty steps with our baggage in hand. There were no porters, so we walked about half a mile, and were met at the hotel by a gentleman in long tails; he looked like an undertaker. He unlocked the metal gates to the hotel, took us up to our room, and left.

One always thinks of Venice in a romantic way but, unless you are interested in history and antiques, it strikes you as being a little like Coney Island. The city is really floating but, over a period of time, it has sunk a couple of feet into the effluent-tainted waters. St. Mark's Square with its surrounding buildings, including St. Mark's Church which is over one thousand years old, is a grand sight worth seeing. Many birds are flying around and orchestras are playing for the crowds.

We took a boat along the Grand Canal, with its many bridges, and other waterways over to a glass factory which proved to be most interesting. The operators of the gondolas sing and serenade the tourists as they paddle along the canals.

On the second day, we checked out of our hotel and took a boat over to the airport, which is about a fifty-minute ride. We boarded our plane for the one-hour flight to Vienna.

Vienna, Austria

Vienna is like a dream come true. Departing Venice for Vienna is like leaving Tijuana, Mexico, and arriving in Victoria, Canada. There is such a vast difference.

The airport is equal or superior to any I have ever seen. The public areas have beautiful carvings, including a marble candle standing about six feet high and three feet around with water slowly flowing down its sides, and a map of the world about two feet in diameter, which has been carved from rock. The furniture has a blue and chrome finish, and all the shops stand like separate islands in the foyer -- a very special architectural design.

The city gives the impression of cleanliness, and it would rank as one of the most expensive places in the world. A hamburger at McDonalds costs approximately thirteen dollars U.S. Meals at our hotel ranged from thirty to forty dollars per person; these meals at home would be about ten dollars each. Our hotel room was more than three hundred dollars Canadian a night for two people. The price of coffee at three dollars and fifty cents a cup was staggering. Eventually, as in other expensive places, one is forced to take it as it is and pay the shot. Of course the locals live by a different standard; our taxi driver told us they could manage on a normal wage.

One unique thing we learned was that a child is always named for the day of the year on which he is born. If your name is Bill, when you meet another person named Bill, you can be assured you were both born on the same day, but not necessarily in the same year.

Vienna was Beethoven's home and Schubert's birthplace. Streetcars run everywhere; you can purchase a day ticket, and get on and off as often as you care to. It would take weeks to see all there is to see, especially the museums, palaces and music halls. The city's famous boulevard, the "Ring", is a large circle surrounded by magnificent buildings, like the State Opera House, the Museum of Fine Arts, the Museum of Natural History, the Parliament, and the City Hall, as well as the monument of Maria Teresa, theatres and, of course, shops. The Spanish Riding School is where you can watch the training of the world-famous Lippizaner horses. We didn't see the Vienna Boys' Choir as it was on Sunday morning; this was most unfortunate for us.

To see the Danube River is like seeing Big Ben in London -- something you have only dreamed about. However, the water didn't seem that blue. One could take a boat ride, but we didn't.

However, while driving around in our taxi, we saw the Hundertwasserhaus, which is an example of unique architecture for modern housing. We also saw the Danube Tower, a symbol of modern Vienna, and the U.N.O. City.

On Tuesday, May 21, 1988, we left Vienna on an Austian Airlines DC9 for Frankfurt, and then on to Bergen, Norway. Iris' note says: *Ham, sausages and scrambled eggs, white rolls, jam, tea and orange juice were served on this very short flight -- 1 hour 20 minutes. (Delicious food)*

Northern Europe

In Frankfurt we left Austrian Airlines and boarded a Lufthansa 737 for Oslo, Norway -- about a two-hour trip.

In Oslo we cleared Customs and boarded SAS for Bergen, for about a forty-minute flight over snow-capped mountains. The scenery was just like in British Columbia, and the on-the-ground June temperature was about seventeen degrees Celsius.

At this time we did not know that Iris' bag had never left Oslo. It took some effort and two days to have it sent to the Royal Viking ship we had boarded in Bergen and was now at Arendal, Norway. We have been most fortunate with all the travelling we have done not to lose any baggage. However, there could not have been a worse place to have it disappear because, if you ever really need your luggage, it is on board ship for all the gala events and cocktail parties.

We sailed on the Royal Viking Sky from Bergen to Arendal, Oslo, Leningrad (U.S.S.R.), Helsinki (Finland), Stockholm (Sweden) and Copenhagen (Denmark).

Bergen, Norway

Bergen is Norway's second largest city, with a population of about two hundred thousand. It has been said that seeing Bergen is like going back in history to an overgrown fishing village in 1070. It wasn't until 1909 that a railway was opened linking Bergen and Oslo. Before that, people could get from Bergen to London more quickly than to Oslo, which made Bergen so different as an ancient trading town.

Arendal, Norway

The town of Arendal originally stood on seven islands. Not too long ago there were no proper streets and no marketplace. Today it is a large exporter of wood pulp and fibreglass boats, as well as being the home of other industries.

Oslo, Norway

The capital of Norway is located at the head of the sixty-mile-long Oslo Fjord. At one hundred and seventy-five square miles in area it is one of the world's largest cities, but it has a small population of approximately five hundred thousand. It has the royal palace, many museums and about twelve hundred miles of ski-touring trails. The royal palace, called the "Slottet" in Norwegian, is currently occupied by King Olav V. It is a grey and yellow stone structure, and is not separated from the public by any fences. Here one can see the changing of the Guards. Our driver told us that the king preferred his modest country home for bringing up his children.

We went to Frogner Park to view the work of the controversial sculptor Gustav Vigeland who, for thirty years, created his own world of human beings and animals in stone, iron and bronze. The assembly of one hundred and fifty statue groups depicts almost every human experience. It is so different and so hard to explain to someone who hasn't seen it. However, it remains in your memories of Oslo forever.

We visited the Holmenkollen ski jump where celebrations take place each winter. More than one hundred thousand spectators attend these gala events.

The Gold Visa Card we have is unbelievable. In Oslo I needed some cash, so I put my card in the slot of the touch-banking system and cash was produced immediately. Most restaurants and hotels around the world accept the card, and, to make phone calls in airports and public phone areas, all you do is slide the card into the telephone slot. You do not need a coin -- just dial your area code and phone number and you're connected to home immediately. Charges appear on your next Visa statement. It certainly beats looking around for coins to put into the slot.

Leningrad, U.S.S.R.

Leningrad, founded in 1703 by Czar Peter the Great, is one of the most historic cities in the world, and was the capital of the Russian Empire for two hundred and five years. It has been called Petrograd, St. Petersburg, and now Leningrad. It is said to have been the birthplace of the Russian Revolution, and is designated as a hero city of World War II. Today it is the second largest city in the Soviet Union, with a population of about four million.

Where the ship docks, there are six hundred acres of walled docks and the largest-ever military base. On arrival at the dock we were welcomed by a twenty-five-piece Merchant Marine brass orchestra, which proved very interesting and enjoyable.

I would highly recommend getting a Russian visa before leaving home; otherwise, if you are on a ship, you cannot even go down the gangplank and walk around the docks. The only way to sight-see without a visa is to take a group bus tour.

When you go on a tour, your passport is surrendered at the dock, and you are given a little Russian book to keep until your return. Before leaving the ship, ladies are advised that they should not take a purse with them or carry any bags. This is not for safety reasons, but to facilitate getting back on the ship. On tour departure you are examined, and have to list everything you are taking ashore, including money and jewellery. It is illegal to make purchases with foreign money; this could get you into a lot of trouble as there is a large black market. You are taken to government stores where you can make purchases. These stores will accept your Visa card, and they are also allowed to accept U.S. cash. On your return, you will not be allowed to take any rupees out of the country.

It is all right to take pictures, excluding anything pertaining to the military or pictures that would be considered degrading to the country.

Not having much interest in art, we did not visit the world-famous Hermitage. Apparently in the interests of education, the Russian people can visit at hardly any cost and consequently it is always overcrowded. Those on our ship that did take the Hermitage tour said it was very hot, crowded and difficult to see much. Originally it was a quiet retreat for the czars and could only be visited by a very few select outsiders. It is undoubtedly one of the world's greatest collections of art, holding some two and a half million individual works. There are eleven hundred rooms open to the public, exhibiting fourteen thousand paintings, twelve thousand sculptures, and four hundred display rooms. It was once calculated that if a visitor devoted one minute to each work of art it would take twelve years to see everything.

Helsinki, Finland

This is a city and country with a long history of wars and Russian control. Although Finland was under Russian rule for some time, it is now independent.

Our first impression was of a very clean city, one you would want to visit again. The people are most friendly and courteous.

Here in Canada Helsinki is remembered for the 1952 Olympics. We visited the area where the Olympics were held, and were very impressed by the statue of Pava Nurmi, Finland's Gold Medal winner.

We also visited a most unusual church, the "Rock Church", which was carved from a granite site and roofed with a copper and glass dome. It was designed by two brothers from a starting point of a rocky outcrop that rises about forty feet above street level. It resulted in an ingenious modern version of a rotunda, with interior walls blasted from bedrock and then spanned by the copper dome.

We purchased some soapstone called "the formation of the Steite Stone two thousand years ago".

Stockholm, Sweden

Stockholm is the capital city, with over a million people. It is a city of islands, canals, bridges, and parks, so, consequently, it is accessible by waterways. A chartered launch will carry you through the islands to see the many historic buildings. There is a good view of the royal palace, which is situated on the island known to Stockholmers as "The Old City". The royal palace was built between 1690 and 1754. It is the only one in Europe where royalty still reside and the public can visit.

Copenhagen, Denmark

Copenhagen is a gracious city, with friendly, hospitable people. It is the site of the most publicized gardens in the world, the Tivoli Gardens. Everywhere one looks there are flowers of all colours and sizes. The city has superb sculptures, a palace, a stock exchange building with four dragons' tails forming its spire, and Rosenberg Castle with its treasures, including the Crown Jewels and regalia.

We flew from Copenhagen to London, England, a flight of about thirty minutes, but, due to tremendous congestion in London, we had to hold for about twenty-five minutes before landing. However, we had been served roast duck which was delicious.

Ten Commandments for a Traveller

1. Thou shalt not expect to find things as thou has them at home, for thou has left home to find them different.
2. Thou shalt not take anything too seriously, for a carefree mind is the beginning of a vacation.
3. Thou shalt not let the other tourists get on thy nerves, for thou are paying out good money to have a good time.
4. Remember thy passport so that thou knowest where it is at all times, for a man without a passport is a man without a country.
5. Blessed is the man who can say thank you in any language, for it shall be worth more to him than tipping.
6. Blessed is the man who can make change in any language, for he shall not be cheated.
7. Thou shalt not worry, for he that worrieth hath no pleasure. Very few things are ever fatal.
8. Thou shalt, when in Rome, do somewhat as the Romans do. If in difficulty, thou shalt use thy good common sense and friendliness.
9. Thou shalt not judge the people of a country by one person with whom thou hast trouble.
10. Remember, thou art a guest in every land. He that treateth his host with respect shall be treated as an honoured guest.

Part 7: <u>GENERAL</u>

" <u>My Family Hall of Fame:</u> It seems that all those entered, and there are few, if any, who are not a member, have mostly stories of sadness, tragedy, sacrifice, and very hard work. I wish I could write more of their happiness; however, they found much happiness amongst the sadness."

<u>My father and I</u>

It is obvious that, being born at a time when education and opportunity hardly existed, my father's train of thought must have been very meagre indeed or, as we assert in this streamlined age, he had a " a one-track mind". I remember quite well some of his outworn arguments, and how difficult it was for me to convince him that things were different in this mechanical and rubberized era. I admit that my father learned a lot during the last fifteen years, as compared to what he knew before. I must say that there is a marked improvement. He is quite intelligent and tolerant towards me now, which only proves that the less-educated can improve as time goes on. Of course, this only applies to certain ideas of his, for I'm still in disagreement with him on many subjects.

Here is an example of his antiquated dogma -- "What is Man? Man is a genus rana, an amphibious plantigrade, hyporetted quadruped, or genus felix. Man is no more than a mosquito. Man sings; ditto the mosquito. What music is more charming, or so touches the feelings, or so arouses a man from drowsiness, as the sweet tone and melodious voice of a mosquito?   Who, on hearing this sweet gentle voice, will not instinctively reach forth and try to gather the singer in, so that he may come in closer contact with him?"

And so my father would go on and on, and would wind up by saying, "Bill Passmore said that Bert Bruce told Slim Dickinson and Harold Bourne and Hugh Francis had said that Frank Fraser and Vic Gilbert had responded to a question which Ron Holtum had been supposed to propound to Art Jackson, who seemed to be satisfied that Stan Martin had never thought that Walter Miles and Pat Mulcahy would be surprised if Maurice O'Connor and Art Poyntz had heard that Jack Price and Herb Sabiston were under the impression that Tod Sanders had remarked to Ed Savannah that Bob Shanks was heard talking to Ed Smith about the remark of Jack Stenstrom to a friend in which Dave Thompson was believed to imagine that Howard Tyrell had suggested that Ron Whittingham might have known that Jack Woodley had said that Hugh Hodgins had told Dr. Charlie that Bob Harris was heard talking about a report in which the Honourable Tom Uphill was heard to repeat the fact that mosquitoes are related to the human family."

<u>Letters from my father</u>

Dear Morris:

A few years ago you employed me to make Carmelcrisp at the Vancouver

Exhibition. You paid me a questionable wage with unlimited hours and I served you faithfully and well. The long hours of mixing popcorn and glucose with a wooden paddle resulted in a damaged sinew to my right hand which developed into a deformity commonly known as a hook. It causes me much embarrassment. I am watched by detectives in department stores with suspicion when my hook finger accidentally hooks merchandise. Shaking hands I find myself hooked. If it be a lady I am easily hooked and find it hard to get unhooked. Some define my hook as a tender hook. When my hook is eyed by others one thinks of a hook and eye.

I am giving you details of my hook so you will fully understand why I am asking for compensation for my hook. Your responsibility as an employer is obvious, and by hook or crook I am going to hook you. A hook is defined as a snare or a trap and there is no doubt in my mind that you were aware that an injury known as a hook would result from the work I undertook in good faith. You took no precautions to protect me from getting a hook. All hooks are dangerous. A hockey player gets a penalty for a hook. It's not my intention to hook you or to let you off the hook and I do not expect you to hook dollars to settle my claim. A hooking compensation of five thousand dollars would stop legal action on my part and at the same time get you off the hook. The whole hooking business settled out of court would be a hooking good thing for both of us. I shall await your reply with anticipation knowing that you would never hook me and would straighten the hook if you had the power to do so.

> *Yours hooking father,*
> *Willie*

* * * * *

The Bottle Battle - written during the South African War:

"Have I been an officer long sir?" "Ever since you wed your sweet wife." We've been married an hour and one quarter, and we've been happy the rest of our life. Shall I tell the tale of bottle battle, where like heroes we made not a fuss, though twenty-four strong was our enemy, and there was only two dozen of us. Then we grasped our bayonets don't you see, we grasped our bayonets whether you see it or not, and then we charged and then we charged some more, and then we charged some more -- we charged somewhat. Then we marched in the honor of England, under the Red, White, Pink and Blue through Blomfonteen and Rumfonteen and the fifteen-cent store too. Did I get the Victoria Cross there, did I get six on a plate, wasn't it me and Lord Roberts that sucked the orange and lemon free state. Was there a man afraid to die, diddley, I die, but fate forbid it, then the General ordered us to Um Fum Fums, we didn't know what he said but we did it. Then the General was wounded in the melee, what part the melee is I cannot say, but he came and took my knapsack for a pillow and said thanks for your loud applause, I can no longer stay, and his head fell forward on the knapsack and he said ask my mother if it is strictly proper to say TO MAY TOES or TO MARTOES, and if it's fried PO-ta-TOES and then I'll say farewell, and die one more time again.

* * * * *

To define Poverty:

To define poverty is like trying to put three scrambled eggs back in the shells. 1Poverty is a state of being deficient of the first necessaries. There is also the poverty of language, and poverty of the soil. The poverty of health, the poverty of personality. In some cases poverty denotes entire dependence on charity. Poverty is when one's income is below a given amount of money, irrespective of the fact that it provides enough to eat and clothe one moderately. Poverty is sometimes a present want that is temporary. Poverty can also be a hopeless degraded state. The cause of poverty is not due to the niggardliness of nature, but to the injustice of man. Poverty is often the stepping stone to success, because necessity is the Mother of invention. In nature we often have a poverty of sunshine and rain, thus a part of life. Now I have a poverty of thought on this subject although there be much more to define this prolific word POVERTY.

* * * * *

Frogs croak:

Your enquiry as to why frogs croak, I shall answer at some length. I studied frogology at a place called Frogsville named after an old Toad called Bill. Frogsville is located one mile south of my retreat in the Sooke Hills, which gave me ample time to study the frog and its activities. The frog is an Amphibious animal of the family "Ranidae" and is capable of making long jumps as far as twenty feet. Leap frog -- this game was played by the frogs hundreds of years ago. Man copied this game for his enjoyment, and school boys today still act as frogs when going to school. The most valuable part of the frog is the hair. A Frogshair coat full length requires 18 hundred and three female frogs and all must be over twelve years of age. The male frog or Bull as it is called, grows coarse green hair and is not suitable for coats or other apparel. Frog language consists of croaks. The high pitched croak is the female, the low croak is the male. I spent considerable time learning their language and became quite efficient communicating with them from my cabin in the Sooke Hills. One croak is like saying "Hi". It is answered by other frogs immediately by two croaks, one high and one low translated means "Who's That" in the key of B flat, three croaks answered in F sharp is "I love you." This conversation causes so much excitement that all the frogs start jumping long distances, which causes the wind to blow through their throats like a flute or saxophone and produces a melody known as the Canadian Band of the Frog Rondelay and is considered a welcome song to man, as it is an omen that Winter is over and Spring is in the air. Trusting this will satisfy your thirst on croaking and that it does not leave you with a frog in your throat for you to join the band.   Froggy Bill

* * * * *

Dear Sir:

In reply to your recent and more recent request to send a cheque I wish to inform you that the present shattered condition of my bank account makes it impossible for me to take your requests seriously.

My present financial condition is due to the effect of Dominion Laws, Provincial

Laws, Municipal Laws, County Laws, Corporation Laws, Liquor laws, By Laws, Brother-in-Laws, Sister-in-Laws, Mother-in-Laws and Out-Laws all of which have been foisted upon an unsuspecting public.

Through all these laws I am compelled to pay a Business Tax, Sales Tax, Amusement Tax, Gas Tax, Water Tax, Excise Tax, Income Tax, Hydro Tax, and Syntax. In addition to these irritating taxes I am forced by the strong arm of the law to get a permit for this thing and a permit for that thing. I am required to get a Business Licence, a Provincial Licence, a Sign Licence, a Dog Licence, a Liquor Licence, not to mention a Marriage Licence.

I am also requested to contribute to every society and organization which the genius of man is capable of bringing into our life, to the Society of St. Jean de Baptiste, the Women's Relief, the Near East Relief, also every Hospital and Charitable Institution in the city, the Red Cross, the White Cross, the Green Cross, the Purple Cross, the Flaming Cross, and the Double Cross.

For my own safety I am required to carry Life Insurance, Liability Insurance, Burglary Insurance, Compensation Insurance and Business Insurance. The Government has so governed my business that it is no easy matter for me to find out who owns it.

Examined, re-examined, informed, required, summonsed, fined, commanded, and compelled until all I know is a lot of money for every known need, desire or hope of the human race, and simply because I refuse to donate to each and all, and go out and beg, borrow or steal, I am talked about, held down and robbed, until I am nearly ruined. I am telling you Mr. Man, that failing a miracle you won't be paid just now, and the only reason I am holding on to life is simply to see what the hell is coming next.

* * * * *

By special request:

A Cockney is a Person born within the sound of the Bow Bells in London. He was conspicuous in his Gaudy Pearl Button suit, and was respected by everyone for his happy go lucky and uneducational ways. The Cockney dialect is unique and often amusing especially when the letter "Aitch" is dropped in the wrong places. An example of this can be appreciated in the following conversation with the telephone operator. Calling the operator for a place named Ealing:

"Will yer give me Healing 32675."

"What place?" asked the operator.

"Healing, you must know Healing," he said.

"No, I don't." said the operator. "Will you abbreviate it."

"Gor Blimey, abbreviate. Well -- E as in 'enry, A - what the 'orses eat, L - what they gives yer, I - that's me, N - that lays Heggs, and G for Jesus, is that plain enough?"

A Cockney Preacher would open his service, " 'e, that 'as hears to 'ear, let 'im 'ear." Then talking about lame horses that pulled heavy loads, he said, "It ain't the 'eavy 'auling that 'urts the 'orses 'oofs, its the 'ammer, 'ammer, 'ammer on the 'ard, 'ard ' 'ighway."

* * * * *

You again seek information from me. This time it is about Mice. After a long study on the Mouse I can now give you my findings, which I hope will satisfy you beyond all doubt. A Mouse is a small rodent of the Genus Mus. Musculuks inhabiting houses and there are many other small animals resembling the Mouse, as the Shrew and the Fitter Mouse. After much research I have concluded that it was a Fitter Mouse that hijacked your strawberries. A Fitter Mouse fits the crime because of his love for the fruit of the Fragaria Viginana commonly called strawberry. It is obvious that the Fitter Mouse fits better than the ordinary Grey Mouse. A study of the Fitter Mouse while I was in the Sooke Hills, I learned the Fitter Mouse travels long distances for food to make him fitter. My most memorial meal concerned two Fitter Mice. Your Uncle Walter Maycock had a shack in the Sooke Hills where he stayed while hunting week ends. A crystal clear stream bordered the shack and from the virgin soil grew the most tasty vegetables. A venison stew was his masterpiece which he allowed to marinate overnight. One Sunday Walter invited me to dine with him which I accepted and filled myself with a large bowl of his delicious mulligan stew. There was a little left in the bottom of the pot that Walter coaxed me to eat, when Lo and Behold there were two well marinated Fitter Mice in the bottom of the stew pot. You will note that my experience has a wide range and you can rest assured that it was a Fitter Mouse that helped himself to your strawberries. I could never understand why the plural of Goose is Geese so why shouldn't the plural of Mouse be Meese. The Tit Mouse is another species of the Genus Mus An interesting article could be written about the Tit Mouse but I will leave that for another day. You can also have a mouse under your eye. Trusting this will explain the strawberry escapade to your satisfaction.

* * * * *

Your meteorological question asking for information about wet and cold months of the past. First may I say that I am an expert on weather, past and present. I spent twenty years in the Sooke Hills where I became famous and known as the Sooke Seer. All atmospheric phenomenon I fathomed completely. I won an award in 1910 when I predicted in February of that year that for the next five months the days would become longer and March with showers. October and November I predicted would have more dark than light hours, the sun would not be warm enough to wear light clothes and sandals. As the Sooke Seer I was called upon many times for advice on meteorological matters. January 12th, 1950, was one of our worst days, wind cold and snow blocked the highways. I predicted this three months earlier, and I was acclaimed the world's outstanding forecaster. I left my crystal ball in the Sooke Hills where it was shot to pieces by hunters who mistook it for a Deer. I am therefore slightly handicapped in giving my former accurate accounts concerning space rockets, satellites and light aircraft. My most notable forecast was on January 2nd, 1913. I predicted a sudden squall, sometime during the day. These uncanny forecasts should give you absolute confidence to your inquiry.

April 24th, 1970 - It was warmer in March, only two warm days.
May 6th, 1964 - Cold to date.

May 8th - Cool and wet.
May 1960 - Wet all month.
May 1962 - Same as 1960.
June 21st, 1968 - Only two warm days to date.
June 29th, 1955 - No warm weather to date, wet and cold.
June 30th - Mortimer comments on weather in Colonist.
July 4th - Weather cool. No warm weather to date.
There was of course many warm months. May 18th, 1950, was 80 degrees. May 30th same year, temperature Hottest day 83 degrees, a record. These are a few of my recordings. I find the Atomic bomb and moon shots are responsible for the bad weather, but have found no reason for the good weather. Hoping you will find these statistics to be enlightening and useful.   The Sooke Seer

Poems by my father, William Kersey

My Allotted Years

Man's allotted years of three score and ten,
I have been very privileged to fulfill,
And my journey through this short lease of life
Has been embellished by so much good will.

At seventy years I can now look back,
The years how they all passed in single file;
Gone -- the glimmering dreams of things that were,
But there were none escaped my grateful smile.

Eight hundred and forty flowery months,
And time has touched me gently with its race;
Two affectionate sons -- a loving wife,
The very best of health -- by God's good grace

Three thousand, six hundred and forty weeks
I learned to live them, so I did not dread
The fateful arrival of Father Time;
Or the grave -- any more than my warm bed.

Twenty-five thousand, five hundred-odd days ,   (25,562 actual)
I cherished as if each were my last;
"All were swifter than a weaver's shuttle" ;   (Job7:6)
I fluttered gaily with them as they passed.

Six hundred and fourteen thousand hours,   (613,488 actual)
Bringing evening when sunset splendours wane,
In my log of life -- indelibly inscribed,
Are those golden hours -- ever to remain.

Thirty-seven million precious minutes,   (36,809,280 actual)
Just a gleam of time, now beyond recall;
A fleeting glance before eternity,
Like a story told -- how I lived them all!

Two billion, two hundred million seconds, (2,208,556,800 actual)
In faultless rhythm -- all were ticked away
By the pulse of time -- and with God the soul,
Now those allotted years are -- YESTERDAY.

* * * * *

Nostalgia (1978)

I lie back in my old arm chair
And try to figure, why I'm still here
And what's my purpose on this earth,
And was my life planned at my birth.

As I lie back in my arm chair
My thoughts float idly, here and there.
I reminisce about things that were
And wonder where I go from here.
I lie back in my old arm chair
Feeling snug and comfy there,
As if I'm in my Mother's arms
And safe from all the world alarms.

I lie back in my old arm chair,
Half in a daze and blandly stare.
I have visions of my uncle Ted,
And others who have been long dead.
I lie back in my old arm chair
And meditate on space out there,
What lifts my arm, what brings a thought,
And how a nasty cold is caught.

I lie back in my old arm chair
In my golden age of ninety year,
Nostalgic thoughts of yesterday
Console my soul, along the way.
As I lie back in my arm chair
Realizing that my end is near,
I've served my time on mortal earth
And received much more than I am worth.

My brother Ray

Raymond was two years older than myself and had a entirely different personality. He went to school for a much longer period of time than I did, and he lived on the farm for some years after I left for Victoria.

When I worked at the Cold Storage plant, they needed fish cleaners. Ray tried his hand at this, but he wasn't too impressed. It was a mighty cold job on the hands, and after work your clothes and hair all smelled fishy -- this was not helped by bathing.

He finally got work with the provincal government, where he stayed for forty-three years, serving in several different departments. He was in an executive position and did his job well. He ended up with a huge pension, which would be very hard to do if one was in business. Depending on your nature, from financial, security, health, and other aspects, I would suggest it is a better life.

Ray was always interested in athletics. Had it not been for the era he grew up in, I would say for sure he would have been an Olympic star. He was in training for long-distance running; some days, while living on the farm, he would run to high school -- a twelve-mile jog.

There was a time when he felt he had had enough of government and would join my peanut-butter company. He gave his notice, and was to start with me in a few days when he had a change of mind, cancelling his notice and returning to the government. I feel this was a good move on his part.

He did work in the peanut-butter and nut plant after hours and, for the fifty cents per hour he made, he was pretty dedicated, doing a top-notch job. He roasted cashews and other nuts in a type of deep fat fryer, using peanut oil. The basket inside the fryer would hold about two hundred pounds of nuts at one time. After cooking was finished, a chain hoist attached to the basket would haul the nuts up about five feet over the fryer to drain and finish cooking. All that had to be done then was to salt them with a flour salt. From there they went to the storage area, where they would be cello-bagged, boxed and shipped to wholesalers.

Ray also roasted peanuts in the shell. These arrived in approximately one hundred and fifty pound bags and, depending on the country they arrived from, were quite dusty. The peanuts from Mexico always had a fair amount of soil on them. The nuts were put into a slowly-revolving gas-fired drum. The dust would be so thick that Ray used a Second-World-War gas mask while roasting them.

Our plant was located on Store Street on the waterfront, and had a driveway going around the entire building. One dark night a city policeman went to investigate, and found the large back doors of the building open and Ray wearing his gas mask. The policeman was actually scared and approached ready to fire, until he discovered what was going on.

Ray also worked in a retail store we owned. Some nights his earnings were pretty meagre but, considering the amount of work involved, I really do not have any guilt feelings, as he was getting as good or better than the going wages. However, I do feel, at this time of my life, I could pay him some back wages, but it is too late, as it is no good to him in his senior years.

Sanitation

When I was a small child on the farm, sanitation was the farthest thing from my mind. The Saturday night ritual of taking a bath was a real work-out.

First, water had to be picked up in ten-gallon cans. We wheeled a wheelbarrow approximately one-half mile each way to our neighbour's pump to bring the water home. Then, after we had chopped sufficient wood, the wood stove would be lit. On the stove top we put a galvanized tub, about four feet in diameter and twenty-four inches deep, until it was warm.

My brother and I lined up. Being the older, he was first. After curling up into a ball he would emerge from the water and proceed to wash with some kind of soap. After he was finished, it was my turn to get into the same water. This water was then put on the garden; this turned out to be very good for growing things.

After the bath we cleaned our teeth with ashes from the stove's fire box. This proved to be far superior to today's toothpaste, and it didn't leave a residue of soap and ingredients in your mouth, which could then go into your intestines.

My personal sanitation started as a slow growth process, and grew to the point in my old age where it has become a fettish -- now taking one or two showers a day and changing clothes more rapidly than the washing machine can handle them.

To me, the designer of the bath certainly had very poor ideas of sanitation -- to sit in a tub of hot water and try to get clean by washing yourself, thus dirtying the water you're sitting in. I can readily see why they invented perfume. My motto is -- if you are going to sit your fanny in a cold tub with hot water, at least have a shower afterwards to clean yourself up.

John Steed

In 1929 Frank Steed from the Channel Islands, an English Navy seaman on the British gunboat Colombo, jumped ship, along with many others, while it was visiting Victoria. He arrived at our farm in Keating and asked my father if he needed any help. Since, in those days the penalty for desertion was very severe, he told us his name was "John" so he wouldn't be identified.

At that time, our farm consisted of a partly-built house without electricity, no water or any facilities, other than a wood stove in the kitchen for heat. The floors were shiplap with knots. You could sweep the floor and push the dust into the unfinished dirt basement. The walls were lathed ready for plastering, which would not be finished for months until enough funds were available. Electricity and plumbing were on the priority list and would be the first things to be done. We also had a strawberry pickers' shed and a barn.

Father told John that he was welcome to move into the shed, and we would feed him in exchange for work on the farm. He proved to be a most reliable, honest, sincere, hard-working fellow, never complaining, and gave a full day's work without remuneration. He became part of the family and, in his spare time, did other odd jobs for pocket money. He helped me cut and deliver Christmas trees during his tenure.

When I was sixteen years old, I left school and got a job at Victoria Cold Storage. I was able to advise John about work in Victoria and he went to work cleaning fish. Due to the twelve-mile distance from our farm to Victoria and the lack of transportation, other than the Flying Line, I moved to town. However, John picked up an old motorcycle to use for his transportation.

About 1933, John decided it was safe to return to England as, after this length of time, he didn't feel he would be charged with desertion. He left our farm, never to be heard from again.

In 1985, my brother Ray decided to see if he could locate him. He wrote a letter to the Channel Islands' newspaper, and enclosed a picture of John. Ray asked them if they knew John's whereabouts. The Channel Islands' paper ran John's picture in their local paper. John's sister, who was still living there, saw the picture and story, and contacted John, who had moved to Hants in England.

John wrote to Ray and, in 1986, we travelled to England with our wives for a reunion. He told us that, on his return to England, he never encountered any difficulties with the authorities, and he went on to serve in the armed forces during World War II.

In April 1989, John came to Victoria with his two daughters to take a second look at what he left behind some sixty years before.

Kersey

Do not miss this village. The heavy woolen cloths known as "kerseys" were famous throughout medieval England, bringing a prosperity that still shows to this day. Late-medieval timber-framed houses line a long street, which dips attractively to a ford at the bottom before rising again to the loftily-placed and very grand parish church to the south.

Just to the north, an Augustinian priory once confronted the church across the valley. Some parts of its buildings remain, but are now private property. It was one of the smaller and later Augustinian foundations, being suppressed as early as 1443-4 in favour of Henry VI's King's College, Cambridge. The college also became patron of the parish church at Kersey. However, it is unlikely that the college contributed to the church's late-medieval rebuilding; this would have been made possible by wealthy parishioners.

Two clear stages in the rebuilding of the church are recognizable. The first predates the Black Death, and was left incomplete in a number of details when the plague visited the parish. It is to the 1330's and 1340's that the unusually broad north aisle belongs. There is no corresponding aisle to the south of the nave, giving the church a somewhat lop-sided feel, which is particularly marked as one enters the building from the north. Next to the altar, a fine set of piscina and sedilia belongs to this period, as does the extraordinary, carved stone cornice located just below roof level. The latter is much mutilated, but is still recognizably designed to tell a long story, the subject of which is not known.

In the second phase of the rebuilding, dating to the fifteenth century, the nave was reconstructed, porches were added to the north and south, and the great tower (a prominent local landmark) was completed. The nave roof is contemporary; it must have been very fine, as originally conceived. The very remarkable panelled roofs of the south and north porches are works of the highest quality, particularly in the south porch. Other features of the late-medieval church are the well-preserved roof-loft stairs and door, the unusually intact portraits (three prophets and three kings) on six surviving panels of the former rood screen, and the original, architecturally conceived, fifteenth-century shaft of the wooden lectern. A fragmentary "St. George and the Dragon" painting has been preserved on the south wall of the church, with many broken mouldings and other bits and pieces collected together (in a haphazard and antiquarian way) in the north aisle.

My wife Iris

I sent the following non-rhyming note to my close friend, whom I was fortunate enough to marry on January 21, 1971. This is, as the saying goes, "a marriage made in Heaven -- a perfect marriage". Iris has been the strength behind me -- not only a perfect marriage, but also a perfect person. I could not have been more fortunate and I know our happiness will live on for many years. In addition to being a terrific cook, partner, helper and all things, Iris has her Pilot's Licence and is most capable in her flying ability. She is also a better-than-average bowler and golfer.

I know for sure how hard it is to be a millionaire and more,
And live within marble walls and have flunkies by the score.
It is the simple things in life that matter.
Time was only made for fools and mad hatters.
Now, if you can scratch an honest itch,
Or if you could dig a ditch,
I invite you to the site of sunshine in full bloom on Seabrook Road.
There, with the frogs and toads, I will stand behind you,
As solid as the trees and the light they invite.

When I say you really, really are the most considerate, kind, loving, prettiest person in the world, with absolute honesty, integrity and all the things there are. This is for today, tomorrow and always. S.N.K.Y.

People you meet

In my garage days Mr. and Mrs. Tom King of Golden, B.C., walked in and wanted to go to Courtenay. A U-Drive would be too costly, so I volunteered to take them up and stay overnight, as I had an aunt and uncle living there. I didn't arrange for any expenses, but I was adequately paid. It was a delightful trip and introduced me to one of the many great friends I have met in my lifetime. Mr. King was the Member of Parliament for the Golden area. He was respected by all, and was a legend in the area he represented. In years to come, when I was in the peanut-butter business, King's General Store in Golden would only handle one brand of peanut butter -- Kersey's -- on his instructions. It was a sad day when he passed on to new pastures. You can be sure Heaven was getting a great person.

My friend Atlee Pearcy, with whom I had worked freezing five-hundred-pound barrels of loganberries at the cold-storage plant, and with whom I first tried out snuff, which almost killed me, had a place at Cultus Lake, B.C. He made me a life member of the International Chowder and Marching Society; meetings are held the sixth Tuesday in each month and the Grand Lodge meets on February 31st. His letterhead was unique.

Another gentleman I met, while working at the Royal Trust Company, was Mr. Herbert Stanton from Pasadena, California. He was very wealthy, and owned several properties in Victoria which I looked after as to rentals, etc., on behalf of the Royal Trust. For some reason, Mr. Stanton thought the sun rose on me. Later, during the days of the depression when I was operating the restaurant, he came in for all his meals during his annual summer trips to Victoria. I visited him in Pasadena and met his wife and family. I also met his married daughter when she came to Victoria to visit us.

He was always saying to me, if I ever needed any money, to please let him know. One day I had a crisis in the restaurant. Walter Fletcher, my landlord's son, and B.C. Electric and all my other creditors were pushing me pretty hard. In desperation I sent an air-mail letter to Mr. Stanton, asking to borrow one thousand dollars for a short period. On receipt of my letter, he wired the money to me and said not to worry about interest or, for that matter, paying it back. I was not going to take advantage of a friend and said I would make repayment.

It was undoubtedly one of the poorest business things I ever did. It topped the list of errors. By the time I paid my creditors something on account, including the rent, I was no better off, and now owed a thousand dollars. Against Mr. Stanton's wishes, I paid two dollars per week to the Royal Trust, on account for the debt. I eventually paid it off, at no interest. I vowed never to do anything like this again, no matter what the circumstances were.

To me it is remarkable how some people will help others. For this thousand dollars, I signed no note, nothing. Mr. Stanton remained a dear friend until his passing away.

In the depression days, running a cash business was not always cash. After eating, a certain number of customers arrived at the desk without any money. Usually we had them sign the food slip and they would pay the next day. Others would run up a small bill and pay on payday. There were a certain few who were never any good as far as paying their bills. These slips would accumulate over the month; most of them we threw away as they were uncollectable.

However, there were wealthy Victoria customers who just wouldn't pay. There was one particular young fellow, who lived with his parents in an exclusive apartment house, the Marine Chalet in Oak Bay. He owed about twelve dollars and refused to pay. In Victoria, however, there was a gentleman named Mr. de Macedo, nicknamed the "Sheriff's Pup", who rode around on his bicycle collecting bad debts. His fee was one-half of the money collected. One morning about ten o'clock I asked him if he could collect the twelve-dollar debt for me. Within an hour and a half he was back to give me my half of the money, and I asked him if he had any trouble collecting. His answer was that, in an exclusive place like the Marine Chalet, all you do is knock on the apartment door and stand in the hallway shouting as loud as you can about the bad debt. All the while the family is trying to invite you inside to pay you. Then he added that, in James Bay, you can shout as loud as you like, but it will do no good.

Frank Paulding of the Y.M.C.A. ran a public-speaking class every Thursday night at the Y. Many young and some older fellows belonged to this group. It had only about two dozen members, but it was a great educational programme. Each Thursday night everyone in attendance had to give a speech on something. You may be asked to prepare a subject of your choice for the next meeting or, at a meeting, you would pick a subject out of a hat, get up on your feet, and talk spontaneously about the subject for three minutes. Hecklers' night was when you ran for a public office of your choice, and were heckled. Strange as it may sound, these meetings were very interesting, with all the different subjects you would hear. In those days there was no TV to watch; this type of thing took its place. Motivation today is difficult for most to acquire, although years ago everybody seemed motivated.

About the turn of the century, a model horse was beautifully constructed from a wooden frame covered by plaster and burlap. This model was almost perfect. About 1946 it came to my attention. It was first seen in Victoria at Wades Saddlery Shop on Johnson Street; it was then moved to Norris Leather Goods on Government Street, where it was in the window for many years.

I would often go to Norris Leather to have them repair leather belts from our nut-manufacturing machinery. On one of my visits it appeared that Norris Leather was going to close down. I was asked if I would like to purchase the horse.

"You can have it for twenty-five dollars."

I said, "What would I do with it?"

When the gentleman said, "Give me fifteen dollars", I bought it and had it moved to our nut plant. I christened it "Peanuts". I had no idea of its true value. I had bought the model to get it out of the owner's way, without any thought of selling it. Within a few weeks I was getting phone calls daily from people wanting to buy the horse. Offers ranged from thirty-five dollars from a collector in Duncan to several thousand dollars from people in other parts of B.C. Every parade organizer in Victoria and up-island wanted either to borrow it or buy it. Bob Shanks of Indian Motorcycle fame had gone real "horsey" and opened a saddlery shop on Douglas Street. I put the horse in his shop for many years, where it was a tremendous advertising medium and certainly enhanced his business. When Bob was retiring, he arranged to send the model to the B.C. Forestry Museum in Duncan.

Cars

Over the years I feel inflation on automobiles has been far greater than on most things. Early in this story I mentioned the 1906 Buick which I paid five dollars for, and was sold by my father for fifteen dollars many years later.

Father provided a 1920 Dodge touring car for our limited use in hauling Christmas trees to Victoria.

After the necessity of my moving from the country to Victoria, I purchased quite a few cars with the income derived from night contracting work I was doing after my day job at the Royal Trust Company. I owned a 1920 Buick in partnership with my brother Ray; it was a four-door touring with convertible top, purchased from Mr. Swengers of Mc and Mc and Prior Hardware. I cannot recall the price, but it would have been less than one hundred dollars. However, it proved too costly to operate -- a tire was worth the price of the car -- so it was sold.

I purchased a Model T Ford of some vintage for fifty dollars. In those days, if you didn't know the dealer, you were sold a "bill of goods". The rear end would be filled with heavy grease and sawdust. After a few hundred miles the rear end was gone.

In the depression I had a 1929 "pregnant" Buick which cost one hundred dollars. It was a really great car. The reason they called it "pregnant" was because the four doors were designed to oval out. I owed our bookkeeper at the restaurant about one hundred dollars, and I agreed to give him the Buick for one hundred and fifty dollars. He gave me fifty dollars and a receipt for the bookkeeping. The next day, with the fifty dollars, I bought a Whippet that was a real "dog". I returned it and received my fifty dollars back. I then asked the bookkeeper to sell me back the Buick, which he did. I do not remember the details of the finances, but it worked out OK.

A little later the Studebaker salesman sold me an expensive car which I should never have purchased. It cost the Buick as down-payment and thirty-five dollars per month. There was no way I could pay this out of the restaurant earnings, so, within two months, I signed a release claim and gave the car back to the dealer. I was now without a car. This was my first experience with assignments; I collected nothing, and lost my Buick and the payments that had been made.

In 1931, I purchased a 1929 Chevrolet convertible for one hundred and fifty dollars. A nearly-new one in 1931 could be bought for about six hundred dollars.

I sold the Chevrolet in 1934 and purchased a very elegant, used De Soto convertible, which had two wire wheels mounted in the fenders. It cost about one hundred and fifty dollars. By this time, I had left the Royal Trust Company, and was operating a garage and doing some U-Drive car business. The U-Drive business in those days really only operated in the evenings; hardly anybody would rent a car in the daytime. If I ran out of cars for rental, I would rent out the De Soto. Although it was not licensed for rental, it wasn't too much of a risk to take. One night I rented it to a sailor, the fee would have been about three or four dollars from six p.m. to midnight. At that time in Victoria there was not one single stop-and-go light, and the corner of Yates and Douglas was the hive of excitement every night. The sailor made a left-hand turn at the intersection without giving a hand signal. For this I received a ticket from the police to appear in court, and had to plead guilty as the offence would have been far worse if I had told the judge that I had rented out the car illegally. I was given a severe talking-to by the judge about the way I drove, and was fined five dollars.

Many young fellows used to admire a Dusenburg that belonged to a Mr. McDermott (Mr. Mc to us). He lived at the Empress Hotel, so we presumed he was very wealthy. He would park the car on Douglas Street where you could park for as long as you wished. The car was the envy of all the young fellows, and we carefully inspected it any time we saw it parked. Bill Sylvester kept it washed and polished for Mr. Mc. I do not know what happened to Mr. Mc or his car, but the car today would be worth millions of dollars. Clark Gable had one like it, and his is now valued at fifteen million dollars.

In 1945, after the war, I purchased a beautiful Packard sedan with two mounted wire wheels. It cost about two hundred dollars and proved to be a good car. It was worth that amount later when I sold it.

In 1946 our peanut-butter company had a small truck that was not too suitable for our business. While playing bridge with Gordon Law, Manager of Weston Bread Company, he told me they had a Chevrolet station wagon that was too small for them and suggested we make a trade, sight unseen, which we did. However, I do not know who got the better of the deal. The Chevrolet had over one hundred thousand miles on it and needed constant repair, but it sure looked classy for displaying our peanut-butter advertisements.

To give you some idea of inflation on car prices, I purchased a new 1946 Buick convertible for three thousand dollars. It was one of the nicest cars they ever produced. In 1988 such a car was selling for over thirty thousand dollars.

I finally ended up winning a 1954 Cadillac convertible at a one-hundred-dollar-a-plate charity dinner. Since then I have been most fortunate to be able to own and drive a Cadillac. However, the thrill is not the same now as it was in those early days of driving my first cars.

Looking back sixty years it seems so easy -- if I had just kept in storage the first six automobiles I purchased, at a total cost of approximately seven hundred dollars, they would have been worth upwards of one hundred thousand dollars in 1988.

                    *
                        *
                            *
                                *
                                    *

Now, as I motor down the highway in my 2001 Corvette, I often reflect on my journey through life. I've gone from the era of the horse and buggy to the ultimate speed machine -- the Concorde -- which carried Iris and me across the Atlantic Ocean in less time than it took to come from Victoria to my first Central Saanich home.

My life, with its trials and tribulations.......I would like to have seen a video of my future from cradle to grave. Knowing what I've learned in eighty-eight years, there would only be a few changes.

"Man's brain was not designed to understand God."

The text of this book was word-processed, from Morris Kersey's original manuscript, by Susan Woods, a good friend who spent numerous hours on the computer.

Printed in the United States
by Baker & Taylor Publisher Services